Food and Beverage Management

Food and Beverage Management

A selection of readings

Edited by
Bernard Davis and Andrew Lockwood

BUTTERWORTH
HEINEMANN

Butterworth-Heinemann Ltd.
Linacre House, Jordan Hill, Oxford OX2 8DP

A member of the Reed Elsevier plc group

OXFORD   LONDON   BOSTON
MUNICH   NEW DELHI   SINGAPORE   SYDNEY
TOKYO   TORONTO   WELLINGTON

First published 1994

British Library Cataloguing in Publication Data
Food and Beverage Management: Selection of Readings.
  I. Lockwood, Andrew   II. Davis, Bernard
  III. Series
  647.95068

ISBN 0 7506 1950 3

Composition by Genesis Typesetting, Laser Quay, Rochester, Kent
Printed in Great Britain by Clays, St Ives plc

Contents

Preface

Food and Beverage Management: A selection of readings is designed to bring together current research and major issues of continuing concern to the wide field of food and beverage management within the context of the hospitality industry.

Building on the successful publication of *Food and Beverage Management* by Davis and Stone in 1985 and 1991, which has been widely accepted by universities and colleges for their degree courses in the UK and overseas, and by the HCIMA as a standard textbook for the Professional Certificate and Diploma and Distance Learning Courses, this text provides specially selected material to further the student's understanding of food and beverage operations and their management. The text includes a wide range of issues and opinions from leading academics, senior industry professionals and international consultants. It is intended that this will provide a springboard for continued research in the field.

The text is aimed at final year students following degree programmes in hotel and catering, hospitality or food retailing management and at postgraduate students in these fields. It will also be of interest to managers in the industry.

The introductory chapter gives an overview of the scope and structure of the food and beverage industry within the UK. The following chapters need to be read with an awareness of this context.

The book is then structured in five main sections covering the key areas of a food and beverage manager's responsibilities as shown below.

- Strategic considerations
- Planning and design
- Managing operations
- Controlling operations
- The view from the industry

We would like to take this opportunity to express our sincere thanks to all the individuals who have contributed to this publication for the time and effort they have devoted to the project and for their considerable expertise and experience. Without them this publication would not have been possible.

We would also like to thank Kathryn Grant, Jacquie Shanahan, Caroline Struthers and all at Butterworth-Heinemann for their continual support and encouragement.

Bernard Davis
Andrew Lockwood

Contributors

Nicholas Alexander is a Lecturer in Retail Management in the Department of Management Studies, University of Surrey. He was previously Coca-Cola Retail Research Foundation Lecturer in Retailing, Edinburgh University. He is an Associate Editor of the *Service Industries Journal*. His research interests include information technology and international retailing.

Francis Buttle is Senior Fellow in Services Management at the Manchester Business School. He has over twenty years' experience in marketing management, research, education and consultancy and has lived and worked on three continents. He has published over 100 items including a widely-adopted hospitality marketing management textbook.

David Capstick On graduating from the University of Surrey, David worked for the retail catering division of Allied Breweries in both operations and systems with responsibilities to branded restaurants. As a Management Consultant with Peter Burholt's, work was undertaken on catering projects both in the UK and abroad. He is currently project managing and implementing a computerized food and beverage system at the House of Commons, Westminster.

Colin Clark is Regional Hotel Services Adviser for the South West Thames Regional Health Authority.

John Connell lectures in marketing and is course leader for the Post Graduate Diploma in Hospitality Management in the Department of Hospitality, Tourism and Leisure Management at Glasgow Caledonian University. For his PhD he is undertaking a phenomenological study into the extension of a UK-based hotel brand into a foreign market.

Bob Cotton is Director of Corporate Affairs for Gardner Merchant, one of the largest contract caterers in the UK and internationally. Having graduated from the University of Surrey in 1970, he spent time with Hawker Siddeley and Chrysler in their employee services departments.

He then joined Gardner Merchant where he worked in operations before becoming Personal Assistant to Garry Hawkes in 1980. In 1986 he also took on the responsibility for public relations and corporate affairs in general. Following the recent management buyout of Gardner Merchant from Forte, he finds more of his time actively spent in the area of corporate affairs.

Bernard Davis is formerly Senior Lecturer in Food and Beverage Management in the Department of Management Studies at the University of Surrey. He is author and co-author of many textbooks and papers on hotel and catering management, including *Food Commodities* and *Food and Beverage Management* with Sally Stone.

Anita Eves is a Lecturer in Food Science in the Department of Management Studies at the University of Surrey. She studied Food Science at the University of Reading and worked at the Leatherhead Food Research Association prior to joining the department.

Luigi Ferrone is Senior Lecturer in Food and Beverage Operations in the Department of Service Industries at Bournemouth University. He has a strong research interest in the application of information systems to food and beverage management.

Cliff Goodwin is a Surrey graduate with fourteen years' industrial experience. He is currently Senior Lecturer and Management Area Leader at the University of Brighton. His extensive consultancy work has focused on management issues in food and beverage operations. He is an external examiner for the HCIMA and the author of their 'Operational Management' distance learning module.

Yvonne Guerrier is a Senior Lecturer in Human Resource Management at the University of Surrey. Her current research interests include the development of managers' skills and knowledge within the hotel and catering industry.

Mike Henderson is Catering Development Controller for Greenall Inns. Since graduating in 1971 he has spent all his time working for brewers and pub retailers. He has been Operations Director for large tenanted and managed estates for two regional brewers and is currently responsible for the policy and development of catering within Greenall Inns – an estate of approximately 400 company catering outlets.

P. J. Houghton is Area Manager, Scotland (South East) for Chef and Brewer, Whitbread Plc. He was formerly an Assistant Area Manager with

Tennents Taverns (Scotland) and a Unit Manager for Allied Lyons. He has been responsible for adopting retail practice in high-volume food and beverage outlets and is currently involved in new option developments.

Haydn Ingram is a third-generation publican, having been the licensee of a large west London pub for fifteen years after training in hotel management. He is currently Senior Lecturer at Bournemouth University and owns a hotel in the city of Salisbury, but finds time to write books and articles on operations and strategic management for the hospitality industry.

Keith Johnson is a Principal Lecturer at the University of Huddersfield and is an active member of the Hotel and Catering Research Centre located there. He is the co-author of the UK and International Hotel Group Directories and sits on the editorial board of three major hospitality journals.

Peter A. Jones is Head of the Department of Service Industries at Bournemouth University. He has a background in developing computer systems for managing food and beverage operations.

Peter L. M. Jones is Head of the Department of Service Sector Management at the University of Brighton Business School. Before starting teaching, he worked for six years in the hotel and restaurant business. After management positions with Trusthouse Forte in the UK and Allied Lyons in Belgium, he opened and managed his own restaurant in Brussels for two years. Since 1981 he has been the author, co-author or editor of six textbooks and numerous articles dealing largely with operational issues in the hotel and foodservice industry. As well as writing, he has been an active consultant for public and private sector organizations in the UK and overseas. He is on the executive committee of CHME, the founding president of EuroCHRIE, a fellow of the HCIMA, and serves on the education committee of IFCA. His first degree was in economics and education, and he has an MBA from London Business School.

Amanda Kemp is a Senior Lecturer in the Department of Food, Nutrition and Hospitality Management at the University of Huddersfield. She was joint chief author of *Management of Fast Food Operations* published in 1992, a contributor to Jordan's *Survey of Britain's Fast Food Industry*, and is currently involved in catering business development within the retail estate of a major brewer. She is also completing a PhD in the field of hotel and restaurant design and is on the editorial board of the *Journal of Consumer Marketing*.

Michael Kipps is Senior Lecturer in Food Science and Deputy Head of Department in the Department of Management Studies at the University of Surrey. He has research interests in the areas of food hygiene and HACCP, and has numerous previous publications on these topics.

David Kirk, who is Head of Department of Hospitality Studies at Queen Margaret College, Edinburgh, has developed an interest in catering design over a number of years, both in Edinburgh and at Sheffield Hallam University, where he played a key role in the development of computer assisted catering design through the CATERCAD project.

Tim Knowles is Lecturer in Hotel Management in the Department of Management Studies at the University of Surrey. His research interests are in the field of food safety legislation. He is the author of the recently published *Hospitality Management: An Introduction*.

Jonathan Langston is a graduate of the University of Surrey. He is an Associate Director of Horwath Consulting, a leading firm of international hotel and tourism consultants and a division of Stoy Hayward, chartered accountants and business advisers. He specializes in undertaking market demand and financial feasibility studies and strategic planning for hotel and tourism projects. He has undertaken projects throughout the UK and Europe (including the former Eastern bloc) as well as Turkey and in North and East Africa.

J. John Lennon is a Senior Lecturer in Hospitality Management in the Department of Hospitality, Tourism and Leisure Management, Glasgow Caledonian University. He has worked for a number of hotel companies in the UK and Europe. His current research interests relate to privatization strategy and retail applications in the hospitality industry. He has acted as a consultant to national and international companies and institutions.

Andrew Lockwood is a Lecturer in Hotel and Catering Management in the Department of Management Studies at the University of Surrey. Following graduation in 1974, he gained managerial experience with Trusthouse Forte and Grand Metropolitan before managing his own hotel. Now an experienced teacher and researcher, he has written numerous books, papers and articles on aspects of hotel and catering management. His long-term research interest lies in managing quality in hospitality operations, a topic on which he has run many courses for hospitality managers in the UK and as far afield as Cyprus and Bali.

Colin Masters is Purchasing Director of Compass Services Ltd, one of the largest independent contract catering companies operating in the UK and Europe. He was previously a trading manager with Tesco and has worked for Sainsbury and Ford. He has an MBA from Cranfield and is a member of the Chartered Institute of Marketing.

Paul Merricks graduated from the University of Surrey with a degree in hotel and catering management. He worked for several years for British Transport Catering Operations before becoming a lecturer in hotel and catering management. He is now a principal lecturer in management at Middlesex University.

Alex Noble is a Lecturer in Financial Management in the Department of Management Studies at the University of Surrey.

Jim Pickworth is the Academic Counsellor in the School of Hotel and Food Administration at the University of Guelph, Canada. He teaches in the areas of human resource management and operations analysis. In addition, he is responsible for the development of the School's Co-op programme. His research has focused primarily on productivity measurement and improvement. Besides writing case studies, Jim has published articles in various journals on topics relating to managerial responsibilities, service delivery systems and human resource practices in the hospitality industry. He has been involved in management development in the UK, and was an Area Operations Analyst for Hilton International.

Abraham Pizam is Professor of Tourism and Hospitality Management in the Department of Hospitality Management at the University of Central Florida where he has previously served as the Chair of the department and the Director of the Dick Pope Sr. Institute for Tourism Studies. Professor Pizam has held various academic positions in the USA, UK, France, Austria, Australia, New Zealand, Singapore, Israel and Switzerland and is the author of numerous scientific publications in the field of tourism/hospitality management.

Stuart Price holds an MBA from the University of Bradford. He is a consultant and analyst with Stoy Hayward Franchising Services and used to manage Britain's only Fast Food and Restaurant Database at the Hotel and Catering Research Centre, Huddersfield University. He has considerable knowledge of the foodservice industries, having conducted repositioning and rebranding consultancy projects for foodservice companies, food suppliers and champagne houses. He is the author of over thirty articles and reports on the global food service industry.

Geoffrey Pye graduated from the Hotel and Catering Management Department of the University of Surrey in 1967. Most of his career has been in personnel and training in a variety of service businesses including hotels, restaurants, multi-site retailing and pubs. He is a fellow of the HCIMA and a fellow of the IPM, and currently holds the position of Personnel Director – Operations for Forte Plc.

Darrell Stocks was educated at Doncaster Grammar School and graduated from the University of Surrey with a BSc in Hotel and Catering Administration. Following extensive management experience with Crest Hotels, he joined Courage where he created and developed Harvester Restaurants, moving with them to become Managing Director following their purchase by Forte. He became Executive Director – Catering with Forte Hotels in 1992 and is currently with Whitbread.

Barry Ware-Lane is a graduate of the Department of Management Studies for Tourism and Hotel Industries of the University of Surrey. He has over twenty years' experience in the hotel, catering and leisure sectors, having held senior positions with Hilton International, Forte, Pizzaland International and the Rank Organisation. As well as undertaking numerous consultancy assignments, he has lectured and acted as external examiner in food and beverage management. Additionally he was Managing Director of a privately owned outside catering company and has opened several restaurant and leisure establishments. He is currently Director – Higher Education for Chartwells, part of Compass Group Plc.

Introduction

1 An overview of the scope and structure of the hotel and catering industry

Bernard Davis and Andrew Lockwood

Introduction

The term 'hotel and catering industry' embraces the economic activity of undertakings which aim to satisfy the demand for accommodation, food and drink away from the home (Medlik, 1978).

The industry in the UK is large but extremely difficult to quantify with any precision (EIU Special Report No. 2169, 1993). Statistics on the industry frequently cause concern to students, academics and management in the industry when researching the industry in any depth, as accurate statistical data has not been collected over the years. It is not uncommon to find surprisingly large differences, for example, in the number of units and in the turnover of most sectors of the industry, when attempting to verify and correlate data produced by different research organizations.

Weaknesses in the collection of accurate data include:

1 The characteristics of this industry are that it is relatively new, has very diversified ownership and is made up of very many small businesses, many of which are not even registered for VAT.
2 The importance and size of the industry has only been seen to be of any major relevance to the government and the economy since 1948, when it was first included in the Standard Industrial Classification (SIC).
3 The SIC was not established until 1948 and updated only in 1958, 1968 and 1980. The classification does not adequately cover the total industry as it is today.
4 Many catering units operate within companies for which catering is not that company's main business and hence separating out data for collection becomes difficult if not impossible.

5 Units do not have to register in any way unless they require a liquor licence or are large enough to pay VAT. It is hoped that with the new Food Premises (Registration) Regulations 1991, requiring the registration of all food premises, that a more accurate base for data may be available in the future.
6 Attempts at correlating data from the main sources such as those produced by the government, major market research organizations and by the professional and trade bodies are frequently frustrated as these sources tend to use their own definitions and base for data produced.

A classification of the industry

As mentioned earlier, the government classifies the industry according to the standard industrial classification of 1980. This classification is now somewhat outdated. For example, many restaurants now have a takeaway element to their business, some takeaway units offer a delivery service for consumption of food at home, some takeaway units offer facilities for the food to be consumed on the premises, etc. Data on major sections of the industry are also not clearly classified by the SIC and so definitive statistics are not available. For example, the SIC fails to clearly identify all forms of travel catering, wine bars, hospitals, etc.

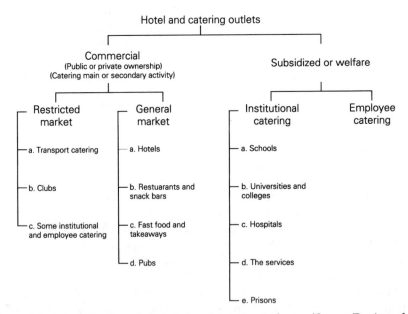

Figure 1.1 A classification of the hotel and catering industry (*Source*: Davis and Stone, 1991)

A classification for the main sectors of food and beverage outlets was published by Davis and Stone in *Food and Beverage Management* in 1985 and later in 1991 (Davis and Stone, 1991). As shown in Figure 1.1, it is based on several clear distinctions that can be made between the many different types of food and beverage outlets. An example of the problems involved in any classification is that of overlap between areas. An area of significant growth in recent years has come from the catering contractors, who conduct their business activity across both the commercial and non-commercial sectors. How accurately data are collected and apportioned and whether at times some of the data are counted twice are of concern.

The importance of the industry

The hotel and catering industry has been widely recognized in recent years as the largest single employer in the UK, representing 10.9 per cent of the employed workforce. It is a bigger employer than education, all types of engineering combined, and even retail distribution (HCITB, 1988).

The industry is also of significant importance to the country in that:

1 Tourism as a proportion of the gross domestic product (GDP), which is the measure of the total output of goods and services in the economy, has remained between 3.1 per cent and 3.8 per cent since 1977.
2 The value of tourism spending as part of total consumer spending shows that all tourism spending represents about 6 per cent of all consumer spending, worth £20.2 billion for 1990 alone.
3 To the above figure a further £5.2 billion needs to be added. This represents the amount calculated for spending by domestic leisure day visitors – making a total for tourism-related spending in 1990 of £25.4 billion.
4 The hotel and catering industry attracts 45 per cent of all tourism expenditure (HCITB, 1988).
5 The largest amount of expenditure is in accommodation (35.0 per cent) and eating out (23.2 per cent) (BTA, 1991).

The size of the industry

The industry is normally seen to be in two broad divisions, each containing specific sectors of the industry. The broad divisions are between those sectors of the industry that operate on a commercial basis and those that operate with some form of subsidy.

Those that operate on a commercial basis tend to be in the private sector of business, where profit is a main objective, serving the general public and for which the service of food and beverages (and at times accommodation) is the main activity of the business (e.g. restaurants, public houses, hotels, etc.).

The subsidized institutional and welfare, or cost, division consists of those businesses which are in the public sector, where the provision of food and beverages (and at times accommodation) is only a secondary activity of the business, where profit is not a main objective and for which the market for customers is normally restricted (e.g. hospitals, schools, industrial canteens, prisons, etc.).

Analysis of the commercial division is somewhat easier, as statistics are more readily available because of the major interest in profit and of the

Table 1.1   Breakdown of catering businesses by turnover, 1990

Turnover (£000)	No. of businesses	Per cent
23–50	33,705	27
51–100	41,848	33
101–250	38,348	30
251–500	8,760	7
501–1,000	2,716	2
1,001–5,000	1,354	1
Over 5,000	254	*
Total	126,985	100

*Less than 0.5.
Source: Butter Council/Key Note Publication (1991). Crown Copyright. Reproduced with the permission of the controller of Her Majesty's Stationery Office.

government interest in businesses that are required to pay VAT. An analysis of commercial catering businesses in 1990 by turnover (Table 1.1) identified the following:

● This division of the industry is made up of a very large number of small locally based single outlet businesses owned mainly by sole proprietors (37.5 per cent) or partnerships (39.2 per cent) (Key Note Publication, 1992).
● Ninety per cent of all businesses had a turnover of £250,000 or less, and 60 per cent averaged less than £100,000.
● Conversely, there were only 1,608 businesses with a turnover exceeding £1 million, i.e. 1.3 per cent of the total of 126,985.

An analysis of the commercial catering division by the number of UK catering businesses, 1980–90 (Table 1.2) shows an overall growth of some 14.1 per cent.

From 1986, significant growth has been made by contract caterers, holiday camping and caravan sites and eating out places (EOPs) including restaurants, cafes and snack bars. A decline in the number of public houses has been due almost totally to the 1989 Monopolies and Mergers Commission report restricting the number of pubs that a brewer could own.

Table 1.2 Commercial catering – number of businesses ('000) by sector, 1980–90

	1980	1986	1987	1988	1989	1990
Hotels and other residential establishments	14.3	12.9	13.0	13.6	14.0	14.4
Holiday camps, camping and holiday caravan sites	1.6	1.6	1.6	1.6	1.9	2.0
Restaurants, cafes and snack bars selling food for on-premises consumption	11.5	14.3	15.2	16.3	17.3	17.8
Fish and chip shops, sandwich and snack bars selling food partly or wholly for consumption off the premises	22.7	28.4	28.7	29.1	29.9	30.9
Public houses	40.6	42.9	42.9	42.1	41.3	40.2
Clubs	17.6	18.0	17.8	17.3	17.3	16.8
Catering contractors	1.2	1.7	1.9	2.2	2.5	2.7
Total	109.5	119.9	121.1	122.3	124.3	124.9

Source: Business Monitor PA 1003. Crown Copyright. Reproduced with the permission of the Controller of Her Majesty's Stationery Office.

This resulted in the big brewers selling or leasing pubs to get their numbers down with the least profitable pubs being unsaleable and closing down (Davidson, 1992). A decline in the number of clubs over the same period repeats the general decline in the number of clubs during the early 1980s recession (Key Note Publication, 1992).

An analysis of the commercial division by annual turnover, as given in Table 1.3, shows growth in all sectors over the period 1980–90. Of particular note here is that:

- The average turnover of catering businesses more than doubled during the period.
- The total turnover of catering businesses increased by 2.47 times.
- Public houses had the largest turnover of £10,648 million, followed by hotels with £6,370 million.
- Catering contractors had the largest increase in turnover of some 3.58 times.

It should be noted that the above data only refer to those businesses that are required to register for VAT and do not include those thousands of small businesses that are excluded from paying VAT.

A further indication of the size of the commercial division is given in *The UK Catering Market* (Key Note Publication, 1991). According to this report, the total number of meals served by this division in 1990 was 5,558 million, the average number of meals served per outlet was 23,350, and the division served 61.4 per cent of all meals served by the industry.

Table 1.3 Commercial catering – turnover of catering establishments (£mn, inc. VAT) by sector, 1980–90

	1980	1986	1987	1988	1989	1990
Hotels and other residential establishments	2,483	4,279	4,781	5,514	5,892	6,370
Holiday camps, camping and holiday caravan sites	405	567	590	696	843	939
Restaurants, cafes and snack bars selling food for on-premises consumption	1,431	2,260	3,064	3,192	3,588	3,906
Fish and chip shops, sandwich and snack bars selling food partly or wholly for consumption off the premises	1,103	2,435	2,826	3,377	3,682	4,162
Public houses	4,857	8,043	8,274	8,716	9,712	10,648
Clubs	1,570	2,203	2,288	2,387	2,401	2,587
Catering contractors	575	1,183	1,288	1,525	1,642	2,059
Total	12,424	20,971	23,111	25,406	27,760	30,672
Average turnover of catering businesses (£000)	113	175	191	207	223	246

Source: Business Monitor PA 1003. Crown Copyright. Reproduced with the permission of the Controller of Her Majesty's Stationery Office.

Analysis of the non-commercial, cost or welfare and subsidized division of the industry is more difficult (Table 1.4). This is because the activity of providing food and beverages (and at times accommodation) is only a secondary activity of the business, turnover and profit are not main objectives and the market for customers is normally restricted. Of note here

Table 1.4 Non-commercial catering – number of catering businesses by sector. 1991

Sector	Total	Sector	Total
Staff catering		*Public services*	
Self-run/industrial/commercial	12,630	Armed forces	426
Contracted	7,100	Prisons	108
National/local government	4,220	Young offenders	39
Off-shore canteens	40	Police stations	575
Total	23,720	Fire stations	375
		Total	1,523
Health care			
NHS		*Welfare feeding*	
Hospitals/clinics	2,440	Local authority	219
Homes	4,945	Voluntary	1,310
Sub-total	7,385	Total	1,529
Private		Grand total	82,397
Hospitals/clinics	290		
Nursing homes	3,010		
Residential homes	11,260		
Sub-total	14,560		
Total	21,945		
Education			
Nursery	1,275		
Primary	22,905		
Secondary	4,650		
Special	1,710		
University	46		
Polytechnic	30		
Further and higher education	494		
Sub-total	31,110		
Private education	2,570		
Total	33,680		

Source: Marketpower (1991). Crown Copyright. Reproduced with the permission of the Controller of Her Majesty's Stationery Office.

is that there is very little movement, either of growth or decline, in the non-commercial division, as suggested by Davis and Stone (1991, p. 5).

A further indication of the size of the non-commercial division is given in the previously mentioned Key Note Publication (1991), where it is stated that the total number of meals served by the division in 1990 was 3,492 million, the average number per outlet was 42,240, and that this division served 38.6 per cent of all meals served.

The Consumer

Age structure

It is important for executives in the industry to be fully aware of the age structure of the UK population and of the population changes by regions, as an aide to forward planning. As can be seen from Table 1.5, there has been a growth in the number of persons age over 65 years of some 1.7 million in the period 1971–91, with a further gradual increase forecast to 2011. In

Table 1.5   Structure of UK population (millions), 1971–2011

	1971	1981	1991	1996	2001	2006	2011
Under 16	14.3	12.5	11.7	12.3	12.6	12.5	12.1
16–39	17.5	19.7	20.3	19.9	19.3	18.4	18.0
40–64	16.7	15.7	16.5	17.1	18.1	19.5	20.2
65–79	6.1	6.9	6.9	6.8	6.7	6.7	7.0
80 and over	1.3	1.6	2.2	2.4	2.5	2.6	2.7
Total	55.5	56.4	57.6	58.5	59.2	59.7	60.0

Source: Office of Population Censuses and Surveys (based on 1989 projections). Crown Copyright. Reproduced with the permission of the Controller of Her Majesty's Stationery Office.

comparison, the under 16 age group has shown a decline of some 2.8 million over the same period. Further to the above, it should be noted that the ethnic minority population, that makes up some 2.6 million of the total population, has shown an almost total reversal of this trend, with the vast majority being in the under 16 age band.

The counties with the fastest growing population between 1981 and 1990 were Buckinghamshire and Cambridgeshire, at 1.3 per cent per annum. Belfast and the Islands of Scotland experienced the largest fall in population, both of 0.7 per cent per annum. In general, there was a movement of the population from metropolitan areas to non-metropolitan areas (Social Trends 22, 1992).

Household structure

One of the most significant features in the past twenty years has been the increase in the number of single- and two-person households (Table 1.6). The increase in one-person households includes not only those over pensionable age (12–15 per cent), but those under pensionable age (6–11 per cent), particularly men, where numbers have risen from 4 per cent to 7 per cent. With 26 per cent of the population now being one-person households, there is clearly an important marketing opportunity for the hotel and catering industry.

Table 1.6   Households in Great Britain by type (%) 1971–91

	1971	*1981*	*1991*
One-person households			
under pensionable age	6	8	11
over pensionable age	12	14	15
Two or more unrelated adults	4	5	3
One-family households			
married couples, no children	27	26	28
1–2 dependent children	26	25	20
3+ dependent children	9	6	4
non-dependent children	8	8	8
Single parent with			
dependent children	3	5	6
non-dependent children	4	4	4
Two or more families	1	1	1
Total	100	100	100

Source: Social Trends 22 (1992). Crown Copyright. Reproduced with the permission of the Controller of Her Majesty's Stationery Office.

As seen in Table 1.6, the proportion of households with dependent children (married couples and single parents) declined between 1971 and 1991 from 38 per cent to 30 per cent of total households, reflecting the falling birth rate from the mid-1960s. This information is of some importance to the fast food and EOP sectors of the industry.

Expenditure on food

The average expenditure on household food and on meals eaten away from home (£ expenditure per household per week) has shown increases over the past ten years mainly as a result of inflation, increases in income and a small increase in eating out (Table 1.7). The total average expenditure on food per household increased by 76.35 per cent between 1979 and 1990, with the average expenditure on household food per household per week increasing by 62.1 per cent, but the average expenditure on meals away from home increasing by 163.1 per cent. Of note here to the industry is that expenditure on meals eaten away from home has grown from 14.1 per cent of the total expenditure on food in 1979 to represent 21.0 per cent by 1990.

Table 1.7   Average expenditure on household food and on meals away from home (£ per household per week), 1979–1990

	1979	1984	1989	1990
Household food*	21.83	26.07	32.99	35.39
Meals away from home	3.58	5.36	8.68	9.42
Total expenditure on food	25.41	31.43	41.67	44.81

* Includes soft drinks, chocolate and sugar confectionery.
Source: Family Expenditure Survey/Social Trends 22 (1992).Crown Copyright. Reproduced with the permission of the Controller of Her Majesty's Stationery Office.

Of further interest is the average amount of money spent on alcohol away from home compared with the amount spent on meals away from home analysed by bands of household weekly income. A higher percentage of the total expenditure is spent on average on alcohol until the £426–476 household income is reached (Table 1.8).

The gross weekly earnings of full-time employees in 1990 given in Social Trends 22 (1992) was £295.60 (mean) and £258.20 (median) for all male employees, and £201.50 (mean) and £177.50 (median) for all female employees.

Eating out

The frequency of meals eaten out away from home depends on two main factors, the socioeconomic grouping and the size of the household. Data on the meals eaten away from home in Table 1.9 show that the economic climate has made most groups cut back on the frequency of eating out, with the exception of the E1 and E2 groups. Expenditure on meals away from

Table 1.8 Average expenditure on meals and alcohol consumed away from home (£ by household weekly income), 1990

Income (£)	Alcohol	Meals
Under 60	2.17	1.58
60–80	2.23	1.43
81–100	2.90	1.92
101–125	4.37	2.99
126–150	4.43	3.92
151–175	5.91	4.44
176–225	7.48	6.37
226–275	9.67	7.76
276–325	10.31	9.04
326–375	12.15	10.24
376–425	12.13	10.83
426–475	13.39	13.09
476–550	14.49	15.66
551–650	16.63	16.39
651–800	20.88	21.05
800 +	24.46	28.87
Average all incomes	10.01	9.42

Source: Family Expenditure Survey (1990). Crown Copyright. Reproduced with the permission of the Controller of Her Majesty's Stationery Office.

Table 1.9 Meals eaten away from home, by socioeconomic group

	Average number of meals per person per week		
	1987	1989	1990
A1	5.42	6.23	5.11
A2	4.70	4.89	4.64
B	3.97	4.27	4.15
C	3.57	3.95	3.83
D	3.13	3.33	3.16
E1	2.09	2.45	2.83
E2	2.64	2.57	2.75

Source: Household Food Consumption and Expenditure Survey (1990). Crown Copyright. Reproduced with the permission of the Controller of Her Majesty's Stationery Office.

Table 1.10   Patterns of consumption of meals eaten away from home by socioeconomic group, 1990

	Average number of meals per person per week		
	Midday meal	Other meals	All meals
A1	2.58	2.53	5.11
A2	2.40	2.24	4.64
B	2.16	1.99	4.15
C	2.04	1.79	3.83
D	1.76	1.40	3.16
E1	1.09	1.74	2.83
E2	1.31	1.44	2.75
OAP	0.81	1.20	2.01

Source: Household Food Consumption and Expenditure Survey (1990). Crown Copyright. Reproduced with the permission of the Controller of Her Majesty's Stationery Office.

home rises with family income, such that households with a gross income in excess of £800 per week will spend 18.2 times as much as those with an income of less than £60. Similarly, the figures for combined alcohol and meal expenditure show that households having a gross income in excess of £800 will spend 14.2 times more than those with an income of less than £60.

Table 1.11   Frequency of eating out (%), 1991

	Men	Women	All adults
Never	23	22	22
Less than once a year	18	18	18
1–2 times a year	9	15	12
A few times a year	18	21	20
Once a month	16	13	15
Once a fortnight	6	5	5
Once a week	6	4	5
Several times a week	3	1	2
Total	100	100	100

Source: Butter Council. Crown Copyright. Reproduced with the permission of the Controller of Her Majesty's Stationery Office.

Further analysis of the data for 1990 (Table 1.10) shows the breakdown between the midday meal and other meals. Midday meals, with the exception of the E1, E2 and OAP groups, are a major element of the total of all meals consumed away from the home.

The frequency of adults eating out in 1991 is shown in Table 1.11. Significant here is the fact that 40 per cent of adults eat out less than once a year and 52 per cent eat out only 1–2 times a year, with only some 12 per cent of adults being able to be classed as regulars – those eating out more than once every two weeks. The opportunities available to caterers, particularly in the commercial division of the industry, are self-evident.

Leisure time

Of importance to executives in the hotel and catering industry is the amount of leisure time available to people in a typical week. With the trend in the past twenty-five years being towards a gradual reduction in the basic working hours per week and an increasing entitlement to paid holidays, more free time is available for people to pursue activities which they had not time for previously. In 1990, nine out ten full-time employees were entitled to more than four weeks' holiday and three out of ten were entitled to at least five weeks' holiday. (Social Trends 22, 1992).

As can be seen from Table 1.12, the amount of free time per week is surprisingly large. However, existing and potential customers do not have

Table 1.12 Time use in a typical week by employment status and sex, 1990–91

Weekly hours spent on	Full-time employee		Part-time employee	House-wives	Retired
	Male	Female	Female		
Employment and travel[1]	48.3	42.6	20.9	0.3	0.7
Essential activities[2]	24.1	39.6	52.1	58.4	33.0
Sleep[3]	49.0	49.0	49.0	49.0	49.0
Free time	46.6	36.8	46.0	60.3	85.3
Free time per week day	4.5	3.3	5.4	8.4	11.6
Free time per weekend day	12.1	10.3	9.5	9.3	13.6

[1] Travel to and from place of work.
[2] Essential domestic work including shopping, child care, cooking, personal hygiene and appearance.
[3] An average of 7 hours sleep is assumed.
Source: Social Trends 22 (1992).Crown Copyright. Reproduced with the permission of the Controller of Her Majesty's Stationery Office.

an expanding amount of disposable income, and it is how they wish to spend their money with an increasing amount of leisure time available, and with increasing competition from all types of leisure businesses, that will be part of the challenge in the near future, particularly to commercial caterers.

Employment in the hotel and catering industry

The difficulties faced in identifying reliable statistics to define the size and structure of the industry are, if anything, even more complex when trying to establish the dimensions of employment in the industry. This does seem a rather sorry state of affairs for an industry that, by any definition, must be one of the top five employers in the UK economy.

According to the *Tourism Intelligence Quarterly* (1993), tourism-related industries employed an estimated 1,412,200 people in December 1992. In addition, the industries had around 183,000 self-employed. Taking self-employed and employees together, this total of employment represents just over 6 per cent of all the employed labour force in December 1992.

The above definition of tourism related industries is based on the SIC classification and includes SIC 661: restaurants, cafes and takeaways, SIC 662: public houses and bars, SIC 663: night clubs and licensed clubs, SIC 665 and 667: hotels and other tourist accommodation, as well as SIC 977 and 979: libraries, museums, art galleries, sports and other recreational services. This last sector alone accounts for around 400,000 employees but does not represent a large part of food and beverage employment. Neither does this figure take into account the non-commercial sector of the hotel and catering industry. An estimate of employment in the hotel and catering industry is given in Table 1.13.

This table is a composite from a number of sources as at June 1992 and allows a comparison between the number of outlets in each of the identified sectors and the number of people employed in them. The largest sector in terms of employment is public houses and bars which account for around 26 per cent of total employment with some 325,000 employees. The second largest employer is the hotels sector with a 23 per cent share of employment, accounting for 285,000 employees. In third place, with a 20 per cent share of employment, are restaurants and cafes excluding takeaways. Surprisingly for the largest sector in terms of number of outlets, some 83,000, the non-commercial sector has only an 11 per cent share of the employees at 140,000 people. This does seem to bring into question the accuracy of these figures.

The final column of Table 1.13 uses the data supplied to calculate the average number of employees per outlet and once again there seem to be some anomalies in the data. The highest number of employees per outlet is in the restaurants and cafes sector, with an average of eight employees per unit. This does seem comparatively high for a sector composed of a large number of very small units. The hotels sector also consists of units of very small size, but an average overall of only five employees per unit seems rather low, especially when compared with the public houses and bars sector which averages the same number. In comparison, the non-commercial sector tends to include some very large units, but the average number of employees per outlet barely reaches two. The accuracy of the data is

Table 1.13   Hotel and catering – Outlets and employees, June 1992

	Number of outlets (000)	Per cent share	No. of employees (000)	Per cent share	Average emps/ outlet
Restaurants, cafes, etc.	33	11	250	20	8
Takeaways	17	5	55	4	3
Public houses and bars	62	20	325	26	5
Hotels and other tourist accommodation	60	19	285	23	5
Other commercial (clubs, leisure, etc.)	55	18	190	15	3
Non-commercial (schools, canteens, hospitals etc.)	83	27	140	11	2
Total	310	100	1,245	100	4

Source: Marketpower/Key Note/*Employment Gazette*. Crown Copyright. Reproduced with the permission of the Controller of Her Majesty's Stationery Office.

questionable, but until a better statistical base for the industry is found then they are the best we have available and at least form a basis for comparison.

Table 1.14 shows the trend in employment from 1986 until 1990. It shows a period of sustained and considerable growth in employment across most sectors of the industry. In particular, the restaurants, cafes and snack bars sector showed the strongest growth, moving from 224,000 employees in 1986 to 310,000 in 1990 – an increase of some 38 per cent. Public houses and bars showed a 29 per cent growth over the same period, while hotels managed 21 per cent growth. The picture after 1990 is not as rosy. The recession had by then begun to take its toll and Table 1.15 shows that every sector had lost employees following a peak in 1990. Some return to growth is, however, evident in the period 1991–92 in the restaurants and public

Table 1.14 Employment in hotel and catering by sector ('000), 1986–90

	1986	1988	1989	1990	Per cent change 1986–90
Hotels	249	265	288	301	21
Restaurants, cafes and snack bars	224	262	288	310	38
Public houses and bars	259	295	327	334	29
Nightclubs and licensed clubs	138	141	142	145	5
Total commercial	870	963	1,045	1,090	25
Contract caterers	156	142	153	162	4
All industry	1,026	1,105	1,198	1,252	22

Source: Key Note Publications Ltd/Department of Employment, (1991). Crown Copyright. Reproduced with the permission of the Controller of Her Majesty's Stationery Office.

houses sectors, with the hotels sector holding steady but clubs still continuing to fall.

The pattern of reduction in the number of employees has not been consistent over all sectors of the industry, neither has it been consistent across all regions of the country. According to Church and Bull (1993a, 1993b), hotel and catering employment lost 23,000 jobs nationally, a decline of 2 per cent, between 1989 and 1991. Thirty-eight of the sixty-six counties and regions of the UK showed this downward trend, but surprisingly at a

Table 1.15 Employment in tourism-related industries ('000) in Great Britain, December 1992

SIC group	1989	1990	1991	1992	Per cent change 1991–92
Hotels and other tourist accommodation	280.4	293.8	271.2	271.3	*
Restaurants, cafes and snack bars	297.0	306.3	287.9	294.8	+ 2.4
Public houses and bars	338.2	338.4	320.9	329.1	+ 2.6
Nightclubs and licensed clubs	143.9	147.7	140.4	137.3	-2.2
Total	1,060	1,086	1,020	1,033	+ 1.2

*Less than 0.5 per cent.
Source: Employment Department, 1992. Crown Copyright. Reproduced with the permission of the Controller of Her Majesty's Stationery Office.

time when total national employment fell by 3 per cent, twenty-eight counties or regions showed an expansion in hotel and catering employment. A detailed analysis of the regional breakdown of employment patterns is outside the scope of this review and can be found elsewhere (Bull and Church, 1993).

Another aspect of the variability of employment in hotel and catering concerns the seasonality of employment in different sectors. Figure 1.2 shows the seasonal pattern of employment by quarter through 1989 to 1991 for three sectors of the industry.

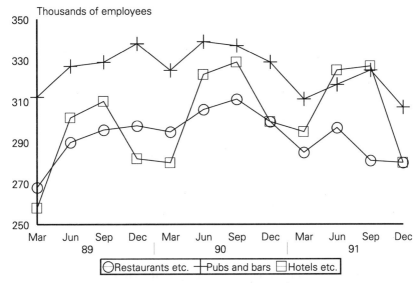

Figure 1.2 Seasonal patterns of employment in three sectors of the industry (*Source: Employment Gazette*. Crown Copyright. Reproduced with the permission of the Controller of Her Majesty's Stationery Office)

In general terms, the first quarter of the year is the lowest for employment but there is a sharp rise into the second quarter. The third quarter shows the peak level of employment, while the last quarter drops away but not as far as first quarter levels. Taking each sector in turn, the public houses and bars sector shows the lowest level of variation across the year and a somewhat moveable peak. In 1989 the peak quarter was the last quarter, in 1990 it was the second quarter but the third quarter in 1991. The restaurant sector shows a slightly more pronounced seasonal pattern but less of a fall in the last quarter as restaurants are geared up for the pre-Christmas rush. The hotel sector shows the strongest pattern of seasonality with a much greater range than the other two sectors. The most likely explanation for this is the seasonal nature of domestic tourism which still forms a major part of hotel demand.

Another dimension of employment patterns is the breakdown of employment by gender and by full time versus part time employment. Table 1.16 shows this breakdown for the restaurants, snack bars and cafes sector by way of an example.

Female employees make up nearly two-thirds of all employees in this sector of the industry with a total of 185,700 out of a total of 296,500 employees. Male employees account for 110,800 of this total or around 37.4 per cent. Of the total number of employees, around 121,800 are employed on a full-time basis, while 174,700 or 58.9 per cent are employed on a part-time basis. This pattern is not consistent, however, between male and female

Table 1.16   Employment in restaurants, snack bars, cafes, etc., in Great Britain ('000), November 1992

	Full time	Per cent	Part time	Per cent	Total	Per cent
Male	68.8	23.2	42.0	14.2	110.8	37.4
Female	53.0	17.9	132.7	44.7	185.7	62.6
Total	121.8	41.1	174.7	58.9	296.5	100

Source: *Employment Gazette* (1992). Crown Copyright. Reproduced with the permission of the Controller of Her Majesty's Stationery Office.

employees. Of male employees, 62 per cent are full time and only 38 per cent are part time. On the other hand, 41 per cent of female employees are full time and 59 per cent are part time. Similar patterns can be found across most other sectors of the industry.

Conclusions

The picture painted above is of an industry composed of many different sectors, each with its own particular approaches and concerns. Techniques and procedures that are successful in one sector of the industry may not seem to be appropriate for other sectors. However, it is possible to identify a number of characteristics which are common to all sectors of the industry (Lockwood 1993):

1 *The central importance of the customer.* Hospitality cannot be delivered without the presence of the customer who also provides the source of

revenue for the continued financial success of the operation. The customer is directly involved in many aspects of the delivery of the food and beverage service. The combination of all customers determines the demand pattern for the operation. One customer forms part of the environment for all other customers. The customer is the final arbiter of satisfaction with both the service and product elements and therefore the judge of the quality of hospitality provided. Given these factors, it is perhaps surprising that some hospitality providers still think they know better than the customer.

2 *The criticality of capacity utilization.* Achieving a satisfactory balance between demand patterns, resource scheduling and operational capacity is one of the most difficult tasks facing food and beverage managers. Managing customer demand to result in the optimum volume at maximum value is extremely complex. Too few customers overall, and the cost structure of the business ensures financial ruin. Too many customers without the required capacity or resources, and the quality of the experience suffers and customers leave dissatisfied. Customer volume can be bought by discounting prices at the expense of value per customer. Not discounting can scare potential customers away to the competition. Yield management is crucial, both for accommodation and for food and beverage operations. Scheduling of resources is also critical. Too many staff on duty to cover anticipated demand, and productivity and profitability suffer. Too few staff on duty, and service levels fall along with staff morale. The key here would seem to be effective forecasting and yet little progress has been made in unravelling demand patterns to provide accurate predictions. Many operations still rely on the equivalent of a wet finger.

3 *The complexity of operation.* All food and beverage operations require a combination of manufacturing expertise and service skill in a business which operates around the clock, 365 days a year, and is busiest when most other businesses are not. To consistently deliver an appropriate level of product and service to each individual customer requires the efforts of many different teams of staff who must be co-ordinated to deliver to standard every time. Catering for the needs of a single customer may be difficult enough, but catering to the needs of many different groups of customers all with slightly different requirements multiplies the complexity of the problem many times over. The importance of a co-ordinated team effort between the different functional groups of employees is self-evident and yet the industry maintains organizational structures and occupational boundaries which directly contradict this objective.

4 *The reliance on service contact staff.* However well planned and designed the hospitality operation is, and however well scheduled the resources, in the final analysis the success of any customer experience will be determined at 'the moment of truth' – the interaction between the customer and the

service provider. A highly skilled chef can spend many hours preparing the finest dishes and yet they can be ruined by the lack of care of the waiter. The point of contact between the customer and service provider is also an opportunity for the operation to sell its service and to generate additional revenue. Service staff significantly increase the profitability of their operations by upselling – encouraging customers to trade up to more profitable and probably more expensive menu items. Referral of business from one operation in a chain to another can also provide added revenue. It is all the more surprising then, that given the key role the service provider has in ensuring customer satisfaction and in improving revenue and profit levels, they still remain some of the least well paid and least respected members of staff (Guerrier and Lockwood, 1989).

In terms of these key dimensions, the similarities between the various sectors of the industry may well be stronger than the differences.

References

BTA (1991), Tourism Fact Sheet. London: British Tourist Authority.

BTA/ETB Economic Research (1993). *Tourism Intelligence Quarterly*, **15**(1), 27–28.

Bull, P. and Church, A. (1993). The hotel and catering industry of Great Britain during the 1980s: sub-regional employment change, specialization and dominance. In C. P. Cooper and A. Lockwood (eds), *Progress in Tourism Recreation and Hospitality Management*, Vol. 5. Chichester: Wiley, pp. 248 *et seq*.

Butter Council/Key Note Publication (1991). *The UK Catering Market*. London: Key Note Publications Ltd.

Church, A. and Bull, P. (1993a). Uneven industry job losses. *Caterer and Hotelkeeper*, 21 October, p. 28.

Church, A. and Bull, P. (1993b). An unlikely spot for a boom. *Caterer and Hotelkeeper*, 28 October, p. 30.

Davis, B. and Stone, S. (1991). *Food and Beverage Management*, 2nd. edn. Oxford: Butterworth-Heinemann.

Davidson, H. (1992). Beer orders fall flat as prices soar. *The Sunday Times*, 11 October.

EIU Special Report No. 2169 (1993). London: Economist Intelligence Unit, p. 1.

Guerrier, Y. and Lockwood, A. (1989). Core and peripheral employees in hotel operations. *Personnel Review*, **18**(1), 9–15.

HCITB Research Unit (1988). *A Growing Force*. London: HCITB.

Key Note Publication (1993). *Restaurants – A Market Sector Overview*, 8th edition. London: Key Note Publications Ltd.

Key Note Publication (1992). *The UK Catering Market*. London: Key Note Publications Ltd.

Lockwood, A. (1993). Hospitality concerns. Paper presented at conference on 'A Geography of the British Hospitality Industry', Birkbeck College, University of London, 16 September.

Medlik, S. (1978). *Profile of the Hotel and Catering Industry*. London: Heinemann.

Social Trends 22 (1992). London: HMSO.

Tourism Intelligence Quarterly (1993). BTA/ETB Research Services. London: BTA/ETB.

Part One

Strategic
Considerations

2 Towards a theoretically based, but practicably workable model of strategic decision-making

Haydn Ingram

Introduction

To what extent should managers adopt a scientific and systematic way of making decisions? The primary managerial role *is* to make decisions (Mintzberg, 1973) and those decisions, in turn, affect performance and people in the business organization. All managers are involved in strategic decision-making at various levels in their organization (Johnson and Scholes, 1989) and so need to be aware of the ways in which decisions are made.

This chapter will explore a systematic model of strategic decision-making in food and beverage operations and consider its value to the busy professional practitioner.

What are decisions, anyway?

The *Concise Oxford Dictionary* defines decision-making as a mechanism for the resolution of a question or choice between alternatives which involves the judgement of the decision-maker(s). Decision-making is, therefore, an active and conclusive process to which a commitment to a new course of action is made.

Strategic decisions are important decisions which permit an organization to determine and implement policies which enable it to achieve its goals and objectives (Bowman and Asch, 1989), but management decisions may be categorized differently. Each functional manager will be faced by different types of decisions. The personnel manager, for instance, whose prime concern is to manage the organization's human resources will face very different decisions to the company's chef or maintenance manager.

Two important factors differentiate management decisions: structure and dependence. Structured decisions are distinctive and clear, whereas unstructured decisions are ambiguous and difficult to analyse and therefore, to solve.

The other category concerns present decisions which are dependent upon what has been decided in the past. If, for instance, an independent restaurant has borrowed money in obtaining leasehold premises, its trading decisions would be geared up to servicing loan repayments and rent on the property.

Who makes strategic decisions?

Corporate strategy concerns planning for the long term (Merricks and Jones, 1986) and therefore more important decisions are resolved at the higher levels of management. Wider managerial responsibilities usually involve wider scope for making decisions, but, as stated in the introduction, *all* managers make strategic decisions.

Hofer and Schendel (1978) and Ansoff (1979) suggest that strategic decision-making can be classified into three levels, depending upon the

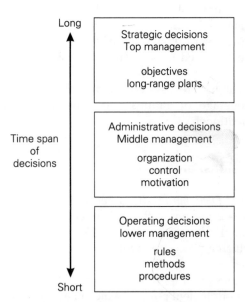

Figure 2.1 Levels of decision-making

nature of the decision (Figure 2.1). Corporate decisions are unprogrammed ones which affect long-term organizational objectives and plans, and are usually conceived by top management. Middle management are concerned with the administration of the business, while lower managers involve themselves mostly with operational decisions.

This 'top-down' approach to formulating strategic decisions implies that decisions taken at higher levels of management are implemented by those at lower levels. Thus, strategic decisions have wide effects throughout the whole organization.

Service industries differ from manufacturing industry in that they entail a greater involvement with the consumer of the service – the customer. Managers in food and beverage units will spend a large part of their working day in interfacing with staff and customers, and the decisions they make will be non-programmed, people-oriented decisions. This explains why managerial life at the operational 'sharp end' is so interesting, and often frustrating.

In what circumstances are strategic decisions made?

Change

> In a changing world, the only constant is change. (Carnall, 1990)

Strategic change follows four basic patterns (Figure 2.2). Henry Mintzberg's studies of organizations over decades suggest that the typical strategic change was an incremental or piecemeal one. Organizations experienced

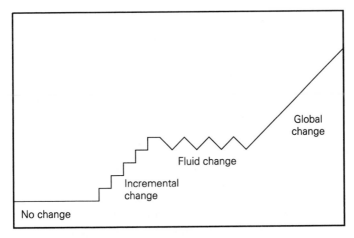

Figure 2.2 Strategic decisions as lines on a graph

periods of continuity, in which there was stability and other periods of fluid, erratic change characterized by strategies which followed different directions.

Global changes in strategies followed major crises, particularly when the company was threatened by the effects of dramatically reduced sales or profits.

The decision environment

Another major factor affecting decisions is the environment in which they are made. Cooke and Slack (1991) define an organization's environment as 'the totality of circumstances under which the organisation operates' and suggest that a successful interface with the environment will lead to increased business performance. The specific environment concerns the regular interface with, for example, customers, suppliers, police, local government offices and perhaps competitors.

The general environment concerns wider issues like the state of the economy, and trends in culture, technology or behaviour.

The strategic dilemma lies in being aware of changes in that environment and being sufficiently flexible to respond to them. For managers in food and beverage operations, the prime responsiveness lies in the determination of the changing needs of customers and of ways of fulfilling those needs. Businesses who do not adapt to these environmental changes may fail.

The task of managers in making decisions is made more difficult when the environment becomes more dynamic or complex (Mintzberg, 1979). In a stable environment, decisions can be based on historical strategies with the outcomes in little doubt, but a dynamic environment brings about uncertainty and makes forecasting more difficult.

Simple environments permit organizations to more easily acquire the necessary knowledge of products and consumers in order to be successful. Where, however, such knowledge has to be more sophisticated or where environmental influences are increasing, the environment is said to be complex.

The decision environment in which food and beverage operations operate at present could be described as both complex and dynamic. Customer expectations and perceptions of value are changing, together with pressures from government bodies, to conform to specific operating and financial standards. Business failure in the sector is growing, due to competition from national and international chains with carefully designed products and service systems.

The typical food and beverage unit, however, is likely to be small and independent, with low sales per unit, and its manager usually spends at least part of his working day 'on the shop floor.' If the view of Merricks and

Jones (1986) is correct, that catering is the last UK cottage industry of the twentieth century, its managers must transcend the parochial view and ensure that they are aware and responsive to this increasingly complex and dynamic environment in the wide world across the threshold.

What makes a good decision?

Prescott (1980) postulates that the quality of a decision may be measured by:

- The achievement of the aim
- The cost of implementation
- The time taken to implement the decision

In addition, the decision must be acceptable to those who may be affected by its consequences and by those who will have to implement the decision. Some stakeholders may be:

- Superiors
- Subordinates
- Unions
- Outside persons (suppliers, customers)
- Outside bodies (regulatory, e.g. Customs and Excise)
- Shareholders

An effective decision, without the benefit of perfect hindsight, could then be defined as the highest quality decision which is acceptable to all the affected stakeholders.

Cooke and Slack (1991) suggest that decision quality should be judged by the appropriateness of the decision process selected and the accuracy of the choice. There are, however, some assumptions made about rationality, rather like those of economic theory. It is assumed that:

1 The decision-maker will act in a rational and logical manner. His preferences will remain consistent.
2 He will be offered clear alternatives to which an outcome will be evaluated and his aim will be to maximize satisfaction by selecting the choice which offers the greatest value.
3 Perfect, unlimited and complete knowledge is available.
4 Each member of a decision-making group will share the same goals and objectives.

These assumptions are clearly just as obtainable as perfect hindsight in advance, but they serve to demonstrate some of the constraints which affect the quality of a decision.

A theoretical model of decision-making

There are distinct stages which are taken in reaching a decision, ranging from the initial motivation to act, through to the review of the results of the decision. All of us, in taking constant decisions in our daily lives, unconsciously go through this process, especially where there are new circumstances which have not previously been experienced. For organizations, strategic decisions are often concerned with the allocation of human and financial resources, the results of which will reflect upon the standing in the organization of those who are responsible for the decision. Small wonder then that some decision-makers reflect carefully upon important decisions and take the view of Mumford and Pettigrew (1975) that the application of rational principles in a systematic framework will lead to improved decision-making and better business performance.

P	Prioritize objectives
R	Recognize problem
O	Organize information search
B	Brainstorm options
L	Logical evaluation
E	Execute chosen option
M	Monitor effects

Figure 2.3 A systematic decision-making process

There are seven stages in the decision process, which can be remembered by using the mnemonic 'PROBLEM', as shown in Figure 2.3. The stages are discussed below.

Prioritize objectives

Organizations must, first, set objectives and such corporate direction is usually effected by those who have the motivation and ability to affect the decision-making process (Gore et al., 1992). This is decision-making at the strategic level which is affected by the managers' attitudes towards leadership and profit. Johnson and Scholes (1989) advance a theory of managerial utility in which managers are concerned, not with pure profit maximization, but with adopting a defensive stance against the threat of take-overs.

Recognize problem

Problem awareness is often sensed by individuals who detect small changes in levels of profit or turnover. Further there may be some customer reaction to price or quality followed by changes in the competitive or economic environment (Johnson and Scholes, 1989).

Organize information search

Once the problem has been recognized and diagnosed, there follows a period when information must be sought in order to put the problem into perspective. What are the objective, quantifiable costs to the business in terms of cost, profit, sales, markets, competition, customers? What are the subjective implications of the problem to the organization as regards image, kudos, skills, power or politics? This stage is an important one, which involves the analysis of the internal and external environments. Frameworks such as PEST (political, economic, social, technological analysis) and SWOT (strengths, weaknesses, opportunities, threats) can assist in structuring environmental analysis. This process of organizational soul-searching is often a painful one which must be carried out in an objective and thorough fashion, which explains why businesses often call in expensive outside consultants to furnish answers which may have been known all along!

Brainstorm options

Once organizations have collected the necessary information pertaining to the problem, they will have a clearer idea of what must be done to achieve the required objectives. Some options will be apparent from management training or previous experience, but these may lack imagination or flair. Brainstorming involves groups of four to eight people who gather to develop ideas, none of which is derided, rejected or pre-judged.

Logical evaluation

This list of possible strategies must now be measured against:

- The firm's objectives
- The probable environmental situation
- The views of important stakeholders
- The organization's attitude to risk

Decisions are taken to create wealth: thus each potential strategy must be measured by the comparative wealth which it can create for the organization. In addition, this equation must be supplemented by an assessment of the likely risks involved.

Decision tree analysis is a technique of quantifying possible payoffs in chart form (Moore and Thomas,1976). In the example in Figure 2.4, a restaurant wishes to evaluate three options to increase trade:

S1 devise and implement a new menu
S2 undertake external advertising
S3 improve internal merchandising

They have calculated the risk that each option will succeed or fail, and the estimated effect of each outcome upon the restaurant's profit.

They calculate that there is a 60 per cent chance that the S1 option will increase profits to £80,000 and a corresponding 40 per cent possibility that £40,000 will be earned. The sum of these calculations will result in an

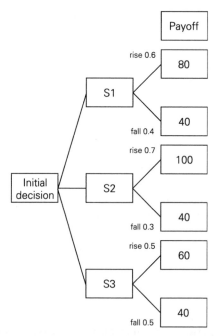

Figure 2.4 Decision tree. The outcome of each option is calculated as the estimated monetary value (EMV) as follows:

$$\text{EMV S1} = (0.6 \times 80) + (0.4 \times 40) = 64$$
$$\text{EMV S2} = (0.7 \times 100) + (0.3 \times 40) = 82$$
$$\text{EMV S3} = (0.5 \times 60) + (0.5 \times 40) = 50$$

estimated monetary value (EMV) for each option. In the example shown, the second option of external advertising (S2) appears to offer the best chance of success with an EMV of 82.

Some other financial techniques used to assist in evaluating and choosing strategies for the future are described below.

Return on investment (ROI)

$$ROI = \frac{Profit}{Investment} \times 100 \text{ per cent}$$

A ROI better than the current rate of interest would be expected by the organization.

Discounted cash flow (DCF)

DCF techniques consider the estimated costs and receipts of an investment over its anticipated lifespan in order to take account of forecasted changes in the value of money.

Breakeven analysis

Breakeven analysis attempts to classify costs into their fixed and variable elements so that expected outcomes may be projected at different levels of activity. These anticipated profits or losses can be expressed graphically to assist evaluation.

Cash flow forecasts

Not all profitable projects may generate sufficient cash to service outgoings, especially in the short term, so cash flow forecasts will predict possible shortfalls.

Sensitivity analysis

Sensitivity analysis is the identification of the effects that such key performance components as sales volume, costs and prices have on bottom-line profit. The wide availability of computer spreadsheets has enabled the value of each component to be changed and the effect of this change upon the other components to be charted.

All of these logical evaluation techniques and models described above assist the decision-maker(s) to look carefully in a formal and systematic way at the possible outcomes of their actions.

In carrying out this process, certain assumptions must be made of, for instance, the future state of the specific and general environments and the ability and willingness of the organization to fund a project.

Execute chosen option

The last section concerned itself with the selection of the optimal strategy, and this one will consider how that strategy should be implemented. It is often at this stage that the systematic rationality may fail due to the influence of that often unsystematic and irrational creature – man.

However well planned, implementation approaches often leave opportunities for discretionary behaviour by middle and operational managers whose task it is to put these strategies into effect in the organization. Those lowest in the management hierarchy spend most on strategy implementation (McCarthy et al., 1983). The major weaknesses of the 'top-down' approach to decision-making are that many managers at strategic level fail to take advantage of the customer knowledge possessed by operational managers and fail to ensure their commitment to the successful implementation of the strategy.

As a result, a good decision may be stifled by the action or inaction of those stakeholders who may be either resistant to change or unconvinced of the decision's merits.

Conclusion

In summary, some of the more quantitative, scientific ways of reaching decisions available to the practising manager by way of management theory have been considered.

In addition, some constraints to this rather too-perfect framework have been identified when uncertainty or humans enter the equation. The practice is often very different from the theory. 'Hands-on' managers in the hospitality industry are typically affected by operational and customer pressures which often appear more immediate than longer term issues.

What then, should food and beverage managers conclude?

● Operations should be 'managed' in an objective and professional way so that the longer term strategic objectives may be attained.
● The potential implications of strategic decisions need to be foreseen so that the major uncertainties can be estimated, as far as is possible.
● In order to be successful, hospitality businesses must interface with, and be adaptable to, their environment, especially where those environments are volatile and uncertain.

- Many practitioners in food and beverage operations do not enjoy the luxury of adequate time, resources and skills to adopt this purist approach. Typically, decisions must be made rapidly without resort to superiors, thus a well-meaning top management strategy may become diluted and diverted.
- The sensible formulation and successful implementation of strategic decisions will only take place when there is communication and co-operation between all managers in the organization.
- Although there is no conclusive evidence in the British hospitality industry that strategic approaches lead to business success, all texts proclaim the virtues of proactive management (Teare and Boer, 1991).
- Systematic models of decision-making are useful to facilitate logical and well-planned decisions, but many small food and beverage businesses thrive through the flair, intuition and entrepreneurial skills of their owners.

Strategic decision-making is, therefore, in itself, not a universal remedy to corporate maladies. Any intrinsic value lies in assisting those who use it to be methodical and systematic in the search for the most effective decision in the circumstances.

References

Ansoff, H. (1979). *Strategic Management*. London: Macmillan.

Bowman, C. and Asch, D. (eds) (1989). *Readings in Strategic Management*. London: Macmillan.

Carnall, C. (1990). *Managing Change in Organisations*. London: Prentice-Hall.

Cooke, S. and Slack, N. (1991). *Making Management Decisions*, 2nd edn. London: Prentice-Hall.

Drucker, P. (1973). *Management Tasks, Responsibilities and Practice*. London: Heinemann.

Gore, C., Murray, K. and Richardson, B. (1992). *Strategic Decision-Making*. London: Cassell.

Hofer, C. and Schendel, D. (1978). *Strategy Formulation: Analytical Concepts*. St.Paul, MN: West Publishing.

Johnson, G. and Scholes, K. (1989). *Exploring Corporate Strategy: Text and Cases*. London: Prentice-Hall.

McCarthy, D., Minichiello, R. and Curran, J. (1983). *Business Policy and Strategy*. New York: Irwin.

Merricks, P. and Jones, P. (1986). *The Management of Catering Operations*. London: Cassell.

Mintzberg, H. (1973). *The Nature of Managerial Work.* New York: Harper and Row.

Mintzberg, H. (1979) *The Structure of Organizations.* New York: Prenctice Hall.

Moore, P. and Thomas, H. (1976). *The Anatomy of Decisions.* London: Penguin.

Mumford, E. and Pettigrew, A. (1975). *Implementing Strategic Decisions.* Harlow, UK: Longman.

Prescott, B. (1980). *Effective Decision-Making : A Self-Development Programme.* London: Gower.

Teare, R. and Boer, A. (1991). *Strategic Hospitality Management.* London: Cassell.

3 Reviewing the performance of corporate food and beverage

Jonathan Langston and Stuart Price

Introduction

The restaurant and its auxiliary services (such as banqueting, bar and lounge and room service) are often regarded as profitable, but secondary in importance, facilities of most hotels (Solomon and Katz, 1981). Despite popular belief, however, the performance of such facilities has declined of late, with profit margins and sales (as a proportion of total hotel turnover) showing decline in North America, Australia and Asia and Latin America. This suggests that managerial focus also needs to redress the balance between accommodation and food and beverage marketing, especially in international hotels where the focus on filling bedroom space may be incongruous with filling dining rooms.

At a macro level, this reflects the level of health of the world economy represented by falling GDP and economic activity in most industrialized countries. Such declines have translated into stagnating or falling hotel occupancy levels due to lower levels of disposable income and a contraction in the budgets of businesses. Slattery and Littlejohn (1991) suggest that a correlation exists between GDP growth and service industry development and activity.

At an industry level, there have also been substantial developments in the nature and extent of competitive rivalry within free-standing restaurants, and increasing industry concentration among supermarkets, which, in addition to providing the customer with wider choice, has resulted in lower propensities for indigenous populations to utilize hotel food and beverage facilities. In key city-centre locations, for example, competition from free-standing restaurants has led to smaller hotel operations geared mainly towards residential use.

Further competition has derived from the expansion of hotel stock within the major markets of the world. In Asia and North America, for example, the concentration of hotel rooms per capita increased from 3,851 to 3,645 people and from 88 to 86 people in 1989–90 respectively.

At a business level, the management of the sales mix, i.e. the range of individual menu items, categories of menu offerings and meal categories (such as breakfast, lunch, dinner), is becoming increasingly complex, often requiring specialist knowledge and sophisticated techniques of analysing food and beverage profitability (Pavesic, 1983; Bayou and Bennett, 1992). This has led some international hotel companies, such as Holiday Inn, Travelodge, Marriott, Omni and SAS Hotels, to form joint ventures with branded restaurant chains, such as Pizza Hut, California Pizza Kitchen and Baskin-Robbins, in an attempt to improve profitability (Schneider-Wexler, 1992), reduce customer risk and capitalize from specialist knowledge of food and beverage management.

Being cognisant of these factors, the purpose of this chapter is to review the performance of food and beverage facilities (i.e. dining rooms, room service, banqueting and bar/lounge) in the main macro-areas of the world between 1989 and 1993. The two adopted measures of performance are the ratio of expenditure on food and beverages to total sales and departmental gross profit margin. These measures reflect activity within the food and beverage departments and, when compared to gross profit margin, are indicative of the extent to which sales have been pursued to the detriment of profits in order to sustain productivity and asset utilization levels. The chapter concludes by proposing a multiple regression model to test hypotheses concerning the influence of market-specific criteria on hotel food and beverage performance.

Sales volume and mix analysis

Table 3.1 shows that European and African hotels derive the highest proportion (31 per cent) of their turnover from food. This is in contrast to the smaller contributions by the North American hotels which generate only 17 per cent. As a proportion of total sales, expenditure on food within hotels in the North American and Asian/Australian markets have all declined between 1989 and 1993. Although the North American hotel food markets have been affected by recession and maturity within its foodservice sectors, the Latin American and most of the Asian economies are newly industrializing and consequently have received substantial new-entrant activity from US- and Canadian-based restaurant companies, thereby increasing competitive activity. Further decline may have been influenced by a fall in the number of visitors deriving from the USA, UK and Germany, but substantial increases from within the Asian and Australian regions. These visitors may have less of a propensity to utilize hotel food and beverage facilities in home markets than those deriving from the western economies, since they have the necessary cultural capital to use indigenous free-standing restaurants.

In contrast, the African and European regions have illustrated increasing food sales as a proportion of total turnover and have seen increased chain ownership within the hotel markets in addition to an increased proportion of guests deriving from outside the EC and USA . Further, in general, these two markets have not received the same degree of attention by US and Canadian restaurant companies as Latin America and Asia.

Table 3.1 Expenditure on food as a proportion (%) of total hotel sales

Region	1993	1992	1991	1990	1989
Africa and the Middle East	31.0	28.7	32.0	26.8	27.9
Asia and Australia	23.1	25.6	24.9	28.8	30.6
North America	17.2	21.4	21.7	20.4	18.6
Europe	31.0	30.1	30.3	29.6	29.5
Latin America	21.9	22.2	22.6	21.5	21.5
Global Mean	24.8	25.6	26.3	25.4	25.6

NB. All figures are medians and refer to chain-owned hotels. Food sales do not include meals charged by hotel management staff.
Source: *The Worldwide Hotel Industry*, Horwath International, various years.

However, the change in sales levels within the food departments has not been uniform. Within the African and Middle East hotels, the proportion of revenue deriving from the restaurant, room service and banqueting facilities has fallen between 1989 and 1993, with bar/lounge services almost doubling its contribution. This may suggest a trend toward greater informality, but is more likely to reflect down-trading, with few free restaurants offering cheaper alternatives. This latter feature is the result of an embryonic food-service industry and, consequently, a lower propensity to utilize non-hotel food and beverage facilities. Although there has been a similar increase in the proportion of revenue deriving from food in Australian and Asian hotel bar/lounge services, it does not account for a similar ratio of total turnover. As a proportion, the Middle East/African hotels generate double the revenues from bar/lounge facilities compared to those in Australia and Asia. Unlike the African/Middle East hotels, however, the proportion of sales deriving from the dining room has increased and those of room service and banqueting decreased. When taken in conjunction with stagnant occupancy levels, the increasing sales deriving from dining room facilities suggest either some form of price discounting and/or greater integration with the local markets.

The North American hotels, in contrast, show a decline in both absolute and proportionate sales deriving from dining room and room service facilities. The fall in occupancy levels (Table 3.2), combined with a

Table 3.2   Annual room occupancy (%)

Region	1993	1992	1991	1990	1989
Africa and the Middle East	60.8	59.7	63.3	65.0	58.1
Asia and Australia	69.7	67.3	70.2	76.6	69.0
North America	60.1	63.0	64.6	65.1	67.4
Europe	60.6	62.3	65.6	67.8	66.3
Latin America	58.7	53.8	67.4	62.6	70.8

Source: The Worldwide Hotel Industry, Horwath International, various years.

deterioration in the average room rate (Table 3.3), suggests that customers may have been down-trading during the period and preferred to utilize free-standing facilities rather than those of the hotel. This would also suggest some inability by the North American hotel restaurants to compete effectively with free-standing units. The ratio of dining room, room service and bar/lounge sales in European hotels have only shown slight decline, with banqueting facilities being the only food department to illustrate growth. The Latin American hotels, however, in spite of their rising average room rate levels have also shown a decline in absolute revenues deriving

Table 3.3   Average room rate (US$)

Region	1993	1992	1991	1990	1989
Africa and the Middle East	65.82	67.71	59.71	70.82	67.79
Asia and Australia	77.93	77.83	65.64	51.12	66.93
North America	55.13	73.62	72.03	64.44	64.33
Europe	77.16	79.35	80.23	68.30	70.73
Latin America	58.05	43.64	51.75	57.29	47.47

Source: The Worldwide Hotel Industry, Horwath International, various years.

from food facilities. Although unfavourable exchange rates may be partially responsible, this decline was particularly evident in banqueting facilities, but was also apparent in room service, possibly as result of declining occupancy levels. Dining room and bar/lounge departments illustrated only marginal growth levels.

It appears from these figures that the two most influential factors on hotel food and beverage sales levels have been economic recession and the growth in stand-alone facilities. The latter is in response to market demand and is, perhaps, iterated by growth in casual eating out evidenced by increases in the proportion of revenue derived from bar/lounge services.

Hotels in developed eating-out markets, such as Europe and North America, strive continually to establish a restaurant formula which will compete successfully with free-standing units. Despite the increasing sophistication of the consumer it appears, from these statistics, that hotels still suffer from a reluctance on the part of the consumer to use food and beverage facilities within hotels. This may be because the demand for hotel products is not mass consumption, unlike fast food and mid-spend restaurants; it consequently requires a more subtle approach to customer targeting and selection than those currently employed and is, in turn, a critical success factor for future profitability. The view of hotel food and beverage facilities as places for residents to eat and as venues for functions still appears to be prevalent, given that banqueting services is the only area to show growth in food and beverage revenues in Europe.

In Africa, where food sales as a proportion of total revenue has increased, it could reflect the perception that hotels are more likely to provide a reliable meal experience in terms of food and service quality as well as in the price/value relationship.

Profit margins

Consequent to the overview of the changing sales mix within hotel foodservice facilities, the following discourse examines whether and where hotels have pursued sales volume to the detriment of gross profits. There are a variety of available analytical models, each with relative merits; however, Kasavana and Smith's (1982) portfolio analysis is used here. Developing from Miller's (1980) methodology, which measures food-cost percentage against sales volume, Kasavana and Smith's model measures sales volume against contribution margin. They define contribution margin as the difference between sales price and direct costs, which is directly comparable with gross profit calculations.

The gross profit margins in general have declined (Table 3.4), reflecting greater competitiveness in the developed markets: in Africa, the decline could be attributed to greater difficulty and therefore a higher cost in

Table 3.4   Gross profit margins in hotel food and beverage departments

Region	1993	1992	1991	1990	1989
Africa and the Middle East	60.8	62.0	64.8	19.6	25.7
Asia and Australia	67.1	46.9	51.0	34.8	32.0
North America	44.1	49.0	49.4	16.5	17.9
Europe	59.5	57.3	59.7	27.8	19.6
Latin America	57.6	61.6	65.0	23.9	27.8
Global mean	57.8	55.4	58.0	24.5	24.6

NB. Gross profit is defined as: (Total revenues from food and beverage less Food and beverage department expenses/Total revenues from food and beverage) × 100.
Source: Derived from *The Worldwide Hotel Industry,* Horwath International, various years.

sourcing new materials. In the North American market, the decline in gross profit margins may be indicative of lower sales volume but rising costs of sales. This latter variable may be of particular significance in the Latin American markets, as food inflation rates have remained consistently in double digits. In Ecuador, for example, the food price index for 1980 was 100, but by 1989 it was 1,828!

The application of Kasavana and Smith's (1982) portfolio approach to menu analysis to the geographic markets shows that the best markets ('stars') are those hotel foodservice facilities which illustrate the highest sales volume as a proportion of total sales and the highest gross profit margins. Due to the divergence in methodologies used in calculating food and beverage expenses in 1989–90 and the remainder of the period, the portfolios given in Figures 3.1 and 3.2 only compare 1991 with 1993.

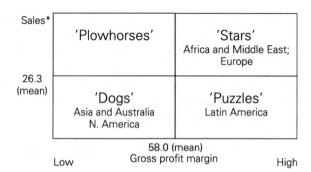

Figure 3.1 Portfolio analysis of hotel food and beverage facilities in 1991
(* = Sales volume as a proportion of total sales)
Source: Horwath Consulting.

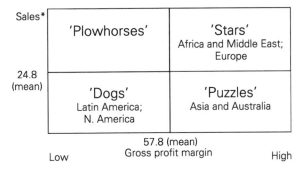

Figure 3.2 Portfolio analysis of hotel food and beverage facilities in 1993
(* = Sales volume as a proportion of total sales)
Source: Horwath Consulting.

The diagrams initially reflect, through the average figures on the axes, the general decline in both food and beverage sales volume and gross profit. Comparatively, however, they show that North American hotel food and beverage facilities have remained low profit/low sales volume players whereas, in spite of the overall decline, European and African/Middle Eastern ones have sustained their position in the high profit/high sales volume quadrant. Latin America's position has changed from being a 'puzzle' to a 'dog', but its position in this latter quadrant is marginal. If the cost of sales in Latin American hotel food and beverage facilities can be altered through tighter financial controls, in the face of further decline, they will resume their 'puzzle' status. In so doing, they would be following a similar trajectory to the Asian and Australian hotels.

Towards a general model

Throughout this chapter the fluctuations in hotel food and beverage performance have been anecdotally attributed to several factors: competition from free-standing restaurants, declining economic performance and activity, occupancy levels, hotel concentration and average room rates, each of which may have had an effect on performance individually or cumulatively. However, in order to measure and establish the role of each variable empirically, a multiple regression model may be used, as follows:

$$P = X_0 + X_1 GDPC + X_2 OCC + X_3 HORECA + X_4 REST + X_5 HOT + X_6 ARR$$

where P = performance; X_0 is a dummy variable; GDPC = annual change in GDP; OCC = occupancy; REST = number of restaurants per capita; HOT = number of hotels per capita; ARR = average room rate.

HORECA is a measure of market size since it represents a per capita estimation of consumer expenditure on hotel, restaurant and catering products. Although GDP has typically been taken as a measure of market size, it is not industry specific. Although *per capita* measures can be misleading in that income/expenditure may be unevenly distributed and there is little distinction of the source (tourist or indigenous) of the expenditure, it is, nevertheless, industry specific.

The hypotheses to be tested are as follows:

H1 Changes in GDP levels are positively correlated to the performance of hotel food and beverage facilities.
H2 Changes in hotel occupancy levels are positively correlated to the performance of hotel food and beverage facilities.
H3 Market size, i.e. domestic expenditure on hotel, restaurant and catering products, is positively correlated to the performance of hotel food and beverage facilities.
H4 The concentration of restaurants per capita has an inverse relationship to the performance of hotel food and beverage facilities.
H5 The concentration of hotels per capita has an inverse relationship to the performance of hotel food and beverage facilities.
H6 The average room rate of hotels illustrates a positive correlation to the performance of hotel food and beverage facilities.

Conclusion

The focus of this chapter has been the impact of external factors on the performance of food facilities in hotels. Although market forces have had some impact on performance, which may be tested using the proposed model, the relative profitability and success of hotel food facilities are not determined by environmental criteria alone. Also of importance are the pricing strategy and product mix of the facilities, in addition to other features such as the nature and extent of branding, design and customer satisfaction monitoring techniques.

In accounting for performance variances, therefore, the inclusion of internalistic factors would permit a more holistic study.

References

Bayou, M.E. and Bennett, L.B. (1992). Profitability analysis for table-service restaurants. *The Cornell Hotel Restaurant Administration Quarterly*, April, pp. 49–56.

Horwath International: *Worldwide Hotel Industry*, 1989, 1990, 1991, 1992, 1993.

Kasavana, M.L. and Smith, D.L. (1982). *Menu Engineering: A Practical Guide*. Michigan: Hospitality Publishers.

Miller, J. (1980). *Menu Pricing and Strategy*. Boston: CBI.

Pavesic, D. (1983). Cost-margin analysis: a third approach to menu pricing and design. *International Journal of Hospitality Management*, **2**(3), 127–134.

Schneider-Wexler, M. (1992). Lease your restaurant to an independent operator. *Hotels*, May, Cahners Publication, pp. 79–80.

Slattery, P. and Littlejohn, D. (1991). The structure of Europe's economies and demand for hotel accommodation. *EIU Travel and Tourism Analyst*, No. 4, pp. 20–37.

Solomon, K.I. and Katz, N. (1981). *Profitable Restaurant Management*, 2nd edn. Englewood Cliffs, NJ: Prentice-Hall.

4 Branding strategies for food and beverage operations

John Connell

Introduction

In order to compete in today's market place, managers need to recognize and capitalize on organizational strengths in relation to market opportunities and competitive offerings. Increasingly, service organizations are targeting market segments that they are best able to serve. Within segments, however, competition is often intense. There are three interrelated conceptual tools which, if properly used, can help to secure success in a crowded market place; these are market positioning, service differentiation and branding. More general accounts of these are given by Kotler (1991a), Lovelock (1991), de Chernatony and McDonald (1992), and Dibb and Simkin (1993). In this chapter these concepts are briefly introduced. Later, issues relating to single unit and chain branding, multiple branding, brand consistency and brand scope are reviewed and discussed. Finally, branding strategies in the licensed retail sector are explored and a brief comparison is made between branding in restaurant and licensed retail sectors. The conclusion drawn is that public house portfolios have yet to benefit from retail branding to the same extent as restaurant chains, although there is some evidence to suggest that softer forms of branding are being used increasingly within the licensed retail sector.

Market positioning, service differentiation and branding

In order to gain preference over competitive offerings, service operations should seek to gain a distinctive and favourable position in the minds of consumers through meaningful differentiation. Positioning is said to take one of two broad forms, that is 'copy' positioning or image positioning and 'real' or product positioning. Shostack (1987) comments that image positioning aims to 'manipulate the consumer perception of reality'. Images produced through advertising which seek to link products with abstract or largely unrepresentational attributes come within this category. In contrast, 'real' or product positioning relates to more objective and functional service components. This latter approach to positioning does not exclude the use of the former. Indeed the two approaches can work successfully in parallel and both can be highly effective.

Burger King, for example, target the mass market for convenient, low-cost restaurant and takeaway meals. The service mix is characterized by the offering of a limited burger-based menu, quick service, busy retail locations, limited peripheral services, courteous staff, and a clean and bright restaurant environment. Burger King compete with other fast food brands offering similar services and have adopted the slogan 'Have It Your Way'. This slogan refers to the addition and subtraction of 'toppings' on certain menu items. This functional differentiating feature has been successfully amplified to create an image of customization and choice within a highly standardized fast food chain.

Levitt (1980) argues that there are no limitations to the choice of differentiation criteria, while Johnston (1989) recognizes that differentiation is commonly based on the range of services offered, price, availability, quality and uniqueness. Kotler (1991b) identifies three broad categories of service differentiation criteria, namely, a differentiated offer – for example an innovatory feature; service delivery – for example through people, the physical environment and through the service process; and image – for example through brand symbols. Typically, services offer a variety of differentiating features and management must decide how many and which ones to communicate. Kotler (1991a) points out that the difference should be important, distinctive, communicable, pre-emptive, affordable and profitable.

Branding is primarily a method of product identification; however, it plays an increasingly important role in market positioning and service differentiation. The brand name represents a set of attributes and is used as a focus for communication with the market. Zeithaml (1991) argues that consumers often find intangible services difficult to perceive prior to purchase and it is recognized by Page (1990) and Onkvisit and Shaw (1989) that branding can help consumers to gain a better mental grasp of intangible services. Branding can therefore simplify and reduce the risk in service purchase. Brand objectives typically include increases in brand preference, loyalty and share. In order to achieve these objectives, the attributes of the service brand need to be meaningful, clearly specified, consistently delivered and correctly perceived by customers.

Research directed at staff and consumers can help to identify service attributes that are especially meaningful to the market and worthy of development and communication but as Lewis and Chalmers (1989) recognize, the research process can be complicated as 'consumers do not always know exactly what it is that forms the basis of their choice'. Attributes can therefore be viewed in three ways. These are salient (those that readily spring to mind), important (those that are given a priority) and determinant (those that determine choice). The intangible aspects of services operations can further increase the complexity of consumer research. A technique known as perceptual mapping facilitates the identification and analysis of service attributes. It is not within the scope of this chapter to examine the technique, but readers may refer to Davies and Brooks (1989), Kotler (1991a), Lovelock (1991) and Lewis and Chalmers (1989). For information on UK sources of food and beverage market intelligence see Connell (1993).

Food and beverage branding strategies

Although branding tends to be viewed as a multi-outlet phenomenon, the principles of branding work equally well in the context of the single unit. Single units can position through differentiation and attain brand loyalty. Indeed, it is not uncommon for large organizations to buy a single operation and replicate the service concept as a branded chain. Quite recently, Stakis plc acquired Sannino's, a Glasgow-based, middle market pasta restaurant operation, and sought to replicate the concept using the original name. Management can achieve significant benefits from building up a branded chain of operations, for example:

● Brand loyalty can be transferred across multiple outlets in different locations.
● The provision of branded as opposed to individually named outlets allows the use of mass media promotional campaigns and the achievement of consumer awareness in mass markets.
● Price discounts can be achieved from the purchase of standardized ingredients and other supplies.
● The introduction of a more standardized operating system can simplify local management decision-making and facilitate increasingly direct inter-outlet comparisons.
● Further internal efficiencies can be gained from being able to focus resources, such as training and product development activities on a single or small number of service brands, rather than a large 'variety' of outlets.

In combination, a branded chain may benefit considerably from consumer response and operational efficiencies, allowing competitive advantage over smaller operations and non-branded chains.

There are today numerous branded restaurants and licensed retail operations. The importance placed upon brands can be seen in the recent management buyout of Wimpy restaurants. Page (1990) notes that the tangible assets of the company amounted to no more than £1 million, but the selling price was £20 million. Companies like Whitbread, Grand Metropolitan and Forte now place branding at the very heart of their corporate marketing strategy, spending considerable sums on the promotion of their branded food and beverage operations (Table 4.1). These same companies

Table 4.1 Main media advertising expenditure of main restaurant chains, 1991–1992

	1991		1992	
	£000s	*Per cent share*	*£000s*	*Per cent share*
Beefeater Steak Houses	61.6	0.2	296.3	0.8
Burger King	4,668.3	13.4	5,302.9	14.3
Harvester Restaurants	856.8	2.45	699.1	1.9
Kentucky Fried Chicken	3,436.0	9.8	3,827.0	10.3
Little Chef	63.3	0.2	3.6	
McDonald's	18,881.0	54.0	19,149.0	51.7
Pizza Hut	3,777.0	10.8	2,577.0	7.0
Pizzaland			599.7	1.6
TGI Fridays	70.3	0.2	105.4	0.3
Wayside Inns	103.9	0.3	29.9	0.1
Wimpy	327.7	0.9	375.1	1.0
Other (inc. public houses)	2,710.1	7.75	4,085.0	11.0
Total	34,956.0		37,050.0	

Source: Register MEAL, London.

have targeted food and beverage operations for continued strategic growth, and as Palmer (1985) shows, some restaurant brands have achieved global proportions (Table 4.2).

Branding can be applied at various levels of service provision. The organization, its outlets and the services and goods offered within outlets can all be branded. Forte, for example, endorse Welcome Break motorway services which offer the Kentucky Fried Chicken and the Granary brands. Within the Kentucky Fried Chicken restaurants can be found branded beverages and branded menu items like the newly introduced Colonel's Classic Burger.

Table 4.2   Selection of British owned/managed branded restaurants and licensed retail operations

---

Forte

Happy Eater	Little Chef	Welcome Break
Wheelers	Distinctive	Harvester
Kentucky Fried Chicken		Sbarro

Allied Lyons

Cafe Classico	Dunkin Donuts	Big Steak
Firkin	Berts Bar	Baskin-Robbins

Whitbread

Beefeater	Pizza Hut	Roast Inns
TGI Fridays	The Keg	Churrasco
Hanrahan's	Brewers Fayre	Wayside Inns
Hoggs Head	Tut 'n Shive	Mulligans

Grosvenor Inns
Slug and Lettuce

Bass

Toby Carving Rooms	Toby Grills	Toby Restaurants
Fork and Pitcher	TJ's	Jeffersons
Drummonds		

Greenalls

Premier House	Millers Kitchen	Hudsons
Quinceys	Traditional Pubs	

Grand Metropolitan

Burger King	Old Orleans	Country Carvery
Country Grill	Country Fayre	Chef and Brewer

Rank Organisation
Hard Rock Cafe

Source: Company information.

Public houses, normally characterized by individual names, are often endorsed by the brewery which manage or operate some form of 'tied' arrangement with them. Young and Co's Brewery of London uses this traditional approach, clearly emphasizing the pub's link with the brewer. Young's position in the market is based largely on real ale and the relatively consistent provision of 'traditional' pub design and atmosphere, including limited use of music and games machines. Young's retail operations have achieved a distinctive position in the market and some brand loyalty. The independently run 135 Club affords the opportunity for customers to visit all pubs within the portfolio (now numbering 180). Brewers also endorse pubs by signage to indicate the availability of their beer brands. Here, it is hoped that loyalty to a branded beer will transfer to loyalty to the retail outlet. A more contemporary approach is to disconnect the link between beer brands or brewery name and to develop and replicate a retail pub concept, using the same name across numerous outlets. Yates Wine Lodges are a more mature example of retail- rather than brewery-based branding. Pubs also brand their internal services; for example, many pub food operations are branded.

Multiple branding is not without problems, as within a given location competition can occur between branded outlets owned by the same firm. This may be viewed as a form of healthy competition, but may also reduce the viability of a unit and lead to its repositioning, rebranding or disposal. Forte recently repositioned the Happy Eater brand in order to distinguish it more clearly from the Little Chef brand. As pointed out by Whitehead and Warren (1991), management can benefit from sharing information on the operation and marketing of different branded outlets, because good practice can often be easily transferred and unproductive competition avoided. Position statements help to clarify and communicate the attributes of the brand in relation to market needs and other brands within the market place.

In order to achieve brand loyalty across a chain of branded outlets, an element of consistency is required in the experience provided. A branded outlet need not be identical to all others within the branded chain. In a hotel chain context, Slattery (1991) uses the terms 'hard' and 'soft' brands to identify levels of consistency in brand replication. Connell (1992) used elements of the services marketing mix proposed by Booms and Bitner (1981) to identify harder and softer hotel brands.

Like hotels, the level of consistency within food and beverage brands relates largely to product and market characteristics. Consistency in the physical environment is more easily achieved when operations are built from new and replicated quickly, rather than acquired and slowly upgraded. In order to achieve consistency in locations, acquisitions or site/location selections need to be carefully considered. In addition, food and beverage operations which offer few peripheral services, low levels of customization and customer contact and rely upon automated production and delivery systems, lend themselves more to standardization and hard replication. A comparison between fast food and middle/higher market level restaurants may help to demonstrate this latter point.

The branded fast food unit meets customer needs by offering a narrow range of simple, low cost but high quality menu items. These are served and consumed quickly with few peripheral services and few adaptations for lunch and dinner services. The customer has little contact with service staff and there is little need to customize to suit individual needs. To deliver speedy service and freshly prepared menu items, the production and delivery systems are often highly automated using computer technology. Outlets are often built from new or fitted within an empty retail shell.

By contrast, middle and higher market level restaurants offer customers a more sophisticated meal experience to meet more social and esteem needs. In order to meet these needs over a longer service duration period, a broader range of menu items are available. The meal experience requires more peripheral services, higher levels of contact with service staff and a more customized service style, allowing more individual needs to be catered for. The meal experience is likely to be adapted to suit lunch- and dinner-time requirements. Sophistication and individual character in the physical environment are valued to a higher degree in the middle and higher market level restaurant operations and outlets can be more easily built around existing architectural features. The branded fast food outlet therefore lends itself to standardization and consistent or hard replication to a higher degree than middle market and higher market level restaurant operations. Hard brands are clearly less able to adapt to local market conditions than soft brands, but benefit to a greater degree from economies of scale in the purchase of standardized ingredients and supplies.

Another important issue in the formulation of branding strategy for food and beverage operations relates to the diversity of market/user segments targeted and the scope of service activities within outlets. Lovelock (1991) identifies five factors, detailed below, which can lead customers to place different weightings on service attributes.

1 The purpose of using the service
2 Who makes the decision
3 The timing of use (time of day/week/season)
4 Whether the individual is using the service alone or with a group
5 The composition of the group

Through customization and adaptations to the service mix, food and beverage managers are able to respond to different customer needs and secure an optimum level of demand. There are, however, operational and market-based reasons for limiting the scope of branded food and beverage operations. First, the production and delivery system is unlikely to be able to cater for customers with highly divergent needs and in trying to do so the operation may not be able to produce core and peripheral services to the specified standard. Secondly, as research by Mintel (1992) shows, customers often interact to form part of the total food and beverage experience. Heskett (1986) uses the terms 'discrete segment behaviour' to describe service situations where different user groups are targeted at different times or within segregated spaces, and 'non-discrete segment behaviour' where a wide range of users consume the service in the same place and at the same time. In both situations, the customer mix should be carefully considered in order to avoid disharmony between users. Thirdly, while it may be beneficial to emphasize different attributes to different user groups, such an approach may fragment and dilute the image of the brand.

Branding strategies in the licensed retail sector

According to a 1992 MORI survey, the British pub is the most important social venue in the country (Brewery Society Report, 1992; Brewers Society Review, 1992). The pub is a long-standing, sociocultural institution and is available in a variety of styles, including the 'traditional' pub, cafe bars, wine bars, 'themed' pubs, family-orientated pubs, high-quality restaurant pubs, games-orientated pubs and disco bars.

Most people have a good choice of pubs locally and choose a pub depending on the occasion and the composition of the group. A large proportion of users adopt a 'local' which they visit more than any other pub. Research by MORI in 1991 shows that hygiene, cleanliness, speed of service and value for money are more important factors in pub choice than the drinks on offer.

Research published by Mintel (1992) shows that in rank order, the main reasons for visiting the same pub are being within walking distance, food availability, congenial atmosphere, prompt service and a suitable mix of customers. The research also identified that the range of beers and the provision of real ale are more important to frequent and male drinkers who constitute an important target group for the brewers.

In marketing their beer products to pub users and the 'off' trade, the larger brewers place great emphasis on branding and mass media promotional campaigns. They have to date, placed little emphasis on the branding and mass media promotion of their retail outlets. There are at least three reasons why the brewers have placed less emphasis on retail branding. The first relates to the diversity in public house portfolios. Bass, for example, have almost 2500 managed houses, but according to their 1992 annual report 'each has its own style and atmosphere' with 'promotions ... tailor made for each pub and its customers' (Bass, 1992). Clearly, without some identifiable element of consistency in the retail experience there is little opportunity to gain brand loyalty across multiple outlets. Secondly, the big brewers had previously been able to expand beer sales through the expansion of their 'tied house' systems. Thirdly, the importance placed upon convenience and the common reliance upon the 'local' reduces the likelihood of brand switching and makes the transfer of brand loyalty across multiple outlets less likely. While many brewers continue to emphasize the importance of their beer products through mass media campaigns and pub endorsement, there is evidence that some brewers are trying to increase beer and liquor sales through market positioning, service differentiation and branding at the retail outlet level.

The reasons behind the shift toward branding are partly structural. Advertising Association statistics show the beer market shrinking and as competition has intensified some regional brewers, like the Greenalls Group, have moved out of brewing to concentrate their efforts on retailing (Advertising Association, 1992). Other regional brewers are continuing their dual role but placing more emphasis on retail operations. The Monopolies and Mergers Commission (1989) report into the Supply of Beer and the implementation of the Beer Orders has led to the partial dismantling of the tied house system. As a result of this legislation, large national brewers like Courage now concentrate on beer production, while Grand Metropolitan concentrate on retailing and property management. Other large national brewers have refocused their effort towards their 'managed house' divisions. These portfolios include many high-volume, city centre operations where retail competition is intense and branding most common.

According to Palmer (1992), possibly the most significant outcome from the Beer Orders has been the creation of a large number of independent multiple retailers. Many of these new companies have been created from the estimated 10,000 tenancied pubs released from the direct control of the big national brewers. Within this new sector are the newly created retail brands, JD Wetherspoon and Slug and Lettuce. Like Yates Wine Lodges, both these brands are operated through the 'managed house' system which provides a higher degree of operational control than the 'tied house' system. The outline strategies of Allied Lyons, Whitbread and Scottish and Newcastle present an insight into current industry practice.

Allied Lyons uses pub categorization techniques which involve the analysis of local markets and the targeting of one of eight different pub styles to fit local demand. By identifying key success criteria of the pub experience across a range of operations, best practice can be easily transferred to other units with similar markets. The company largely retains the individual names of their pubs and endorses them with the names of their divisional brewery supplier. Some pubs are supplemented with internal service brands like Big Steak, a pub food concept, and Mr Qs, a pool/leisure concept with games, video, music and other entertainments directed at the under 30s age group residing in suburban locations. Mr Qs has been introduced to outlets with an under-utilized room, allowing such operations to continue to serve existing users and attract new customers. The company also operate retail-based brands like the Firkin chain and is developing and expanding other branded outlets including Alloa Pubs and Restaurants – Berts Bar, which is now represented in major Scottish towns and cities.

Whitbread's managed house division, Whitbread Inns, operates three trading styles – individual 'community' inns reflecting needs of the local area; 'destination venues' where people make a special effort to use the service, such as city centre bars; and 'pub catering concepts' such as Brewers Fayre and Wayside Inns which offer food in a traditional pub atmosphere. Recently the company developed two new pub brands, namely Hogshead and Tut n' Shive. Through rebranding, these new retail concepts are being introduced mainly in 'destination venues'. Both are being promoted as differentiated pub concepts in markets where competition is more intense and less localized.

Scottish and Newcastle are also involved in retail branding. Here, outlets have been selected for a rebranding process which involves the continuance of the original pub name, but uses the brand name T and J Bernard as an endorsement. The brand attributes of T and J Bernard include a good selection of real ales, quick and courteous service, 'traditional' pub design and a clean air environment.

Interpretation and conclusion

Chain branding has become well established within the restaurant sector. Some of the softer, middle market restaurant brands, like Harvester, have now achieved critical mass, allowing recognition in national markets and other benefits associated with chain branding. In total, branded fast food and middle market restaurant chains have achieved a competitive advantage through operational efficiencies and market response.

Historically, pubs have been characterized by individual names and identities. This has been encouraged by the pub's sociocultural status, emphasizing strong local identity and serving highly localized markets. The regional and big national brewers have traditionally used beer- or brewery-based endorsement to link their diverse portfolios. With beer sales in decline and factors other than beer brand availability important in pub choice, opportunities for retail-based differentiation appear promising, particularly in markets where demand is less localized. The big national brewers, newly formed retail operators like Greenalls and smaller groups like Grosvenor Inns are increasingly branding their retail outlets and internal services without the use of brewery names. As their names suggest, many of these new branded outlets are based on the traditional pub experience.

In conclusion, although the large brewers operating diverse portfolios already benefit from standardization in their operating systems and supplies, they have yet to benefit from branding at the retail level to the same extent as branded restaurant chains. Even though the barriers to pub branding are considerable, soft branding provides a basis for meaningful differentiation in an increasingly competitive retail market place.

References

Advertising Association (1992). *The Marketing Pocket Book*. Henley on Thames, UK: Advertising Association/NTC Publications, p.23.

Bass (1992). Annual Report. London: Bass plc.

Booms, B. H. and Bitner, M. J. (1981). Marketing strategies for service firms. In J. Donnelly and W. R. George (eds), *Marketing Services*. Chicago: American Marketing Association.

Brewers Society Report (1992). *A Consumers View of Pub-Going*. Research by MORI. London: Brewers Society.

Brewers Society Review (1992). *Beer is Best*. Research by MORI. London: Brewers Society.

Connell, J. M. (1992). Branding hotel portfolios. *International Journal of Contemporary Hospitality Management*, **4**(1), 26–32.

Connell, J. M. (1993). *The Users Guide to Hospitality Marketing Literature and Intelligence*. Glasgow: Search Publications.

Davies, G. and Brooks, J. (1989). *Positioning Strategy In Retailing*, London: Paul Chapman Publishing.

de Chernatony, L. and McDonald, M. H. B. (1992). *Creating Powerful Brands: The Strategic Route to Success in Consumer, Industrial and Service Markets*. Oxford: Butterworth-Heinemann.

Dibb, S. and Simkin, L. (1993). The strength of branding and positioning in services. *International Journal of Service Industry Management*, **4**(1),25–35.

Heskett, J. L. (1986). *Managing In The Service Economy*. Boston: Harvard Business School Press, pp.14–16.

Johnston, R.(1989). Developing competitive strategies in service industries. In P. Jones (ed.) *Management In The Service Industries*. London: Pitman, pp.111–126.

Kotler, P. (1991a). *Marketing Management – Analysis, Planning Implementation and Control*, (7th edn). Engelwood Cliffs, NJ: Prentice-Hall, pp.288–309.

Kotler, P. (1991b) *Marketing Management – Analysis, Planning Implementation and Control* (7th edn), Engelwood Cliffs, NJ: Prentice-Hall, pp.462–472.

Levitt, T. (1980). Marketing success through differentiation of anything. *Harvard Business Review*, Jan.–Feb., p.73.

Lewis, R. C.and Chalmers, R. E. (1989). *Marketing Leadership In Hospitality – Foundations and Practices*. New York: Van Nostrand Reinhold, p.282.

Lovelock, C. H.(1991). Positioning a service in the market-place. In C. H. Lovelock (ed.), *Services Marketing*, 2nd edn. Engelwood Cliffs, NJ: Prentice-Hall, pp.109–117.

Mintel (1992). Vol. 1, *Pub Visiting*. London: Mintel Leisure Intelligence.

Monopolies and Mergers Commission (1989). *The Supply of Beer*. London: HMSO.

Onkvisit, S. and Shaw, J. (1989). Service marketing; image branding and competition. *Business Horizons*, **32**(1), 13–18.

Page, T. (1990). Designer label leisure. *Leisure Management*, Sept., pp. 34–37.

Palmer, A. (1992). Industry Report – How The Pub has Changed. *Publican*, 11 Jan., No. 427, pp. 3–44.

Palmer, J. D.(1985). Consumer services industry exports: new attitude and concepts needed for neglected sector. *Columbian Journal of World Business*, Spring, pp. 69–74.

Shostack, G. L. (1987). Service positioning through structural change. *Journal of Marketing*, **51**, 34–43.

Slattery, P. (1991). Hotel branding in the 1990s. *Travel and Tourism Analyst*, No.1, pp. 23–35.

Whitehead, J. and Warren, K. (1991). Beefeater devours Berni as their fortunes are reversed. *Independent*, 4 March, p. 25.

Zeithaml, V. A. (1991). How consumer evaluation processes differ between goods and services. In C. H. Lovelock (ed.), *Services Marketing*, 2nd edn. Engelwood Cliffs, NJ: Prentice-Hall, pp. 39–47.

5 Strategies for expansion – franchising, acquisition and management contracts

Keith Johnson and Amanda Kemp

Introduction

The main aims of commercial businesses are related to the time scale for their achievement. Higgins (1983) regards organizational growth as being 'second only' to profit generation in ensuring the continuation of an enterprise over the longer term. The importance of growth and expansion as key corporate objectives for hospitality businesses is illustrated in the following extracts:

> Our objectives are to spread best practice and, through increased strategic focus, to identify growth opportunities both in the UK and overseas for development in the medium term. (Whitbread Annual Report and Accounts, 1991/92)

> These results demonstrate the strength and resilience of our business portfolios, which have enabled us to weather the prevailing conditions and to produce growth. (Grand Metropolitan Interim Report, 1992)

Organizational growth can manifest itself, and therefore be measured, in a variety of ways. Of these, market size and market share are of particular importance since they are often positively correlated to improvements in return on investment.

Hospitality organizations seeking to expand their market size and share can do so by:

1 Altering their product mix by improving and adapting their existing products and/or introducing new ones.

2 Penetrating new market segments.
3 Following a strategy designed to facilitate 1 and 2 simultaneously.

Of these alternatives, option 3 is the most ambitious and risky. It is more likely that hospitality organizations will plan for growth incrementally by tackling either the product mix or seeking new markets at any one time. However, for any of these options to be sustained, an expansion in the number of operating units is required. This is because hospitality outlets, by their very nature, are restricted to servicing relatively small local markets. Therefore, simply expanding the unit size will not produce the required improvements in market penetration. Similarly, there is a limit to the amount of product development that can be supported from one unit, no matter how large this might be.

Statistical sources, such as the Census of Population and Employment, Mintel and Euromonitor reports, illustrate that, within the UK, both the restaurant and hotel industries are composed of a large number of small businesses. Dominance of such fragmented markets is very dependent upon expansion of the number of outlets controlled rather than growth in the size of individual units. Expanding the area of operation and increasing market share in this way enables an enterprise to remain successful, profitable and dynamic. Consequently, it is this particular form of growth, the expansion of outlet numbers, which is the focus of this chapter.

The growth of outlet numbers is, in itself, regarded as tangible proof of organizational success. Such growth, together with the development of a balanced portfolio of markets, enables operating and investment risks to be spread across a wider base. This form of growth enables market dominance and economies of scale to be realized. It also facilitates the development of an organizational infrastructure, including trained personnel, standardized operating procedures, management expertise and control. It is also one means of developing brand awareness. All of these factors contribute to the feasibility and likelihood of further growth. In short, expansion can fuel further expansion and 'chain' operations can be developed, particularly in the hotel, fast food and themed restaurant sectors. In contrast, recent Monopolies and Merger restrictions have forced UK brewers to move in the opposite direction by curtailing their outlet numbers and forcing them to grow profits and turnover at individual unit level.

The motive for growth will influence the appropriate direction and the methods adopted. An effective choice of growth strategy will play a major role in determining a company's overall survival and success and will be heavily influenced by the stage of development in the company's lifecycle. A correlation or 'fit' between the company's capabilities and the market opportunities is essential. It is on the basis of this 'fit' that any growth strategy should be evaluated. It is to such strategic choices that attention is now focused.

Barriers to growth

Although the expansion of outlet numbers is often desirable, it is not always easily achievable. On the face of it, the simplest way to expand outlet numbers is either to buy some or to build some. However, this approach presupposes that:

- Capital is, or can be made, readily available to finance purchases and/or construction.
- There are outlets in existence which can be bought and readily converted to the style of unit required or that there are suitable greenfield sites on which to develop such units.
- The legal constraints on construction and/or acquisition are surmountable.

Lack of finance, acquisition candidates and greenfield sites, together with legal or other technical constraints, act as barriers to expansion, which limit the speed of growth, or stifle it completely. Indeed, there are a host of potential barriers to growth in addition to those outlined above. The size of these obstacles is often proportional to the scale and complexity of the anticipated expansion. They reach their height when international expansion is contemplated. Simple growth strategies, such as the model outlined above, are too rudimentary to function in all circumstances. Fortunately, other options are available which offer different opportunities to overcome these barriers to varying extents.

The extent to which barriers to growth are surmounted provides another means by which to evaluate expansion strategies.

Expansion methods and options

Expansion options can be categorized on the basis of ownership. All expansion strategies provide opportunities to own:

1 The tangible capital (money, land, labour, buildings, equipment, etc.)
2 The intangible capital (technical, procedural or marketing knowledge)
3 The risks (to both 1 and 2 above)
4 The rewards (both financial and non-financial).

Any organization wishing to retain total control of its operations, withstanding all the risks and reaping all the rewards, may do so by internalizing its growth through full equity involvement. The speed of expansion, by this method, is often limited by the capital outlay required. This may allow competitors to seize expansion opportunities. However, this slower, organic form of expansion does allow control to be complete, the experience curve to develop and any firm specific advantage to be protected. In its most extreme form, greenfield sites will be acquired and outlets designed and built to company specifications.

Alternatively, in exchange for partial loss of control, an organization may share the risks (and rewards) with one or more partners. By doing so it will externalize its growth. This is a fundamental decision in any expansion strategy; either to 'go it alone' or to involve external agencies. The use of third parties to help fuel expansion assumes that potential partners can be found. They may be attracted for many reasons, but are usually seeking to share in the specific competitive advantage enjoyed by the expanding organization. Within the hospitality industry, the differentiation and development of a firm specific advantage is somewhat problematic. Product characteristics of perishability, intangibility and difficulty in standardization, due to labour intensiveness, influence the type of advantage that can be achieved. Nevertheless, the possession of a reliable and reputable brand which can be successfully replicated in new markets is seen as a major attraction for potential partners.

If partners are used, then the extent of their involvement can vary enormously. As a result, expansion methods are commonly represented by a continuum stretching from full equity involvement at one extreme to non-equity involvement at the other. Although any particular method may fall at any point on this continuum, the most commonly employed options can be categorized under the following headings:

- Full equity involvement
- Franchising/licensing
- Management contracts
- Joint ventures

However, an examination of company histories and portfolios reveals that these are merely 'ideal types' and that in reality a mixture of all of these methods can be used to secure the development of one outlet, let alone a chain of them! Consequently, the boundaries between these alternatives are far from hard and fast. Newly emerging forms of funding expansion, such as sale and leaseback arrangements which seek to release capital tied up in a stagnant property market for export to more buoyant locations, are not included in this schema. Nevertheless the schema is still valid since these arrangements are combinations of categories contained within it. Consequently, it is used to structure the remainder of this chapter. Each alternative will be dealt with in turn and will be contrasted to the full equity involvement which has already been outlined.

Franchising/licensing

This has been a popular option in the hospitality industry, particularly within the restaurant sector. It is also gaining ground as a means of hotel chain expansion. Expressed simply, franchising is where the parent company allows others to operate clones of its outlets. More comprehensively:

> Business format franchise is the grant of a license by one person (the franchisor) to another (the franchisee) which entitles the franchisee to trade under the trade name/trade mark of the franchisor and to make use of an entire package comprising all the elements necessary to establish a previously untrained person in the business and to run it with continual assistance on a predetermined basis. (Mendolsohn and Acheson, 1987, p. 1)

Consequently there are three phases to the business format franchise namely:

1 The development of a business concept.
2 A process of initiation to, and training in, all aspects of the running of the business according to the concept.
3 A continual process of assistance and guidance.

As the franchise develops and passes through these phases, resources are required from both franchisor and franchisee. Such resources are usually more considerable than any one individual could reasonably afford or command. Consequently, the relationship between the two parties can be, and needs to remain, mutually beneficial. The relative advantages and disadvantages for each party are summarized in Table 5.1.

In developing a franchise, the following criteria should be considered:

1 The concept must have demonstrated its success.
2 The business should be distinctive both in its public image and in its system and method.
3 The system and methods must be capable of being passed on successfully to others.
4 The financial returns from the operation of the franchised business must be sufficient to enable:
   (a) the franchisor to obtain a reasonable return on the assets employed in the business,
   (b) the franchisee to earn a reasonable reward for his labours,
   (c) the franchisee to make payment to the franchisor of a reasonable fee for the services which he will continue to supply to the franchisee.

Table 5.1 Relative advantages and disadvantages of franchising

Advantages		Disadvantages	
Franchisor	*Franchisee*	*Franchisor*	*Franchisee*
Reasonable profit from low-risk capital	Use of proven business format	Damage from substandard or dishonest franchisees	Loss of total independence
Capital investment by franchisees	Use of brands/ trade names	Loss of control over product and service quality	Royalty payments to franchisor erode profitability
Rapid expansion of brand image over short time	Relatively low risk business development	Recruitment of suitable franchisees	Not free to sell franchise
Motivated and keen franchisees relative to managers	Franchisor support in training, equipment and food purchasing, marketing, promotion, site selection and acquisition	Less profit than from company-owned unit	Tied to franchisor's suppliers
Franchisees can be responsive to local market needs and conditions	Use of standard management, accounting, sales and stock control procedures	Difficulties in removing franchisees	Affected by poor image, practices, etc., of franchisor
Franchisees can achieve personnel and administrative saving	Improved prospects of loan acquisition	Difficulties of obtaining design, decor changes, etc.	Format or contractual changes may be imposed
Franchisor is not responsible for security of assets	Management information	Need for good communication	Difficult to withdraw from franchise agreement
	Privileged territorial rights	Future brand growth may be related to franchisees Preparation of future competitor	

Table 5.2 Fast food franchise growth in USA

	Sector	Year business began	Franchising since	Co Owned			Franchised		
				1987	1988	1989	1987	1988	1989
Kentucky Fried Chicken	Fried Chicken	1930	1952	1,920	1,909	1,910	5,480	5,680	5,707
Dunkin' Donuts	Doughnuts	1950	1955	30	8	8	1,640	1,727	1,841
Burger King	Hamburgers	1954	1954	788	828	873	4,452	4,807	5,083
McDonald's	Hamburgers	1955	1955	2,280	2,434	2,619	7,274	7,621	8,101

Source: Acheson and Wicking (1992).

Once a successful blueprint has been developed which meets all of these criteria, expansion can occur with extreme velocity, as Table 5.2 illustrates. When the data in the Table are reworked in terms of the balance between company controlled and franchised outlets, the pattern given in Table 5.3 emerges.

Table 5.3 illustrates that both Kentucky Fried Chicken and McDonald's seek to maintain around 25 per cent of their portfolio as company outlets. These outlets must have established profit records as they are the 'demonstration' units that are used to attract new franchisees. They also encapsulate, in tangible form, the franchisor's financial commitment to the business concept and provide a forum for testing product and service

Table 5.3   The ownership mix of fast food outlets (%) in the USA

	Company owned			Franchised		
	1987	*1988*	*1989*	*1987*	*1988*	*1989*
Kentucky Fried Chicken	26	25	25	74	75	75
Dunkin' Donuts	2	1	0.4	98	99	99.6
Burger King	15	15	15	85	85	85
McDonald's	24	24	24	76	76	76

Source: Acheson and Wicking (1992).

innovations. Burger King also maintains a constant company to franchised ratio, but at a lower level. Dunkin' Donuts is a smaller, less complex concept and can therefore support a greater ratio of franchised outlets. The initial investment is correspondingly lower and the potential market of franchisees, therefore, that much greater. The need for company-owned demonstration units is less critical in view of the lower outlays, lower per unit profitability and lower risks involved.

Table 5.4 presents the same kind of data for a single year (1990) for the UK. As can be seen Kentucky Fried Chicken maintains its ratio of franchised to owned outlets, whereas the other two do not. Burger King more than doubles its company-owned outlets, while McDonald's moves in the opposite direction to its Stateside policy and franchises very few outlets. One part of the explanation for these differences is that the UK fast food market is at a different stage of development to that of the USA. This affects the risk:benefit ratio attached to equity investment within that market. These factors, in turn, affect the relative attractiveness of franchising *vis-à-vis* other methods of growth. Franchising internationally also raises issues of

Table 5.4   Ownership mix of fast food outlets (%) in the UK

	Company owned 1990	Franchised 1990
Kentucky Fried Chicken	75	25
Burger King	61	39
McDonald's	7	93

communication, cultural adaptation and cost effectiveness that do not arise to the same degree within a home market.

International franchising

As illustrated above, a number of US-based hospitality organizations have expanded internationally using franchising. They have done so by using one or more of the following methods:

1 *Master license*. The firm grants a licence to an individual or firm in the target territory. The licensee then operates all outlets under its ownership and control, sub-franchises within the territory, or adopts some combination of these strategies.
2 *Direct license*. The franchisor grants a licence to the operating franchisee and provides direct back-up and support, sometimes through the presence of direct representation in the target territory.
3 *Branch subsidiary operation*. The firm establishes a direct presence in the area by setting up a branch or subsidiary when it expands in the territory by granting franchises and providing direct services to its franchisees.
4 *Joint venture*. The firm establishes a joint company or partnership with a company or individual in the target territory and grants the on-site partner a licence to operate its own outlets, sub-franchise, or both.

See Mendelsohn (1992) for further explanation of these options.

Two crucial factors often determine the choice of franchising method when a firm expands into other countries. The first is the franchisor's willingness and ability to devote the financial and human resources necessary to provide direct support to its international franchisees. The second is the availability of suitable potential licensees, franchisees or partners in the target territory.

In North America, many franchisees are entrepreneurs with limited capital, but this is not always the case elsewhere. In Japan, for instance, franchisees are often large trading firms that want to diversify into the service sector. This type of franchisee generally prefers to operate under a master-license agreement.

One advantage associated with international expansion involving partnership, such as franchising, is that exposure to a variety of markets may uncover products, processes and ideas peculiar to an individual market. These may then be developed for successful transfer to other markets. The Teriyakiburger, developed by a McDonald's franchisee operating in Japan, is a good example of this.

Domestic companies serving only one market have a much lower level of exposure to such diverse influences. Nor do they usually possess the resources needed to research, develop and introduce new products on such a broad scale.

The common pitfalls associated with the development of an international franchising programme by prospective franchisors are:

- An insufficiently strong home-based business.
- An unwillingness to devote resources exclusively to international development.
- An unwillingness or inability to devote sufficient financial resources to the effort.
- An unwillingness or inability to devote sufficient manpower resources.
- An inability to recognize the amount of time it will take to become established and profitable.

The degree of underestimation by companies of the last three factors can vary between a half to one-third (Mendelsohn, 1992). Early identification of those issues in any franchise development strategy is vital in order to prevent them creating significant problems.

The dynamics of the franchising relationship

A successful franchise system will generate a learning curve for both franchisor and franchisee. The franchisor develops the ability to identify and retain the most profitable franchises. This may encourage a movement towards direct ownership of the most profitable outlets, in the belief that further profit enhancement can be achieved. Similarly, the franchisee, having gained business experience and confidence, may seek to operate more independently by exiting the franchise – again in the belief that greater rewards are possible. Therefore, it may be mutually beneficial for the system to revert to one of direct ownership.

Oxenfeldt and Kelly (1968–69) argue that most successful franchise systems will revert to wholly owned chains, and empirical support is provided by Sasser and Wyckoff (1978) who noted the declining percentage of the US chain restaurant industry operated by franchises as long ago as 1969–76.

Franchising is obviously advantageous to a franchisor in that it uses someone else's capital to increase the number of outlets. This, in turn, can increase brand awareness. The combination of these two factors can lead to rapid expansion and the gaining of critical mass, in effect reducing the period of infancy and adolescence of the enterprise. Once this critical size has been achieved, many economies of scale can be enjoyed. Direct ownership is more attractive when this level has been reached. Consequently, although franchising may still be used to exploit marginal locations, the franchisor's main concern may move from growth to gaining direct control of the more central and important franchises. Full ownership is also more feasible at this stage because of the funds generated from a successful franchise network.

Buying back from franchisees may also occur for more negative reasons. Outlets that are trading problematically and/or poorly have to be turned round in order to protect the brand. The easiest way to secure this is often a buyout, which returns control to the franchisor.

A constant threat to both parties is the danger of 'cannibalization' of the basic business concept. Such a scenario has recently arisen between Peter Morton of Hard Rock cafes and Robert Earl of Planet Hollywood. They are involved in a protracted and extremely expensive law suit following Morton's claims that Earl copied the Planet Hollywood format from the rock memorabilia restaurants and stole trade secrets while he ran the other half of the Hard Rock chain for the Rank Organisation. Earl's Planet Hollywood, in turn, is facing a former franchisee's plans to operate a Paradise Hollywood concept along very similar lines (Sillitoe, 1993). McDonald's provides another good example of a response to this issue. In the 1960s they followed a rule that new store sites in the UK had to serve a population of at least 50,000 residents within a three-mile radius. This policy changed early in the 1970s as a result of market research showing 75 per cent of customers using the outlet in conjunction with some other activity. From then on McDonald's outlets have been located much closer together, in an attempt to capitalize on different customer traffic patterns. At the same time, the greater density of outlets has made it more difficult for cannibalized alternatives to service the same market.

Therefore, franchising is not based on a static partnership. Changes occur as the parties, and the business itself, grow and develop along a lifecycle trajectory. It has become an established means of hospitality outlet expansion within both domestic and international markets. In particular, it has been extensively used in the fast food and themed/concept restaurant sectors. It seems set to continue in these areas and to expand into others, as the current round of franchising hotels into Eastern Europe demonstrates. Management contracts are also used in these circumstances and attention now turns to these.

Management contracts

This is an increasingly popular method of expansion in both domestic and foreign markets. Essentially, an agreement is reached by the owner of an outlet for the operation of that unit, to professional standards, by a third party. More precisely management contracting is:

> An arrangement under which operational control of an enterprise which would otherwise be exercised by the directors or managers appointed or elected by its owners, is vested by contract in a separate enterprise which performs the necessary management functions for a fee. (Sharma, 1984)

This definition requires updating, in that in addition to the fee an agreed profit percentage is usually also levied. The balance between fee and profit varies according to circumstance. For example, in high-risk trading environments the operator will usually demand a substantial percentage of remuneration as a fixed fee in order to ensure a certain minimum level of earnings. Contracts are usually valid for a five- to seven-year period, although the number of UK restaurants and hotels going into receivership and requiring day-to-day management while restructuring and/or disposal takes place has generated shorter time horizons for these contracts. Indeed, the existing staff may even be appointed to run the contract if the receivers believe that poor management was not the reason for the initial failure. Such was the case of Principal Hotels in 1992. Contracts may also be extended beyond the immediate operation of the outlet and into financial and marketing programmes or skills training and management development of the unit owner's own team.

Another extension of the contract is seen in project management agreements where the contractor carries out the design and construction of the property prior to its operation. Technical service agreements such as these are a key feature of the approach of major hotel management contractors such as Hyatt and Sheraton.

Management contracts are still relatively rare in the restaurant sector. This is largely due to polarization of ownership between small independents and company-owned chains. Also, unlike hotels, the property base for a single restaurant operation is unlikely to be substantial enough to warrant uninvolved corporate investment. However, some of the more innovative pub management schemes, for example Grand Metropolitan's Inntrepreneur, have their roots in management contracting.

The advantages to the contractor are:

- Low risk market entry.
- No necessity for capital investment.
- The ability to capitalize on existing management skills, in some cases at marginal cost (for example, marketing and financial control systems).
- A guaranteed income and quick returns.
- Greater operational control than franchising, combined with the ability to retain some aspects of the firm-specific advantage.

In terms of international expansion, contracting avoids confrontation with foreign governments over issues such as land purchase, property developments and usage. It is a useful way of increasing co-operation with local businesses to develop the marketplace. In some parts of the world foreign companies are not allowed to own equity in businesses and hence contracting is a means of overcoming this obstacle to globalization. Contracting also reduces exposure to political risks because it provides an easier 'escape' from unstable or undesirable situations due to the lack of equity involvement.

The client retains the capital appreciation on the property, but is freed from the day-to-day operational problems of making a financial return from it by drawing on the intangible capital of the contractor.

Once again, to attract potential clients the contractor must have a successful 'track record' on which to sell. The management skills on which the relationship is based need to be demonstrated 'up front'. This may require some outlets to be operated under full equity. In this case the skill of contracting is to transfer management expertise from a context of total control to one of only partial control. It is vital for the contractor to establish acceptable scope in which to exercise control and to limit the extent of interference from the local investor into the way in which his investment is being run. Such interference is likely to peak if the contractor has insufficient management resources and marketing insight to exploit the local market fully. Success is dependent upon making a clear statement of what the client can expect and then delivering it.

Fixed term management contracts may be used at the early stages of a joint venture to ensure efficiency of operation and to assist in the process of management development and the transfer of technology and marketing techniques. In short, to prepare the ground for, and reduce the risks associated with, some longer term equity involvement.

Joint ventures

Joint ventures may be a feature of both franchising and management contracting. They involve co-operation among at least two investing parties who may, or may not, be involved in other aspects of the business. As investors seek to spread risk, or to put cash generated from other businesses into longer term developments, so the exact nature of operational involvement and cash return will vary. There is no consistent format for joint ventures, other than that provided by legislation. Many operations may begin life initially as joint ventures. Increasingly, management consultancy companies are being recruited by clients based on their ability to bring capital to the project under consideration. Additionally, cash rich investors may be attracted to take a stake in established businesses, so allowing their owners to release equity built through the business for investment in new locations.

Conclusions

In short, growth can confer profitability and profitability can confer growth and access to a range of methods of gearing equity to achieve it. To maintain this virtuous circle, a company must continue to make sound choices concerning the expansion methods it deploys. These choices will be contingent upon circumstances. Circumstances which are continually altering. A range of expansion methods has been outlined, together with their relative strengths and weaknesses. This provides some insight into the circumstances which are likely to favour a given form of expansion. Of the host of variables which have to be taken into account, the stage of development of the organization is particularly important. This is depicted in Figure 5.1 and below in a manner which is intended to summarize the chapter:

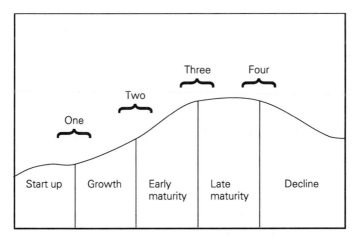

Figure 5.1 Stages of development of an organization

Transition one (start up–growth)

Obtain finance and retain equity. Open outlets and prove success. Companies with less than five outlets have negligible infrastructure, particularly in terms of trained personnel. Establish visibility and viability.

Transition two (growth–early maturity)

Expand nationally by franchising, but retain those outlets which are 'key' in terms of profit and/or capital appreciation.

Transition three (early–late maturity)

Buy back selected outlets. Continue to strengthen the brand via non-equity methods in marginal locations.

Transition four (late maturity–decline)

Expand out of home market through master franchising or joint ventures. Begin to reclaim selected franchises in home country.

References and further reading

Acheson, D. and Wicking, N. (1992). Fast food franchising and finance. In S. Ball (ed.), *Fast Food Operations and their Management*. Cheltenham: Stanley Thornes.

Ball, S. (ed.) (1922). *Fast Food Operations and their Management*.Cheltenham: Stanley Thornes.

Buckley, P. (1985). *The Economic Theory of the Multinational Enterprise*. London: Macmillan.

Casson, M. (1981). In A. Rugman (ed.), the Foreword to *Inside the Multinationals*. London: Croom Helm.

Euromonitor Publications (1990). *The European Consumer Catering Report*. London: Euromonitor Publications.

Eyster, J. (1977). Administering the hotel management contract: an analysis of owner and operator concerns. *Cornell HRA Quarterly*, Aug., pp. 12–20.

Go, F. and Christensen, J. (1989). Going global. *Cornell HRA Quarterly*, Nov., pp. 73–79.

Hibbert, E. P. (1989). *Marketing Strategy in International Business*. Maidenhead: McGraw-Hill.

Higgins, J. M. (1983). *Organisational Policy and Strategic Management: Text and Cases*. Dryden, p. 18.

Holly, J. (1983). Management contracts. *Handbook of International Trade*, Vol. 1. London: Macmillan.

Lecraw, D. J. (1984). Bargaining power, ownership and profitability or transnational corporations in developing countries. *Journal of International Business Studies*, Spring/Summer, pp. 27–43.

Littlejohn, D. (1985). Towards an Economic Analysis of Trans/Multinational Hotel Companies. *International Journal of Hospitality Management*, **4**(4), 157–165.

Mendelsohn, M. (1992) *Franchising in Europe*. London: Cassell.

Mendelsohn, M. and Acheson, D. (1987) *How to Franchise Your Business*. London: Stoy Hayward.

Oxenfeldt, A. and Kelly, A. (1968–69). Will successful franchise systems ultimately become wholly owned chains? *Journal of Retailing*, **44**(4) 69–83.

Rugman, A. (1981) *Inside the Multinationals*. London: Croom Helm.

Sasser, W. E. and Wyckoff, D. D. (1978) *The Chain Restaurant Industry*. Lexington, USA: D. C. Heath.

Scott, B. R. (1971). Stages of Corporate Development Case Number 9–371–291, BP 998 Intercollegiate Case Clearing House. Harvard: Harvard Business School.

Sharma, D. D. (1984). Management contracts and international marketing in industrial goods. In E. Kaynak (ed.), *International Marketing Management*, Ch. 7. New York: Praeger.

Sillitoe, D. (1993). A bit of a beef about burgers. *The Guardian*, Outlook Saturday, 22 May.

6 The application of retailing to food and beverage operations

P. J. Houghton and J. J. Lennon

Introduction

When the term 'retailing' is used, the most common interpretation relates to activities involved in the sale of goods and services to their ultimate consumers (Duncan and Hollander, 1977). Such an understanding suggests a very simple and practical process consisting of merchants buying goods, placing them in stores, and then selling them to consumers. However, consideration of other perspectives somewhat complicates this view. Rogers and Grassi (1988) offer what they term as five universal functions of retailing. These encompass: merchandising, operations, promotion, finance and human resources.

Merchandising concerns itself with all activities relative to the buying and selling of goods. Operations are concerned with the management of the physical plant, overseeing maintenance and bookkeeping. Other activities include customer services, receiving, checking, marking, warehousing of incoming merchandise, and store security. Some larger stores, Rogers and Grassi (1988) argue, have separate property divisions, but in all other stores facilities development is part of operations. Promotional activities include advertising, personal selling, sales promotion, merchandising, public relations, publicity and sponsorship. Finance involves itself with the control of the retailer's assets, with responsibility for ensuring that working capital is available. Other areas of concern centre on the development and maintenance of accounting and record-keeping systems, the control of physical inventory, merchandise and expense budgets. The finance area also produces all required reports both internally and externally. Finally, the human resource element oversees recruitment, training and evaluation of personnel. It administers the compensation and benefits packages and, where necessary, deals with trade unions.

Clearly, these features of retailing outlined by Rogers and Grassi have some application to the scope of this chapter. There remains, however, confusion in the work of Rogers and Grassi, in that the crux of their analysis is not 'managerial' in the strategic sense but more operational, concerning itself with the actual operation. Subsequently, there must be a more suitable breakdown of retailing management. This would appear to be provided by Davidson *et al.* (1988), who classify the classic functions of retailing into three categories.

First, retailing must create 'product and service assortment' that anticipates and fulfils consumer needs and wants. Secondly, retailing must offer products and services in quantities small enough for individual or family consumption. Thirdly, retailers must provide for the ready exchange of value through:

- Efficient handling of transactions.
- Being open for trading at convenient hours and locations.
- Providing information that is useful in making choices.
- Offering products and services at competitive prices.

This analysis lends itself very accurately to broad 'strategic' understanding and is ideal as the retail 'ethic'. However, the basis for comparison and application between retailing and hospitality must be tangible; therefore, it is necessary to determine what 'tools' the retailer has in order to achieve the broad objectives. Davidson *et al.* (1988) appear to crystallize the above requirement and the concerns of other authors by generating the retailing mix. This consists of: location, physical facilities, merchandise, management, pricing, promotion, services, organization, and personnel.

Clearly there remains scope for considerable cross application and strategic development of each of these areas. In the context of food and beverage management, the retailing concepts of merchandise management and display management, will be examined and application considered. This is not to say that other areas are not relevant or appropriate, rather that the scope of this chapter simply could not accommodate such detailed review of primary retail concepts.

Merchandise management

Introduction

It can be argued that a profitable retailing strategy is built around the combination of an effective market strategy and a sound financial strategy

(Davidson *et al.*,1988). An effective market strategy is one which produces a market programme that is highly consistent with the expectations of a target market segment, with fundamentally competitive positioning against the direct competition. A sound financial strategy is one which provides adequate resources to implement the market programme and produces financial performances consistent with the return on investment objectives of the retailer.

Merchandise management is not simply inventory control and stock control, but includes planning the size and composition of merchandise inventories as well as a variety of functions relating to the purchase, promotion and sale of merchandise. The task now, if a potential cross-industry comparison is to be made, is to define merchandise management and expand upon its constituent elements in order to identify potential applications.

Toward a definition

Merchandising, being the primary function of retailing, has been defined by the American Marketing Association as 'the planning involved in marketing the right merchandise at the right place at the right time in the right quantities at the right price'. The right merchandise relates to variances in: models, styles, brands, colours, sizes and so on, that targeted consumers would expect to have available. The right place concerns not only store locations but what merchandise should be carried at each location and where in the outlet that merchandise should be positioned. The right time indicates that the merchandise should be available for consumers to purchase at a time convenient to them. The right quantities are those that allow consumers to exercise the types of choices they desire without having the retailer tie up unnecessary funds in inventory. The right prices refer to those that will attract customers in spite of competition, yet will generate a reasonable rate of return on investment for the retailer.

From these observations, the management of merchandise may be seen to be the planning and control of a merchandise inventory to maintain a balance between the expectations of target customers and the requirements of the firm's financial strategy. The task, therefore, of effective merchandise management is to find and maintain this balance by operating within the two distinct areas of merchandise planning and merchandise control. Merchandise planning entails the establishment of merchandising goals/ objectives and the development of plans indicating how these proposed objectives are to be achieved. Merchandise control involves the monitoring and measurement of actual merchandising performance and the analysis of variances between actual and planned performance. Following on from this element of merchandise control, adjustment in planning results where actual performance greatly exceeds or falls short of the projected performance.

The task now, is to examine the general activities involved in merchandise management so as to ascertain if there is a platform which readily lends itself to the cross-industry comparison. Elements of relevance in this section centre on merchandise content management and stock management. They will be examined in turn, in order to evaluate their respective potential for further analysis.

Merchandise content management

A retailer's merchandise inventory may be viewed as a mix of different types of merchandise. The term 'merchandise mix' refers to the item-by-item content of a merchandise inventory. The management of this mix involves three broad considerations. First, fundamental decisions as to what generic types of merchandise should be carried. Secondly, what styles, models, sizes and price ranges to target. Thirdly, how many units of each item to have in inventory.

Different types of merchandise also impose different requirements upon the operational framework of the retailer. Variances in selling activity, advertising and promotion, store layout and location will all be affected by the nature of the proposed merchandise content. Decisions regarding the size and content of the merchandise mix also have a fundamental bearing on the retailer's financial programme. Merchandise inventories represent one of the largest single assets on the retailer's balance sheet, consequently variance here will have a direct impact on the capital tied up in stock holding. The implementation of a mix of merchandise should take into consideration assortment, specials and seasonality. Assortment involves the range of choice offered among merchandise items that are largely substitutable (consumer demand increases as the number of substitutable items increases). The problem in assortment merchandising is deciding what range of assortment factors are essential to maximize opportunities for satisfying demand, without incurring the adverse consequences of excessive costs or risks of owning and holding too large an inventory. Special promotion merchandise is frequently employed for reasons other than incremental sales. Often they act as a form of incentive or publicity to the retailer. Consequently the retailer must plan stock levels very carefully. Finally, many items of merchandise are seasonal and therefore have a limited shelf life. To maximize returns from such item classfications requires keen planning and control. Once a merchandise mix policy has been accomplished, it is necessary to manage the stock and attribute a pricing policy to that stock. Each function is done in harmony and in no particular order, as inferred by this chapter sequencing.

Stock management

The analysis of stock management may be broken down into two broad categories: stock balance and stock turnover. Stock balance is the fundamental analysis of what merchandise is 'in-store'. Major areas for consideration centre on merchandise variety, the range of categories of merchandise, and merchandise assortment, the choices a consumer will have within any particular merchandise variety (variables here include size and colour). Stock turnover is the yardstick most commonly used when comparing retail turnover with stockholding levels. Clearly, this has a knock-on effect on the 'bottom line'; therefore, consideration is given to the implications of high stock turnover and what may constitute the ideal stock.

Stock balance

It is the task of management to develop a merchandising philosophy appropriate to the individual firm, where due consideration is given to the potential targeted market served by the operation and its own specific operating characteristics. Pertinent to this targeting of effort is the combination of merchandise variety and assortment which determines the strategic level of an operation's inventory specialization. This combination also represents the concept of merchandise content. Some minimum variety of different classes of goods is virtually dictated by trade custom and consumer expectations. Problems, however, may arise from attempting to provide too great a variety of separate merchandise lines without due consideration to assortment factors. This is often a cause of inventory imbalance which can be of damage to a retailer. Also, widespread diversification often leads to a heterogeneous stock of unrelated merchandise. This has the effect of confusing customers and ultimately in the reduction of turnover, presenting new problems to the management.

Once the variety of goods to be stocked has been determined, the assortment within each stock line must be given consideration. The retailer must be selective when assembling stock assortments where the aim is to develop a stock that is in a reasonably healthy balance with sales and to maintain that balance under ever-varying demand and supply conditions.

The principal aspects of a stock-to-sales balance within a particular variety of merchandise class or basic merchandise category may be broken down into three areas. First, the total inventory investment must be reasonable, as determined by the stock turnover rate, in order to secure the many benefits of a healthy rate of turnover without the disadvantages of frequent purchasing or starved stock conditions. Secondly, the breadth of choice within the merchandise inventory must be adequate as judged by consumer demand and the competitive market place. Subsequently, there is a need to provide consumers with a reasonable selection of items within each merchandise category. Thirdly, the stock depth behind each item should be at least reasonably proportionate to the sales importance of the item. Practically, however, this cannot be followed rigidly because it may not be possible to maintain continually the same rate of stock turnover on each item.

Where an inventory exists that meets all the major requisites of balance, it may be considered an ideal stock. The ideal stock is a variable concept, however, relating to the nature of the merchandise to which it is applied. Staple items, for example, with steady flows of sales can have ideal stocks quite easily adopted. Fashion items, however, result in a more general ideal stock philosophy because the exact styles or designs that comprise such items are subject to rapid change. Often, there is little or no reordering of identical goods (the seasonality factor). The problem of establishing ideal stock schedules is dynamic in nature. Plans require review and periodic adjustment in order to maintain a reasonable inventory balance.

Stock turnover

Fundamental to an understanding of merchandising is the concept of stock or inventory control, the method of its consumption and the ramifications of operating at inventory turnover rates that are not normal or reasonable. The rate of stock turnover is undoubtedly the most commonly used measure of the degree of balance between stock and sales. It is simply an index of the rate at which merchandise moves into and out of a store or department.

The maintenance of a healthy flow of merchandise is one of the principal avenues toward profit maximization. Care is required when evaluating the appropriateness of a turnover rate for a given firm, for different lines of business have widely varying turnover rates. This is not a result of some companies being inherently more efficient than others, but an indication that operating characteristics vary from firm to firm.

Thus, any anticipated change in the rate of inventory turnover must be evaluated in the light of its potential impact on all the variables that influence profit.

It is possible that the sales volume component of the strategic profit model may increase with a lower total stock quantity for three reasons. First, the stock is 'fresher' and turning more rapidly. Motivation on behalf of both staff and consumer is likely to be higher when the inventory is fresh and interesting than when the sales organization is constantly being urged to move merchandise that should never have been bought. In addition, a store with a low inventory is always in a good position to increase inventory levels when specific opportunities present themselves. Secondly, a fresher, more saleable stock may also lead to higher realized selling prices, as merchandise losses from physical deterioration, time obsolescence or fashion change are minimized. The result is a larger proportion of sales made at initial prices and a smaller proportion at marked down prices. Thirdly, a higher stock turnover rate can lead to a lower cost of goods sold, just as an open-to-buy position makes possible opportunistic buyouts, manufacturers' close downs and other special purchase situations.

Clearly, the management of inventories is fundamental to retail success. The variety of operations, successes and failures in the retailing industry leave few rules when attempting to guarantee operational continuity; however, following the basic principles of stock balance and stock turnover, many potential operating difficulties can be overcome. The nature of the retailing industry is that, in theory, market forces determine consumer choice, and in such a diversified consumer market, choice assortment seems a never ending continuum.

Display of merchandise

Introduction

When used effectively with other forms of promotion, displays (both window and interior) can, Bellenger and Goldstucker (1983) argue, act as a catalyst to sales. Davidson et al. (1988) expand on this assertion by adding that all displays have two basic functions. First, to arouse interest and stimulate the sale of the featured merchandise; secondly, to reinforce the institution position of the store in the marketplace.

Dramatic and compelling displays of merchandise in the windows and in the departments of the store are often more capable of persuading consumers to identify with fashion themes and styles than advertising or publicity. It is the retailers' belief, Bellenger and Goldstucker (1983) argue, that display forms the vital bridge between mass communication and personal selling. Lowry (1983) supports this view in asserting that visual merchandising includes effective displays that project the proper store image and assist the personal selling effort.

Retailers use window and interior displays to complement their other promotional activities. Unlike advertising, which is generally viewed at a location away from the store, displays are seen in the store. As a result, intentions to buy, argue Lowry (1983) and Bellenger and Goldstucker (1983), can be more easily converted to actual purchases. This makes a properly designed display a forceful selling device that can trigger impulse purchases. A feature of self-service establishments is their prolific use of eye-catching displays in order to tempt the consumer into making impulse purchases. Clearly, the selection of merchandise for display in store windows, open store fronts or special interior displays will be governed by a number of considerations. Davidson et al. (1988) crystallize the common opinions of other authors in this field into five distinct areas.

First, merchandise saleability is crucial to display effectiveness in that attractive and wanted merchandise sells readily, induces more people to come to the store or departmental selling area, and suggests that the entire merchandising operation is progressive. Obviously, an item may be selling well for a number of reasons; seasonality, fashion trends, uniqueness or price being some. However, continuous use of special displays to clear merchandise at special prices may lead shoppers to the conclusion that buying and pricing errors must be the rule rather than the exception.

Secondly, the merchandise for display must have impulse buying potential. An item may have a rapid rate of sale and yet be strictly a convenience demand good, not one that may be purchased on impulse with little subsequent potential for incremental volume. The grocer, for example, has little to gain by using valuable display space for staple items such as sugar and salt.

Thirdly, due consideration must be given to the margin of profit. Since display space is at a premium and must produce a return, the retailer can ill afford to think in terms of sales volume alone, but must also consider the gross profit margin and direct selling and handling costs to form a concept of display profitability.

Fourthly, the merchandise for display should feature tie-in characteristics. Co-ordinating departmental image or collaboration with strong national promotional campaigns by either suppliers or industry groups provides the consumer with an identifiable market position.

Finally, merchandise for display should provide for institutional support. Some displays should aim exclusively at the promotion of the store as an institution with little or no emphasis on specific merchandise. Store character or prestige also may be promoted through the display of goods of very limited demand. For example, a store seeking a reputation for fashion leadership in its community may give window display to expensive high fashion apparel or accessories at the opening of each new merchandising season. This type of promotion can be overdone, which creates resistance among consumers who would otherwise be in the defined market.

Whether the value of displays, particularly window display, is increasing or decreasing a store's profile and sales is debatable, but many retailers hold great value in display as a form of sales promotion. Bellenger and Goldstucker (1983) have noted how certain forces suggest a reduction in the importance of window displays, particularly those of large department stores.

Probably the most important and relevant factor diminishing window display effectiveness, they go on to argue, is the trend toward suburban shopping centres. People shopping in large suburban centre stores typically drive up to a store and enter immediately, which significantly reduces the opportunity to interest them in window displays away from the main entrance. Alternatively, town centre shopping areas with high pedestrian

traffic still get exceptional results from window displays. In this environment, shoppers move within an area from one store to another. Window
displays, therefore, make more sense in these areas. The same is true for
outlets in shopping centres, or malls, which experience a high volume of
leisurely shoppers who pass by their windows. Clearly, there is a sound case
for the use of display in the retail exchange environment. The task is to
identify the key components of an effective display.

Components of an effective display

The academic efforts in the area of displays are weak within the retailing
management discipline. Since the display of merchandise is fundamentally
a structure, assembling component parts into a 'whole' intended for
interpretation by the target audience, perception will have a significant part
to play in determining the relative merits of a display. Clearly, this
introduces an academic minefield as to how to quantify the effectiveness of
individual displays, as the motive and purpose behind every individual
display are likely to be different. However, at this point in time, the review
of relevant literature in retailing management does highlight five components, considered important when developing a display.

First, the display requires planning in order that the appropriateness and
feasibility of a display can be determined without losing the continuity of in-
store display. Lowry (1983) asserts that the display must have a theme and
ensure that this includes due consideration to the overall store image.
Additionally, Bellenger and Goldstucker (1983) suggest that the chosen
merchandise should be in demand, resulting in the projection of a good store
image if the displays show the right merchandise at the right time.

Secondly, the display should have input, or, as Davidson *et al.* (1988)
suggest, be distinctive, dramatic, arousing attention and interest through the
use of colour, lines, props, accessories, lighting and motion. Bellenger and
Goldstucker (1983) emphasize the importance of lighting in creating an
effective display, a view supported by industry practitioners.

Thirdly, the display should be up to date, pleasing and appropriate. A
display may be distinctive and even sensational in the eyes of its creator, yet
be ugly or offensive as perceived by its target market. All the elements
should be in agreement, so that the effect produced is one of unity.

Fourthly, the display should be simple in order to allow the intended
message to be quickly and clearly received and understood. Consequently,
the merchandise must lend itself to being balanced and simple in form as
well as appear neat and clean where appropriate.

Finally, a unanimous sentiment of the authors is that the merchandise in
display should be shown in use, as far as is practically possible. In addition,
relevant information as to price, uses, etc., should be readily available. In

order to maintain the effectiveness of displays, window displays may be changed on a weekly basis in larger city-based stores and more frequently in local stores. This is because the store in a small city or town, located in a compact business district, is likely to have its customers passing its windows more frequently. Clearly, displays inside the store need not be changed as frequently as this.

Types of display

There are two distinct categories of merchandise display: window and storefront and interior. Store windows and open fronts of shopping centre stores are used to invite the customer into exploring the possibilities for exchange to be found inside the store. Initially, the potential value of such display space depends on the circulation or the quantity and quality of the target market traffic that is exposed to it.

For promotional reasons alone, retailers would generally prefer to make display changes more frequently than they actually do. Alternatively, continuous unscheduled changes add expense and require effort; keeping sales staff notified of these changes requires effort (less so now with electronic point-of-sale equipment). Moreover, the floor space that would be required for window or entrance displays is valuable for interior merchandising. For these reasons, many new and modernized stores are planned with minimal emphasis on window display space. They have, instead, visual fronts which make up the store as an institutional type of display, or an enclosed or semi-enclosed front which maximizes the amount of interior wall selling space and enhances the architectural appeal of the exterior.

Interior display, in effect, gives merchandising life to the physical layout of the store and to the merchandise assortment created by the buyers. The term 'interior display' embraces all forms of merchandise exhibition and all promotional signs and decorations inside the store. Included here is everything from small and informal counter displays within a single department to storewide promotions, which in large stores are planned and executed by a central display staff. There are effectively four categories of interior display which Lowry (1983) terms as: closed assortment displays, open assortment displays, point of purchase displays and theme setting displays.

The closed assortment display allows the shopper to view the goods but without handling them. Generally, silverware and fine linens that may be damaged or stolen are often kept in display cases. However, many items that were formerly in closed displays have been changed to open displays in order to make goods more accessible to shoppers. This has been made possible by advancements of in-store security technology by security tagging and other protective devices.

An open assortment display allows shoppers to handle and try on the merchandise prior to purchase. Hang racks of dresses in department stores and the centre aisle displays of sale merchandise in discount stores are examples of open assortments. In self-service stores, exciting open assortment displays are necessary.

Point of purchase materials are a form of open assortment display that are located near the point of sale. The point of purchase displays of most cosmetics are familiar to department store shoppers. These are often prepared by suppliers who seek to draw attention to their goods. Some of these assortments remind shoppers of needed purchases, while others result in impulse buying. Most theme-setting displays are promotions associated with special events, such as 'back to school', graduation or June weddings. In a theme setting, the merchandise is displayed in a particular environment.

Advantages and disadvantages

Both displays and advertising have the fundamental purpose of either selling the featured merchandise or building a reputation over a longer period of time for the store. The advantages of displays in this regard are that they are used at the point of sale, drawing potential customers to the store and specific merchandise. The display presents the merchandise itself; life size, in a natural colour, with fabric texture and other details easier for the customer to see. In addition, Bellenger and Goldstucker (1983) argue that shopping is a form of entertainment. It is possible, they suggest, that good display is capable of creating a strong desire for merchandise, even with the passive customer.

Davidson *et al.* (1988) isolate further advantages of display. Groupings of related merchandise mean more sales; they make shopping easier for the consumer, often serving as reminders of needed items that otherwise might be forgotten. The cosmetic display that features a complete line, including eye make-up, lipstick, creams, etc., is one example of the application of ensemble promotion. As another example, in supermarkets it is common practice to display many houseware items in the food merchandising area, even though each store has a separate housewares section. Generally, such housewares merchandise is featured adjacent to, or along with, food items that are in some way related. Baking trays next to turkeys at Christmas and dishcloths in the cleansing section are examples.

These advantages speak strongly for displays but, because of their fixed position, they are not seen unless people visit the store intentionally, pass the display accidentally or are attracted to the store by advertising or publicity designed to bring them there. Wise retailers use display in conjunction with advertising to gain certain advantages. Displays make it possible to reach customers who have not been exposed to advertising and vice versa. Repetition creates a strong impression on the customer that the store considers the merchandise and themes featured as worth while.

The store's buyers have an incentive to develop bigger and more original promotions when promised the double action impact of advertising and display. Many merchandise managers and promotions directors, Bellenger and Goldstucker (1983) argue, believe that consistent and repetitive emphasis on important merchandise will produce greater sales. Indeed, in an era of self-service merchandising, point of purchase display materials prepared by manufacturers have grown in importance, serving as silent sales people that remind, signal attention and provide reasons for buying. The expanded use of such materials involves the manufacturer more directly in the retailing process and the creation of the exchange environment.

It can be seen that displays form an important factor in the promotional mix. If used correctly they attract customers and present the image of the store to passers-by. They expose the store in terms of its fashion timeliness, quality, creativity and overall personality. Their role is fundamental to many retailers (though not usually the promotional backbone) and should be considered carefully and be congruent with store objectives.

Clearly there is depth of understanding and a sophistication of approach evident which is of vital interest to the food and beverage manager, since inevitably retailers are now competing directly with caterers for disposable income.

The food and beverage context

Display and direct selling of food in the context of buffets, bars and trolley service have been already recognized by numerous authors in the food and beverage field: see Fuller (1974), Lillicrap (1983), Davis and Stone (1991). However, the detailed utilization of retailing principles in this area has not been examined. A key variable in this context is not only perception but also time. The development of one stop shopping, 'convenience' stores, cellular communication systems and fast food all have a relationship with time utilization. Appropriate display and seen evidence of rapid service/consumption have a critical appeal in a society where many working people feel they are deprived of time. In this context, eating out crosses the boundary constantly on what may be defined as leisure (cf. Parker, 1978) or, in a retail context, an essential versus a non-essential functional purchase (Lewison and Delozier, 1987). Eating out for pleasure has become one of the fastest growing areas of consumer spending in the UK (Jordans, 1992). Obviously, display can actively promote food during times of non-essential consumption. Accordingly, seat occupancy can be maximized during 'down' times if active retail promotion is utilized to increase 'impulse' purchases. Food and beverage analysts have much to learn from retailers in this context. Shopping has become a major social activity and a large leisure pursuit.

Most research shows that recreational shopping correlates positively with impulse purchasing. Impulse purchasing is one subject area that deserves further review, but essentially there is general agreement that it is related to a number of factors:

- Social context/environmental (group versus individual purchase)
- Purchase event (gift versus non-gift purchase)
- Physical environment and retail design
- Individual mood variation
- Marketing factors (24-hour retail possibilities)
- Environmental factors (exchange rates)
- Cultural aspects (attitude and lifestyle)
- Personality traits (e.g. materialism, sensation seeking).

Although non-essential shopping occurs less in the UK than shopping for essentials, it is of enough significance to warrant retail research in this area. Clearly the application to non-essential catering purchasing is clear. Food malls perhaps suggest the beginning of a response, but both in merchandising and display terms they require further development. There are, however, isolated examples of good practice that have occurred more as a reaction to accepted catering know-how rather than by looking at cross-application of retail principles. JD Wetherspoon, the pub operating company, has simply concentrated on traditional settings and quality produce. In focusing on strict design principles (real ale and no juke boxes) it has shown incredible growth since conception in the 1980s (Bolger, 1992). A pre-tax profit of £2 million on sales of £21 million were reported in 1992 and prospects for continued growth appear good. This pub chose to utilize a number of simple retailing concepts:

1 *Brand image.* Pubs trade under distinct brands, JJ Moons, Moons Under Water and White Lions of Mortimer, all branded with the JD Wetherspoon logo.
2 *Product mix.* In addition to a number of 'real ales', one low-priced beer is offered and careful attention is given to food.
3 *Decor/environment.* Traditional bar counter, hand-pull pumps, welcome atmosphere, unthreatening environment.
4 *Wide target market.* For example, the low price attracts students and pensioners (individuals with low discretionary income but who are potential high-volume customers).

5 *Location*. JD Wetherspoon has been willing to research potential locations in detail. Conversion of existing retail units to pubs was undertaken where locational research and competition analysis dictated.

What is important in the case of JD Wetherspoon is the utilization of retailing principles/concepts to create a successful chain with growth potential. Wetherspoon have recognized (as many retailers have) the key importance of captive/commuter custom and accordingly they operate in locations such as Liverpool Street railway station and Heathrow Terminal 4.

The physical confines of such locations present selling advantages. Travelling for many individuals will bring disorientation and will move people away from daily routines (Menzies, 1990). In this context, people are more susceptible to impulse purchasing. Retailing or catering in this context must emphasize speed of service, convenience and quality display to act as a catalyst for impulse buying. Although sensitive to passenger flows, prime locations such as airports and main line stations are less sensitive to price and high returns are feasible. However, catering operations must directly compete with retailers in this context. Accordingly, caterers should attempt to identify operational sites (e.g. railway stations with restoration potential) which are as yet under-exploited.

Airport retailing and catering are now, of course, major revenue generators but increasingly sophisticated retail mall developments, utilizing state-of-the-art display and merchandising techniques, would appear to be eclipsing the catering functions. Given that the 'duty free' market is so important in this context, it is interesting to see how, with the general abolition of fiscal frontiers, retailers are anticipating market change. The implications here for food and beverage locations are considerable. Since privatization in 1987, British Airports Authority plc (BAA) has considerably expanded its retail operations. It should be noted that much of the produce already for sale is not of a duty free nature. Accordingly, units survive as normally operating retail outlets. Its operating division, British Airports Services (BAS), has developed catering provisions. For example, the Gatwick Airport development of both the Avenue and Village Malls shows considerable investment in food and beverage units, which is encouraging. Whether it will remain competitive in the future is an area worthy of further examination.

Retail consultancy: a growth industry

Work in the field of merchandising, and display improvement in food and beverage operations, has provided a valuable revenue stream for consultants and in-house retail trainers. Breweries, in efforts to improve revenue generation, have been attempting to instil, in licensees, a retail approach to their operations. However, such work is fairly fundamental in its approach and rather simplistic in orientation. Normally pub managers or tenants are given simple information on retail concepts. For example, a basic classification of customers is undertaken to describe pub image by dominant consumer types. A current sample of this type of material is shown in Table 6.1.

Such consumer-related information is at best basic and at worst directly misleading. Clearly such material does not begin to consider the detailed work conducted on gender and social consumption (Deem, 1986; Hey, 1986), but rather represents an uncritical and rather banal operational approach to what is in essence a complex field.

Table 6.1 Sample 'retail'/pub consumer classifications for taverns: classification utilized by a major UK brewer

DOMINANT CONSUMER TYPES

1 Regular (predominantly male), middle-aged, after-work, group drinkers
2 Down-market, older (predominantly male), 'local' drinkers
3 Young, up-market singles, drink after work before moving on
4 Young mobile singles
5 Mature, habitual, local pub visitors
6 Infrequent drinkers

CONSUMER PROFILE

● Greater proportion of females
● Mixed age range with younger bias, and higher than average income
● Higher than average proportions of middle management, administrative and professional, and junior managerial, supervisory and clerical
● High proportion coming from work at lunchtime and early evening
● Local customers, especially at night
● Average travel is longer, due to lunchtime and early evening trade
● Shorter visits (lunch break and quick evening drink), and less frequent (larger repertoire)
● Product range needs to be wider to cater for range of consumers
● Hand-pulled cask ales preferred
● Catering is important, at lunchtimes and sometimes evening
● Quality of decor and facilities is important – traditional atmosphere, not fashionable
● 'No threats' and 'a place that's a bit special in its area' are important – not too busy
● Relatively even spread of trade throughout the day
● Often a suburban traditional pub, accessible to offices, business and private housing
● Quick, efficient service required

Source: Momentum Training (1991a).

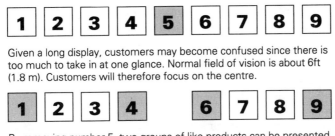

Given a long display, customers may become confused since there is too much to take in at one glance. Normal field of vision is about 6ft (1.8 m). Customers will therefore focus on the centre.

By removing number 5, two groups of like products can be presented. Now customers will take in each group at a glance. The majority of customers look from left to right, so positions 1 and 6 will be fairly strong and 4 and 9 will be very strong. Most retailers position brands they want to sell to the right. If this were a bar with two displays and a till in the centre, 6 would be the strongest position.

Figure 6.1 Sample grouping products for effective merchandising (*Source*: Momentum Training, 1991b)

The approach to display is also fairly fundamental (see, for example, Figures 6.1 and 6.2). Perception and areas such as colour, product linkage and zoning are ignored, whereas (in this case) fairly simple display techniques are advanced. When compared with approaches common within the retail industry (detailed earlier), the lack of sophistication and detail is evident. Areas such as window and shelf display are simply not given prominence beyond the most cursory approaches to producing 'visual impact'. Action checklists are utilized frequently by consultants in this type of training (Table 6.2) as *aides-mémoire* and active learning tools. However, despite such efforts the approach is at a very low level and does not begin to comprehend the complexity of merchandising and display.

When products are brought to the front edge of a shelf they have good impact. The impact diminishes when the leading edge is lost.

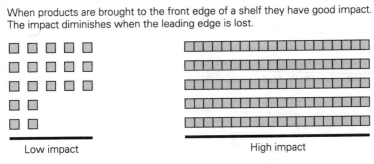

Low impact   High impact

If the shelves are too deep, leave the back empty and concentrate on the leading edge.

Figure 6.2 Sample leading edge display technique (*Source*: Momentum Training, 1991b)

Table 6.2 Sample action checklist for managed pubs

	No	Yes

Entering the pub
Does the pub look demonstrably open?
Can we see in?
Is the entrance warm and welcoming?
Is the external lighting correctly used?
Is the back door as inviting as the front?
Is the exterior clean and presentable?
Does the lobby offer helpful advice?
Can we have an impression of what we are walking into?
Are gardens and car parks tidy and presentable?

Inside
Is there background music?
Does music and atmosphere match customers?
Does it match expectation created from the outside?
Does furniture layout match the groups of customers arriving?
Has customer flow been carefully planned?
Are toilets and other amenities clearly signed?
Is light appropriate to time of day?
Is pub warm and inviting for first customer?

Source: Momentum Training (1991a).

Clearly not all approaches to applying retail principles in food and beverage are so simplistic. The pub company, JD Wetherspoon's intuitive business approach and the type of interactive merchandising and training used by the TGI Friday chain are good examples of more sophisticated directions being taken.

Location strategy for food and beverage: some examples of practice

In food courts the linkage with retail is clearly of a functional service nature. Eating out becomes a part of the shopping experience and major elements of the gross leasable area of many malls are let to caterers (Menzies, 1991). In this context, food preparation and service are often clearly visible and in better operations almost of a theatrical nature (for example, Faneuil Hall in Boston, Massachusetts, and Ghiradelli Square in San Francisco, California). In such an operation (literally a food mall), crowds are drawn to watch a master chef/baker at work. However, the variety of food experiences available in a food court can often be a reason for failure. This is not just because of the closeness of competition, but also the labour intensive nature of manning a multi-unit food court. In order for it to remain open and staffed, there are little opportunities for management to make operational labour savings when demand is low. Location and level of catchment are also key areas which may result in failure in food court terms. However, location can create an independent dynamic. Milburns, a small catering company with a reputation for quality food and service, has targeted some of the UK's finest visitor attractions as locations for food and beverage outlets (Milburns Restaurants Ltd., 1992). The Milburns rationale for this is a simple understanding that food and beverage can extend the visitor stay and improve the visitor experience of a quality attraction such as the Victoria and Albert Museum, London (Sutton, 1990). Thus the integration of food and beverage within visitor attractions and as a part of retail malls is extremely important and has been well demonstrated by Disney in its theme park operations in the US, Japan and France. For example, Main Street is the major thoroughfare through which all visitors to parks enter and exit. This area sees optimum integration of food and beverage and retail outlets which are strategically located and effectively promoted. Again, a formula of extending visitor stay with a view to maximizing revenue potential is in operation here. Similar trends are occurring in the sports and recreation and leisure fields. Developers are grouping individual leisure attractions together to realize:

● Economies of scale
● Variety of base attractions
● Increased retailing opportunities
● Increased food and beverage potential

This pattern is obvious in UK shopping mall developments (e.g. Newcastle upon Tyne's Metro Centre and Sheffield's Meadowhall Complex), wherein retail is located with leisure facilities and both integrate food and beverage facilities.

Conclusions

In theory then, one might assume that food and beverage operators are utilizing retailing strategy. In practice, however, it is clear that the thorough application is not great and the level of theoretical appreciation is weak. For example, in terms of feasibility for a food and beverage operation, if one applies retailing strategy the planning processes should include:

1 Investigation of catchment area (with reference to existing and future development, gender balance, demographics, lifestyle, disposable income, chronological profiling, etc.).
2 Site evaluation.
3 Competitor analysis (not merely in terms of food and beverage but in terms of any competitor targeting of disposable income).
4 Concept development, that is appropriate for the target market.
5 Projecting sales, costs and profitability in relation to floor space utilization. Further examining payback and return on investment in terms of location and asset base.
6 Analysing potential market/sales variation based on market type and size assumptions.
7 Qualitative market research.
8 Quantitative market research.
9 Identification of product mix, either food, beverage or more broadly catering leisure/retail.

Food service and production could provide a fulcrum link between retail and leisure, since it is becoming an increasingly important part of the shopping and leisure experience. However, until caterers recognize the advantages of utilizing retail principles in the sale and provision of food and beverage, their success rates and their future potential will remain poor. Such techniques can be applied to small operators as easily as larger groups. A retailer such as Matches (Garnett, 1993) utilizes computer-based sales analysis to review purchasing for what is essentially a small, up-market 'designer' clothing store. Matches' computer system can accommodate a 9000 customer mailing list which can build in personal preference and customer taste, as well as gift purchase specifications. The customer base is quantified and allied to strict design criteria. All units are small (approximately 600 ft^2, 56 m^2) and are refurbished at a cost of approximately £70,000. Customers are offered complimentary coffee, wine and beer and staff are paid on basic salary plus generous sales-related bonuses. Matches operates on a 38 per cent gross margin, with a sales growth of 15 per cent per year. Thus, if even a small retail operator can utilize technology and principles to secure a market position and profit-based growth, there should be no excuse for the sluggish reluctance of many caterers to adapt. The strategies are in existence; the application is the task of the food and beverage company of whatever scale – to ignore this area may well have serious long-term consequences.

References

Bellenger, D. N. and Goldstucker, J. L. (1983). *Retailing Basics*. Illinois: Irwin.

Bolger, A. (1992). Finding the way to the right bar. *Financial Times*, 29 August, p. 30.

Davidson, W. R., Sweeney, D. J. and Stampfl, R. W. (1988). *Retailing Management*, 6th edn. Chichester, UK: John Wiley.

Davis, B. and Stone, S. (1991). *Food and Beverage Management*, 2nd edn. Oxford: Butterworth-Heinemann.

Deem, R. (1986). *All Work and No Play? The Sociology of Women's Leisure.* Milton Keynes, UK: OU Press.

Duncan, L. and Hollander, T. (1977). *Modern Retailing Basic Concepts and Practices*, 9th edn. Illinois: Homewood.

Fuller, J. (1974). *Chef's Manual of Kitchen Management*, 3rd edn. London: Batsford.

Garnett, N. (1993). From rags to riches. *Financial Times*, 22 May, p. viii.

Hey, V. (1986). *Patriarchy and Pub Culture*. London: Tavistock.

Jordans (1992). *Britain's Catering Industry.* Bristol: Jordans.

Lewison, D. M. and Delozier, M. W. (1987). *Retailing*. New York: John Wiley.

Lillicrap, D. (1983). *Food and Beverage Service*. London: Edward Arnold.

Lowry, J. R. (1983). *Retail Management*. Cincinatti: South Western Publishing Co.

Milburn's Restaurants Ltd (1992). Sales and Marketing Brochure. Bath, UK: Milburn's.

Momentum Training (1991a). House Marketing and Merchandising Plan (Training Materials). Edinburgh: Momentum Training.

Momentum Training (1991b). Retail Marketing and Merchandising (Training Materials). Edinburgh: Momentum Training.

Parker, S. (1978). *The Sociology of Leisure*. London: Methuen.

Rogers, D. S. and Grassi, M. (1988). *Retailing: New Perspectives*. London: Dryden Press.

Sutton, A. (1990). A quality image for museums. *HCIMA Year Book 1989–1990, pp. 326–327.*

7 Restaurant company financial performance analysis

Alex Noble

Introduction

Several years ago, I was discussing financial performance with a friend who was about to open a restaurant. He had decided on a location, on the principle of finding a street which already had several successful restaurants and doing something slightly different from them, but within the same genre. We discussed all the usual criteria – the financial and operating ratios he could use to monitor performance, the limitations to borrowing as part of his initial capital, and so on. He duly opened the restaurant, achieved only modest success, but certainly preferred it to working as deputy chief accountant (to me) in the City. He later told me that the financial rewards were less – certainly when considered as an hourly rate – but that factor was easily outweighed by 'quality of working life' considerations such as being his own boss, making his own decisions, having a regular clientele who were not just customers but friends, and so on. I have lost touch with him recently, but so far as I know his modest success continues and he is perfectly happy in his career.

One of my local streets is a bit like the one in which Hassan set up in business. During the past decade it has changed character dramatically, from being a very mixed suburban high street, through a period when every second property was occupied by an estate agent, to the current incarnation when the estate agents are being replaced by restaurants. The classic adage of 'go where the competition is' is working with a vengeance, and there are now almost twenty restaurants in a half-mile long street which originally had only four, including two rather dubious cafes. Several have clearly caught the mood of the time and are extremely busy; most others have busyish weekends but are largely deserted during the early part of the week. There are two, however, which are worth reflecting on. They occupy corner sites, with nothing to distinguish those sites from the rest of the street, at first glance, anyway. On these sites, in contrast to the rest of the street, restaurants have come and gone, lasting anything from three months to two years; one site has had four different owners and styles, the other five. It doesn't seem to matter whether the style is wine bar, bistro, up-market restaurant or whatever; it doesn't seem to matter whether the same style is working elsewhere in the street; it doesn't seem to help that the owners have previously been successful with restaurants in other parts of the area. Restaurants simply do not survive in these locations.

These introductory comments may seem a long way removed from the financial performance analysis required by the heading to this chapter. They do serve to create a context, however. Many writers on financial appraisal have hinted, implied or even said outright that finance and thus financial appraisal are the be-all and end-all of any business enterprise. They are not. Financial *solvency* is (of course) essential, but many other factors come into play in the real world, and maximizing profit may well be some way from the top of the list. Again, it is worth emphasizing the old principle that performance analysis provides information and enables questions to be asked. It only rarely provides the answers; it never takes the decisions stemming from these answers. That is the role of managers or owner/ managers according to context. It also has a less common function in providing basic information when a business is about to start, and it is this aspect that will now be focused on.

Decision time

An individual may decide on a restaurant career explicitly to make money. Many more will be in the business for a variety of vague or ill-defined reasons connected with an enjoyment of cooking, meeting interesting customers and having a perception of a glamorous way of life. Many in these latter categories pay scant attention to the financial aspects, and have some vague idea that the venture will be profitable so long as they can more than half-fill the restaurant on average. A very large proportion of these enterprises fail within the first few months, and it may be argued that if the owners had considered some elementary financial statistics before they started, they might well have done things differently, or maybe not started at all.

Every elementary text on finance will contain a chapter or chapters on the interpretation of accounts, which will include details of the measurements which may be taken and notes on the meaning of these measurements. It is not intended to reproduce these exhaustively here, and the reader is referred to such texts as Kotas (1986) and Coltman (1979) for a treatment of the main ratios (in particular) normally used in the hospitality industry. We will use these measures to look at a possible approach to opening a restaurant by a newcomer to the business.

Before embarking on that task, we can perhaps review the main types of measurement in common use, and look at how they might be applied in circumstances such as these.

Types of measurement

The normal classification of information is into *financial ratios*, using money figures which (in an established business) will normally be derived from the accounts, and *operating ratios*, such as seat turnover, which are derived from non-financial information, or from a mixture of the financial and non-financial. Also valuable in this context will be an understanding of the nature of the costs we are dealing with, particularly their changeability with volume of business. In other words, are individual costs fixed, variable, or somewhere in between?

Any two figures can be used to produce a ratio, of course, since we define 'ratio' as the relationship between two figures. It follows that some ratios have no meaning at all, and others are only relevant in specific circumstances. A number are of almost universal application, and are used as indicators of general well-being.

The measurement most often used as a touchstone is the *return on capital employed*. This suffers from various definitions, all differing in detail, but most commonly along the lines of

$$\frac{\text{Net profit}}{\text{Equity + Loans}}$$

From the point of view of our budding restaurateurs, this is of value mainly in comparison with other enterprises once they have got going (are we doing as well as they are and we should be?)

More to the point at the planning stage is the potential *return on equity*. This is measured as

$$\frac{\text{Profit after interest}}{\text{Owner's equity}}$$

The logic of this is as follows: the owners will have put a significant sum of money into the business. This is clearly risk capital, i.e. they will almost certainly lose it if the business goes wrong. But they do have a choice; they could put their money (effectively risk free) into a building society and obtain a return on it there. They could also (we will assume) go to work for another restaurateur and obtain a salary for doing so. We can now take the remaining profit after interest has been paid, adjust it for the salaries which the owners would have received had they been in comparable employment, and look at it as a return on their investment. An example may make this clearer. Suppose we are projecting a profit after interest of £40,000 for a restaurant in its first year, the owners having put in £200,000 of their own money. This therefore represents a return on equity of 20 per cent, which on the face of it is reasonable. The accounts will not allow for owners' 'salaries', however, but we know that a husband and wife managing a similar restaurant elsewhere will jointly earn about £30,000. It follows that the comparable return on equity is only £10,000 or 5 per cent, which most of the time is less than the rate available from a long-term building society account, and far less than the expected return from an investment in equities carrying a similar level of risk.

There are many reasons why such a return may be acceptable, of course. Many people prefer to work for themselves for a lower return rather than maximize their income as an employee; the return is a one-year figure, and future profits *may* be higher; the income is to a degree related to effort put in and may therefore be controllable, with harder work being directly rewarded; short of bankruptcy there is probably more security – or at least decisions are in their own hands ... and so on. The point is that this kind of analysis tells them what decisions they need to take and gives them the basic information on which to take them. *How much* do they value the freedom of their own business – would they still go it alone if the potential return on investment were negative, for example?

If they were to approach the position in a calculated manner, they would work out the return required on their capital investment on a basis of expecting the risk-free return as from a building society, plus a premium for taking the greater risk involved in this type of business. If the risk-free return were say 8 per cent and they wanted a risk premium of 7 per cent (begging the question of how this is to be calculated for the moment), they would then want a net profit after interest and notional salary of £30,000, i.e. £60,000 *before* the notional salary is deducted. Whether they went into the business would then turn on whether they could realistically expect a profit of that level.

Risk premium

Returning to the question of risk premium, there is a wealth of published work on the subject; it has a been debating issue among accountants and financial economists for many decades. Much of the theory is (at first glance) less than useful to the small business, since it is derived from portfolio theory and large public companies. It takes the position of the investor as investor rather than as owner manager; it assumes that those investors are prepared to move in and out of investments to obtain a 'balanced portfolio', so spreading (and thus minimizing) their risk. It is undoubtedly sound in its overall precepts, but with still some life in the debate and uncertainty round the edges. Its principles are also surprisingly versatile, and are by no means inapplicable to the small organization if this is carefully done. The more rigid theorists may blanch a little, but this they have done since Noah protested that a 300-cubit ark couldn't float unless the elephants were left behind!

The principles behind the theories are these.

1 Risk (for this purpose) is measured as the standard deviation of the expected returns from the investment. It follows that for an investment such as a government stock, where a precise return is stated at the beginning, guaranteed by a sovereign authority, risk is at its lowest possible value. It may then be taken as zero and all other situations related to that.
2 Any other investment carries some risk in comparison. This risk is generally held to contain two components – *business risk* and *financial risk*. Business risk relates to the variability of the likely return arising from the nature of the business, financial risk to variability of return arising from the presence of prior calls on that money – broadly on the gearing of the business.

It seems logical that the business risk of a delicatessen will be higher than that of a small supermarket selling staple foods – the sales and thus the profits of the former are due to marginal purchases, the latter are core items and thus more stable. It further seems logical that investors will prefer the stability of the latter unless they can anticipate a higher average return as compensation for taking the extra risks of the former.

If a business runs partially on borrowed money rather than equity, the return to the lenders is a charge on profits prior to the owners' calls on that profit. The result is an amplification of the fluctuations in return. If, for example, profit before interest changes from £100m to £120m, that is clearly a change of 20 per cent. If there is a prior charge of £50m in interest, the profit attributable to the shareholders changes from £50m to £70m, a fluctuation of 40 per cent. A degree of gearing is normally beneficial – if money remunerated at 10 per cent can earn pre-tax profits of 15 per cent that has to be good for the owners – but again, as with business risks, the extra financial risk may be expected to carry a penalty in the extra return required by the owners for taking it.

A great deal of theoretical work has been done in this area by, *inter alia*, Modigliani and Miller (1958), on the relative costs of debt and equity, by

Markowitz (1952) on portfolio selection, and by Sharpe (1964), Lintner (1965) and Mossin (1966) on market equilibrium under conditions of risk. It is suggested, however, that the non-specialist reader refer to a distillation of their work if deeper elucidation is required, rather than consulting the original papers. Such a summary is found in several texts on company finance, including Samuels *et al.* (1990) and Brealey and Myers (1991). The essence of the matter is that, for shareholders, a large proportion of the risks can be eliminated through diversification. Certain parts of the risk – 'unique risk' – are specific to any given share, and by a judicious selection of companies that part of the risk can be offset and thus cancelled out. The residual part of the risk – 'market risk' – cannot be so eliminated, as it is inherent in equity investment and thus present in all shares. Investors will not be able to seek a risk premium for that part of the risk they can eliminate, but can legitimately expect to be compensated for bearing the market risk. An extension of this is the so-called Capital Asset Pricing Model of Sharpe, Mossin and Lintner, who pointed out that while the market risks affected all businesses, it did not affect them all equally, and that the risk premium required would not be the same for all companies – thus agreeing with the position noted through basic common sense. From their work a well-known formula has been devised, which expresses the market risk of a given company as a multiple of the average market risk for all companies (giving a factor known by the Greek letter beta, β) and uses that to calculate the expected rate of return.

The logic is as follows: the return expected on a share will be the risk-free return plus a risk premium. The risk premium will be found as beta times the average risk premium for all companies. An example may make this clearer.

Suppose the risk-free rate is known to be 9 per cent, and the average return being earned by all quoted shares is 15 per cent. The market is a free market, which will adjust the price of shares so that the actual money return gives the rate deemed right for those shares. It follows that the market expects an average risk premium of 6 per cent, i.e. the excess return over the risk-free rate. If a particular share has a beta of 1.5 (being regarded as 1.5 times as susceptible to market risks as the average share), the risk premium expected for it will be 9 per cent, and the overall expected return will be 9 + 9 = 18 per cent. In general, the expected return on a security will be

$$R_s = R_{rf} + \beta(R_m - R_{rf})$$

where R_s = expected return on a security, R_{rf} = risk-free return, R_m = average market return, and β = beta.

For large quoted companies the calculation of beta is normally done *ex post facto* based on historical data, basically saying that this tells us what beta *was*, and is therefore the best approximation to what it *is*. It is inevitable in such circumstances of empirical assessment that different analysts produce slightly different figures for the beta of an individual company. The emphasis, though, should be on the word 'slightly'.

The application

In our assessment of compensatable risk we have moved from a measure based on the standard deviation of the expected returns to one based on those risks which cannot be diversified away, on the grounds that a rational investor is risk averse, will hold a risk-minimizing portfolio of shares, and thus will neither seek nor be entitled to compensation for those risks which can be diversified away. To repeat, however, most of the work in this field focuses on large, quoted companies with a ready market in their shares and (largely) identifiable risks. It is of no direct relevance to the circumstances we are considering, but it does provide a benchmark to which our small restaurateur can relate his affairs.

How, then, do we apply it? Various organizations calculate betas, frequently as part of an investment service and for a fee. We can look at a selection of betas for the kind of business we are interested in, i.e. restaurant companies, and thereby see what the market thinks of those large companies. There are two minor difficulties here – there are few quoted businesses which are *solely* restaurant based, and there are considerable variations in the betas of individual companies within any classification, reflecting the market view of their individual exposures. We can use 'industry average' betas, though, which will get over at least one of the problems. Even industry average betas change over time, but by relatively little, given that they are being measured in relation to the market as a whole, which (by definition) has a beta of one. We find that some typical industry betas are in the region of:

breweries	0.85
food retailing	0.80
food manufacture	0.90
leisure	0.95
tobacco	1.15

As we would expect, staple businesses like food retailing are safest, and therefore command less of a premium than riskier ones. Leisure is regarded as safer than the market average, but not by very much. Tobacco is unusual in this regard, but no doubt the perceived health risks contribute to that.

As a result of that, we could decide on an appropriate beta for our restaurant company. Possibly it equates near enough to 'leisure', and using the market beta of 1.00 would be a fair measure of risk.

This is a baseline. It would only apply if our company were both large and typical and, like all calculated betas, it assumes the company is geared to the level of the average company of that type. It would be lower for an ungeared business, to allow for the smaller financial risk, but the calculation of the resulting 'ungeared beta' is beyond the scope of this reading.

If the potential restaurateurs accept that analysis they would be looking for a return of the same as the average for the Stock Market as a whole, although they would be wise to consider that a minimum, given the extra risks of a small company. In recent years that would produce an expected return of some 5 per cent over the risk-free rate.

This will allow a focus on a particular minimum level of profit and forces consideration of the main parameters of the projected profit and loss account, and of the validity of the underlying assumptions. The level of sophistication of the analysis will depend on the time and skills available, of course, but even a rudimentary check will unearth a number of practical figures which will have a ring of plausibility (or implausibility as the case may be).

At the most basic level, the measures of *average spend* and *gross profit margin* can be combined. The type of restaurant is obviously known, and experience or local knowledge can be brought to bear on the question of the likely size of the average customer's bill. Again, local or industry knowledge can be utilized to project a gross profit percentage for the type of establishment. For example, an average spend of £15 and a gross profit percentage of 60 per cent will give a gross profit per meal of £9. At this basic level, average spend can be regarded as marginal revenue, food and beverage cost as marginal cost, and therefore gross profit per meal as contribution. All other costs are treated as fixed. If these come to say £60,000, the required contribution is that plus the notional salary of £30,000 and the 15 per cent return on investment (also of £30,000), a total of £120,000. It follows that about 13,350 meals have to be sold in the year to achieve the necessary income and profit.

Is that plausible? Will the restaurant sell 45 covers a night? Will the good weekend takings make up for Monday when the place is almost deserted? Should they close on Monday and avoid some of the costs? This analysis will direct their minds to the questions, but not solve them.

Conclusion

All that is a far cry from my local street. Restaurants come and go, high hopes fade and starry eyes dim – or dreams are fulfilled in reality, all with no obvious reason for success or failure. Many factors are at work, and in the end gut feeling or basic instinct may be as good a guide as anything. All the same, there might be just a few less catastrophes if some paid a little more attention to the financial fundamentals, even if it did get briefly in the way of brooding over whether cassoulet was quite suitable to the ambience, or whether only lobster thermidor would do.

References

Brealey, R. A. and Myers, S. C. (1991). *Principles of Corporate Finance*. New York: McGraw-Hill, Chaps. 7 and 8.

Coltman, M. M. (1979). *Financial Management for the Hospitality Industry.* Van Nostrand Reinhold, Chap. 2, pp. 12–40.

Kotas, R. (1986). *Management Accounting for Hotels and Restaurants*. Guildford, UK: Surrey University Press, Chap. 15, pp. 259–276, Chap. 16, pp. 277–288.

Lintner, J. (1965). The valuation of risk assets and the selection of risky investments in stock portfolios and capital budgets. *Review of Economics and Statistics*, **47**, 13–37.

Markowitz, H. M. (1952). Portfolio selection. *Journal of Finance* **7**, 13–37.

Modigliani, F. and Miller, M. H. (1958). The cost of capital, corporation finance and the theory of investment. *American Economic Review*, **48**, 261–297. This article opened a lengthy debate on the subject, which lasted more than a decade and gave rise to a formidable body of theory on the subject.

Mossin, J. (1966). Equilibrium in a capital asset market. *Econometrica*, **34** 768–783.

Samuels, J. M., Wilkes, F. M. and Brayshaw, R. E. (1990). *Management of Company Finance*. London: Chapman and Hall, Chaps 8 and 9.

Sharpe, W. F. (1964). Capital asset prices: a theory of market equilibrium under conditions of risk. *Journal of Finance*, **19**, 425–442.

Part Two

Planning and Design

8 Location analysis and market feasibility

David Capstick

Introduction

Location analysis and market feasibility represent two critical issues at the planning and design stage of any project. An unfavourable analysis of the location and the infeasibility of operating within the bounds of the market should terminate the project. Accepting that the study of these two areas is an essential part of any project, it is difficult therefore to contemplate that a completed project should fail.

However, the reality of the situation is very different. There are many factors which contribute to either no study being undertaken at all, or only a partial study having been conducted. Factors as diverse as relying purely on 'gut feeling' through to short sighted cost cutting in not providing sufficient financial resources to conduct an adequate study are often quoted examples. Personal confidence alone in a project is not enough; experience has shown that researched data to confirm initial reactions are indispensable.

This chapter will illustrate the importance of thorough location analysis and a well-researched market feasibility study. By reference to factors that require consideration when developing a food and beverage operation, a recommended approach to location analysis and market feasibility will be presented.

The areas of study are both wide and varied. When assessing location and market, the implications and ramifications of the issues covered in the other contributing chapters of this book are also valid. It would be impossible to proceed with this stage of the study without considering, either broadly or in detail, strategic issues, operational policies, marketing strategies, financial aspects, etc., as all these factors contribute to the overall product. Many of the areas of study and issues raised in a feasibility study are directly associated with marketing issues. A number of the points discussed under location analysis and market feasibility also appear in marketing topics.

The food and beverage operation is a combination of the product, the price, the location and the market. Ascertaining how these factors fit together is critical to the success of any food and beverage operation.

In essence, the topic for discussion is no more complicated than examining a straightforward approach to feasibility studies. There is not, and it is probably not possible, to define a comprehensive, all-embracing framework for a feasibility study. Any study will be dependent on a format which is tailored to be particular to the exercise in progress. Buttle (1986)

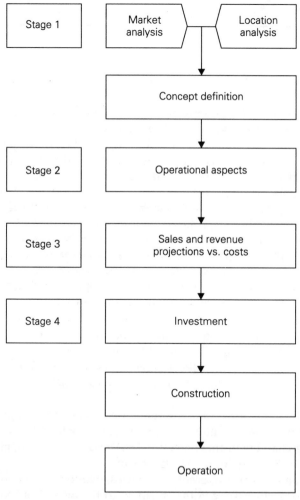

Figure 8.1 Outline of a feasibility study (*Source*: Buttle, 1986)

illustrates diagrammatically in detail the scope of issues reviewed, while undertaking a feasibility study. The broad approach to a study is identified in Figure 8.1 to reflect the relative importance of location and market from the outset when considering the global perspective of a feasibility study.

A study is naturally progressive and therefore becomes staged. In this simplistic model the initial stage reflects location and market assessment together with preliminary marketing aspects and concept definition. The second stage considers and encompasses all operational criteria and requirements, while financial considerations represent the third stage. The final phase accounts for action, i.e. investment, construction and eventual 'live' operation of the facilities.

It is important to remember that a feasibility study is only relevant for the time period during which it was conducted. Like a food and beverage product, the study has a shelf life and requires updating. A feasibility study is, and can only be, a snapshot of the situation for a designated period of time.

It is therefore established that location analysis and market feasibility are an integral part of a formal feasibility study. It is difficult to discuss location and market separately, and so too is it impossible to conduct feasibility studies without considering these two aspects.

What is the relationship between location and the market?

Location and market are intrinsically linked. Location is, by definition, site specific. The site can range from a plot of land or a building through to a larger physical geographical area, for instance a city or region. Ultimately for food and beverage operations a specific and defined location or site will require precise identification in order to ensure an objective study.

A location can exist in its own right, irrespective of the presence of a market for a defined food and beverage product. Traditional intuitive feeling and experience will always contribute to the identification of a location; however, the success of the location is critically dependent on the market.

The market, and all those factors which make up the market, are flexible and moveable. The market surrounds and encompasses the location. The market exerts both direct and indirect pressures and influences on the location.

The market therefore has to be identified and measured. First, the proposed food and beverage offer requires definition in order to identify the target market. Without determining the food and beverage offer it is difficult, or impossible, to assess the market.

Any proposed operation at a specific location, however, would be unable to survive without an identified market. There are many examples of situations where operations have opened with insufficient research having been undertaken and closure has soon followed. Similarly it should not be forgotten that markets change and/or move; therefore, future developments should be considered from the outset. A location cannot change – it is a fixed site and an appreciation of this fact is critical from the beginning.

In considering location and market, three key aspects should be examined. These are the present situation, changes that can be foreseen and the effect of these changes on the future success of the operation. Understandably a degree of modelling and assumptions require to be initiated.

A feasibility study provides the framework to establish the inextricable link between location and market. In order to assess the two factors and base a decision on the findings of the research, a predetermined method of approach should be identified. Food and beverage operations are no different to other businesses in terms of initial research.

What is feasibility?

Feasibility means 'being possible', 'able to be done'. A study is undertaken to examine all options, and where possible to account for all eventualities, to assist in the decision-making process of proposing a recommendation. In terms of opening a food and beverage catering operation, the recommendation would be based on the viability of such an operation.

Ward (1989), with reference to hotels, states that the 'purpose of a feasibility study is to provide an objective, independent appraisal of an opportunity, providing sufficient information . . . to make a decision as to proceed or not'. The key to the success of a feasibility study is assembling relevant information in order to make a balanced decision.

Why conduct a feasibility study?

It is important to realize that feasibility studies are conducted for a variety of reasons. The size and scope of food and beverage feasibility studies vary dramatically and are not necessarily only applicable to new build scenarios. Businesses, in normal trading circumstances, are under continual review and this inevitably leads to a form of ongoing feasibility study.

Greene (1993) and Ward (1989) highlight a number of reasons for the initiation of such a study. The reasons, which are common and standard, fall into three broad identifiable categories:

1 *Financial*
   - to support applications to raise finance
   - to establish trading levels, culminating in cash flow and profit forecasts
   - the determination of pay-back periods

2 *Operational*
  ● to define the operation
  ● to attract potential operators
  ● to calculate optimum land use
  ● the preparation of planning permission documentation
3 *Marketing*
  ● location analysis
  ● market identification
  ● concept definition
  ● competition analysis
  ● strengths, weaknesses, opportunities and threats analysis

Catering operations are traditionally characterized by a variety of features. A short cycle of operations aligned with the unpredictability of volume of business offering a highly perishable product are but a few examples. Although these factors can be managed at the operating stage, it is important to assess their future impact at feasibility level.

The above-mentioned points reflect the main areas of study, but, the list is by no means comprehensive. The actual areas of study will be defined in the terms of reference of the report. Identifying location and market are thus shown to be essential to the study.

Types of feasibility study

The reasons for conducting feasibility studies have been identified above. The application of location analysis and market feasibility varies within different types of food and beverage feasibility studies.

It is possible to identify a minimum of five food and beverage operation study types:

1 *New projects.* The most commonly experienced and most comprehensive type of study. Various options are reviewed from a new building, a new site, or a new idea/concept to new areas of business.
2 *Existing, operational facilities.* The units may be currently operating as a food and beverage outlet or a site may be considered for a change of use to catering. An advantage to this type of study is that there is an amount of previous trading history in the current market to be reviewed.
3 *Existing, non-operational facilities.* There are a variety of units which fall into this category. Previously trading units, now closed, are an example. The reasons for failure are often blatantly apparent. In some instances sites may be an integral part of an overall scheme with catering being designated, in a preconceived form, to a particular location. Shopping centres are a prime example.

4 *On-going expansion and rollout programmes*. Large organizations such as fast food operators with established concepts continue with rollout programmes which have largely become standardized. Studies follow defined patterns and are not necessarily less detailed. There are inherent dangers in this type of study, as the objectivity of the exercise should not be lost. Sites are unique and consideration should be realistic.

5 *Feasibility studies within feasibility studies*. The situation arises where food and beverage operations are a part of an overall concept or project, for example Center Parcs in Europe. The catering element requires separate analysis within the overall study. In this example the location and market are defined.

As it has already been established that each feasibility study is unique, this list of possible food and beverage feasibility types is unlikely to be comprehensive. However, the type of study illustrates the differing location and market considerations.

The feasibility study

In theory, the application of a feasibility study should be standard in terms of approach. However, the criteria used and areas examined should be particular to either the operation envisaged or the objective of the study. For example, a study into a pizza home delivery operation will be different to that of a city centre cafe bar operation.

There is neither a right nor a wrong way to approach location analysis and market feasibility. It is essential, though, that there is a methodology to the study. A methodology will provide three benefits:

- A quality study and report
- A better development process for the next stage of the project
- An improved overall recommendation

It can be assumed that there is a broad framework within which to work. There are identifiable features to a feasibility study which are essential to achieving the above-mentioned points. First, there must be a clearly defined objective. Secondly, complete access to full information on the project should be permitted. This information must be relevant and directly related to the study. Thirdly, a structured approach is a prerequisite. These points all contribute to the methodology. The published references at the end of the chapter identify this need for a methodology.

Feasibility studies, and in particular location analysis and market feasibility, are the first stage of a longer project if the recommendation of the report is to proceed. It is therefore imperative to remember that this report is a critical first step; an incorrect interpretation at the feasibility stage will lead to a disaster at project termination.

Approach

The approach will be variable, to account for the situation. The first step will be the appointment of a feasibility study team. The second step entails establishing the terms of reference. In normal circumstances these will be set by a steering committee.

The format of the study will be guided by a number of factors. Feasibility study definition will include time and manpower resources available, identification of areas to be addressed, available information, etc. The report structure will be defined and a programme of events to include reviews and progress presentations agreed. The culmination of the whole exercise will be the final report presentation. The recommendation is the outcome.

The diverse nature of types of feasibility study, depending on the food and beverage product under consideration, or the stage in the product's lifecycle, will ensure flexibility in the methodology.

Following the appointment of the study team and the terms of reference, the next step will be the assessment of the location and market. Kendall (1982) suggests a phased project development process. The process proposed is applicable to food and beverage operations. The identifiable phases are:

(i)   Preliminary concept
(ii)   Market study
(iii)   Revised concept
(iv)   Revised costings
(v)   Financial evaluation report
(vi)   Sensitivity analysis
(vii) Financing arrangements
(viii) Detailed design and planning

Although market feasibility and location analysis can be identified as two distinct aspects of the study, the overall effect of the two issues is made apparent and emphasized in the above process. Specifically the market study stage will research location and market.

Undoubtedly market research by its very nature will always throw up anomalies. The purpose of the report is to provide concise and precise information pertinent to the study. An objective evaluation of the location and current market will be undertaken. If the recommendation is to proceed, then stages (iii) to (viii) will naturally follow.

Catering feasibility studies are initiated for a number of reasons. Many studies can be termed pro-active, as information is a major requirement in order to assess the potential of a location. These types of studies form the base from which to provide specific information, for example to financial institutions, main boards, etc.

A study will not guarantee the future success of a project, but it will substantially reduce the risk of error. For example, siting a traditional family restaurant requiring car parking facilities and access to residential neighbourhoods in a city centre is a patently obvious error. However, some aspects of a study are less clear and require confirmation.

Data

Initial raw base information provides a nucleus from which to formulate ideas and to base decisions. A food and beverage operation is measured by key performance indicators and at the feasibility stage an attempt will be made to calculate the potential performance. Market and location are prime providers of this information.

Pedestrian counts, traffic counts, occupancy levels of existing food and beverage operations, population densities and socioeconomic groupings are all sources of raw data. Analysis of existing menus and pricing structures, together with product mixes, will provide broad information on spending patterns. Standards of current operations will also be reviewed.

The above types of information will provide sufficient data to conduct preliminary analysis. Primarily a view can be established as to whether the market is currently under-catered for or over-catered to. By examining the mix and type of catering offered, opportunities can be identified. Analysis of numbers of catering outlets, the offers served (sandwiches/takeaway, ethnic, coffee shop, etc.), the places of unit operation, the levels of trading (peaks and troughs of business, seasonality), and the hours of opening will paint a clear picture of the overall catering market in that geographical location.

For operators without a concept, this type of information will assist in identifying opportunities in the market. Existing operators or those with a defined concept looking to expand will apply specific criteria particular to the type of catering offer to be introduced to determine levels of business.

The standard operating performance indicators will be applied to assess both location and market. Understandably the figures have a definite financial orientation. Central to the whole issue is the expected volume of business.

The expected/forecast number of meals to be served will be determined by a number of factors in addition to market size; for example, number of seats available and projected seat turnovers. In-depth analysis will use variables to enhance the accuracy of calculations. Variables based on trading patterns and opening hours will reflect on the overall volume of business. Accuracy or inaccuracy of raw data will manifest eventually.

Spends per head based on menus and sales mixes ultimately determine revenue levels. Analysis of hourly, daily, weekly and annual trading patterns requires to be undertaken. Consideration to margins will determine contribution levels. Profitable levels of business will be a known factor; achieving this at a specific location with the resident market requires proving. Achieving the desired level of turnover is paramount, whether to attain break even or return on capital invested.

It is inappropriate to project one year's trading in isolation without considering the long term; the report must be dynamic. Food and beverage operations perform very differently in year two and subsequent years compared with the first year of trading. Established companies with a number of units operating are in a far stronger position when it comes to short- and medium-term forecasting. Accurate historical information provides an advantage to these companies.

Location analysis

Location is a key element of the food and beverage marketing mix and should be reflected accordingly in studies.

Location, as previously determined, can be independent of a market, but the financial success of a location is market dependent. The adage 'location, location, location' is synonymous with the hospitality industry. A number of factors are particularly relevant, for example accessibility and visibility.

An element of intuitive reaction can be applied to location analysis. First impressions are important and experience will initially direct the views of the principals involved at the project commencement. Time and money might be saved at an early stage by the observations of a professional caterer. An initial site/location visit is essential. Immediate responses to the location would be considered and a decision as to proceed or not would be agreed.

A process of selection and elimination must exist or a great deal of time and misspent resources will accumulate. Companies, whether large or small, will conduct desk research initially to establish whether a geographical area is appropriate and able to support an operation of the style and size proposed.

Once a suitable geographical location and finally a specific site have been established, the process of preparing a feasibility study is then able to commence. A favourable decision on location has to be made prior to continuing with the study.

There will be straightforward logistical location problems, for example, as to the availability of suitable premises to accommodate the catering operation. The physical size of the building may not conform to the minimum requirements of the site specification. Similarly, prime high street locations may not be available and therefore alternative secondary locations have to be considered.

Location is critical to the market of food and beverage operations. The catering operation is unlikely to have no competitors; if this was the case, it would only be for a short period of time if the operation proved to be a success. Therefore, location advantage over current or future competitors is necessary.

The importance of planning for the future and anticipating change was previously discussed. A detailed feasibility study can be justified for this reason alone. The location has to be viewed from both a short-term and long-term aspect. Only on-site analysis will identify changes to road networks, such as one-way systems or bypasses, relocation of offices and industry. Any one of these factors may have a dramatic effect on a food and beverage operation.

Visibility and accessibility are two essential features of location selection. Communication to the market takes varying forms in order to inform the customer as to the existence of the operation. Once the customer is aware of the product, accessibility becomes important. Not every operation is fortunate enough to rely on reputation alone.

When studying location, account should be taken of the competition. Competition does not always manifest itself in the form of direct competitors, for example other restaurants or catering operations. Competitors extend to operations that attract the potential customers' disposable and discretionary incomes, for example cinemas, ten pin bowling centres and other leisure activities. However, it is not uncommon to turn competition to an advantage in attracting new business from existing market sources. An example is where leisure interests are grouped in a specific location and catering interests survive alongside, providing the market with greater choice.

Additionally there are restrictions regarding locations. A prime example are motorway service areas in the UK. Sites are predetermined and numbers controlled. Airports illustrate particular access restrictions in areas which have full public access, landside, and those that are restricted to passengers, airside.

Once a location is accepted it cannot be moved, despite any change to the surrounding environs and market. Therefore, careful attention should be attached to the attributes of the site and the local and national influences that will be exerted both directly and indirectly in the future.

The above are examples of factors that can be specifically applied to location. Other aspects are entwined with marketing issues.

Market feasibility

Contrary to statements made above, in the natural order of progression some market research will have been conducted, usually desk-bound, prior to location selection. The acceptance of a possible location for the operation will initiate the full feasibility study.

Market feasibility considers many subjective issues. There are unquantifiable aspects of a market feasibility study which defy measurement. Intuitive feelings are a good example. Many factors taken alone prove difficult to accurately measure; however, collectively a form of measurement is possible.

It is not always necessary to commence a study with a defined product or target market in mind. Many projects examine the total catering market of the location purely to produce a report that can be sold to interested parties as an identification of catering opportunities. Companies operating branded restaurants would consider independently produced reports to reduce initial costs on unsuitable locations.

There are a number of sources for location and market reports compiled for a varying number of reasons. Trade publications over a range of professions, for instance chartered surveying, provide data either globally or specifically on locations or by business activities. Although not directly related to catering, the publications do provide valid information on differing aspects of the market. For example, residential, commercial, future plans and so on. Any study on the catering market will include an assessment of the overall market characteristics.

The market

The market can be studied from two different angles. First, determining what the actual market is of the area under study. Secondly, calculating the envisaged market of the food and beverage offer under consideration.

In practice it is difficult to examine one without the other, because there are obvious cross-overs in the same way that there are between location and market. In the final analysis the second aspect will require resolving, as this determines the final conclusion and the purpose of a feasibility study.

Determining the total market

It is imperative to research the total market, i.e. the market that physically exists. The level of depth is variable, reflecting the requirements of the study, but it should suffice to enable the formation of a valid assessment of the market.

Areas of market study are relatively standardized, and Doswell and Gamble (1981) provide a comprehensive framework for a typical hotel feasibility study. The areas of the study are not dissimilar to those conducted for a pure food and beverage operation.

The standard areas of a study aim to quantify and qualify some basic, but nevertheless vital, information. As a base, it is essential to establish a platform from which to extend further and more detailed studies.

Once the statistical data, such as population size, age distribution, socioeconomic groupings, employment levels and so on, have been gathered it is then necessary to analyse and interpret the findings.

Care should be exercised when reviewing the information; statistics should be current as outdated information is potentially dangerous. Following data accumulation, confirmation of the research would be undertaken to agree the statistical data with observed patterns of market behaviour at the site. It is not uncommon to experience a situation where the market and other related factors appear ideal on paper, but in reality circumstances are somewhat different. The local market may not have changed and is as identified in the statistics, but the actions of the population make it infeasible to proceed.

Trading patterns and levels of trading can change quickly. Improved transport networks and levels of car ownership will contribute to new destination points. A high street food and beverage operation aimed at the day shopper market may suffer at the expense of a purpose-built out-of-town retail complex.

By reiterating the importance of local site research, the above negative features of operation can be minimized. Research can take place in many formats, ranging from full competitor surveys through to traffic and population counts. Information extracted from these types of investigations provides real data on the market. Research has to be complete; partial information is misleading. All trading periods will be monitored, including day/evening and weekday/weekend periods.

Although not altogether scientific, personal reaction from site/location visits is extremely important. First-hand pertinent and relevant information particular to the operating environment gained is invaluable. Accurate source information will form a sound base on which to formulate desk analysis.

The aim is to calculate the total catering market in order to gauge the size of the expected market. The feasibility study recommendation will be based on the market.

Conclusions

Location and market are two key and separate issues that require to be quantified and qualified in a food and beverage market feasibility study. These two aspects need to be considered jointly in order to provide an overall impression of the operating market. It is impossible to consider either subject totally independently. Similarly, it is true to state that there are equally important other areas of a feasibility study that also require detailed consideration.

References

Buttle, F. (1986). *Hotel and Food Service Marketing: a Managerial Approach*. London: Holt, Rinehart and Winston.

Doswell, R. and Gamble, P. R. (1981). *Marketing and Planning Hotels and Tourism Projects*. London: Hutchinson

Greene, M. (1993). Let's be feasible. *Caterer and Hotelkeeper*, 4 March, pp. 37–38.

Kendall, P. J. (1982). Recent experiences in project appraisal. *Tourism Management*, Dec., pp. 227–235.

Ward, T. J. (1989). The hotel feasibility study – principles and practice. In C. P. Cooper (ed.), *Progress in Tourism, Recreation and Hospitality Management*, Vol. 1. London: Belhaven Press, pp. 195–205.

9 New product development in food and beverage operations

Tim Knowles and Barry Ware-Lane

Introduction

New product development is a constituent element of the marketing process which includes the product lifecycle, segmenting the market into target groups and developing the desired market position (Kotler,1991). Future growth depends on developing and introducing new products to the marketplace, while at the same time acquiring maximum market share to achieve economies of scale.

Definition

New product development (NPD) can be considered as the development of the individual elements making up the total product or the development of the total product itself. Furthermore, NPD can be viewed either in terms of its newness to the company or to the marketplace (Booz et al., 1982).

Food and beverage operations can be regarded as a combination of products/services within a total product system. In this context, three levels can be determined within the total product system:

- The core product, i.e. food and beverage
- The tangible product, i.e. decor, furniture, fittings
- The augmented product, i.e. service quality, added value

Each level can form part of NPD in isolation or as a totality. The concept of an augmented product refers to the way in which the buyer views the total consumption, a fundamental issue recognized by Graham Campbell-Smith (1967) in his book *Marketing of the Meal Experience*. Product augmentation not only refers to the tangible aspects of the product, but also the intangible aspects such as customer service and atmosphere.

Added value can be extended to the core food and beverage product with, for instance, widening the provision of coffees and teas, or the addition of vintage wine by the glass, whereas other operators may provide valet parking or children's entertainment. Food and beverage operations such as TGI Fridays, Planet Hollywood and the Hard Rock Cafe introduce an element of *theatre* to the concept in terms of ambience, service and customer care. Essentially this process of product augmentation involves adding value to the core product and allows the operator to differentiate itself from its competitors.

Total concept

The total product system must be viewed within the wider environment of the:

- *Market feasibility study* involving investment returns, demographic and socioeconomic factors, and location, as discussed in the previous chapter.
- *Type of business operation* whether it be independent or company development, franchise, management contract or partnership. Each type is influenced by the availability of finance and the business relationship which in turn affects NPD.

The development of a total food and beverage concept focuses in the first instance on the style of operation in terms of the production system and service style. Such decisions will have implications for both production and service staff levels and will influence pricing policy.This will be dependent on the particular target market the operation wishes to attract. Consideration should also be given to the design and decor of a particular operation.This involves both interior and exterior design, including signage and staff uniforms, and complimentary printing and promotional material.

Taken together, the feasibility study, type of business operation and style of operation form the total product or concept. It is the total concept that creates the brand or brand image. A brand is therefore a standardized product system capable of rapid expansion to the targeted market on a regional or national basis and engenders security and value for money. Typical examples of successful brands include McDonald's, Pizza Hut, Beefeater and Harvester.

Elements of the concept

As opposed to the creation of a total product system, one can also consider new product development in terms of the individual elements making up a food and beverage operation. These elements, some of which have already been referred to, are considered in more depth below.

Service style

The classification of service methods has already been identified by Davis and Stone (1991) into three main categories: self-service, waiter service and special service arrangements.Through the process of NPD, extension of these service methods has now evolved, an example being Movenpick's Marche Restaurant, Leicester Square, London. In this particular example, both the food production and service method have been adapted within a free flow restaurant environment. Food and beverage are prepared, displayed/merchandised and served at various levels of the server/ customer interface; for example, food selected and prepared to order in front of the customer, traditional counter-assisted service, and finally self-selection of wine by the customer. In addition, the decor has been designed to create a number of eating experiences within one restaurant.

Another example of service method development can be seen within the pizza sector. Traditional waiter/waitress service pizza restaurants have evolved into takeaway and home delivery outlets, utilizing whole pizzas with new product accompaniments, to a new product development stage of assisted self-service pizza slices, e.g. Pizza Hut Express, Perfect Pizza. Alternatively The Deep Pan Pizza Company combine waiter/waitress service with an 'as-much-as-you-can-eat' self-help buffet at a fixed price, thus demonstrating a combination of service methods.

Menu items

There are two main types of menu development:

1 The introduction of a totally new product such as non-alcoholic beer, Tab (Coca Cola Schweppes), Vegetarian Burgers, Quorn and a number of other examples of retail-led manufactured products which are normally supported with major advertising expenditure.
2 The extension or adaptation of individual menu items such as Butterfly chicken breasts, and numerous prepared products chilled or frozen (eg. as demonstrated by the trend to prepared ethnic dishes). In this case, both customer demand for innovation and ease of preparation for the operator are satisfied.

Examples of menu development include McDonald's (Feltenstein, 1989) who have in the recent past extended their menu beyond their traditional core product of burgers, to food items such as salads, pizza and speciality products normally associated with food themes. This approach combats menu fatigue associated with a limited product range. It is also important to note that food trends such as healthy eating have influenced menu development, e.g. leaner cuts of meat, vegetarian dishes and the growing demand for mineral waters.

Shifts in the UK's population profile will bring with it demands for new eating out experiences. Reductions in younger age bands and corresponding increases in older groups, be they young families or the more affluent retired sector, will influence the type of food and beverage provision.

As international travel has developed, food and beverages, commonly available abroad, have been introduced into the UK. In this context one can observe the introduction of Mexican and Japanese food and individual menu items such as deli-type sandwiches, frozen yoghurt, quality hot dogs and doughnut varieties.

Food products such as ice cream have been further developed by Häagen-Dazs (Grand Metropolitan Group), with an emphasis on quality ingredients and sophisticated marketing allowing a premium price to be charged.

Technology

The style of operation can be considered in terms of its use of technology, be it catering equipment or electronic point-of-sale systems. Current trends include the use of hand-held order-taking key pads linked to kitchen terminals, allowing the server more time to attend to the guest. In addition, computer software allows management access to information relating to sales mix trends and food and beverage control. Other uses of catering equipment technology can, for instance, be seen in airline catering together with systems such as vacuum packing, modified atmosphere packaging and sous-vide preparation.

Development of new product concepts

A prerequisite for most new concept development is the need for a feasibility study. It would clearly be inadvisable to undertake substantial investment without seeking to establish that the catering unit will offer an attractive product to its intended market and that the level of utilization will provide an acceptable reward for the resources it employs (Gamble, 1980). However, NPD is evolutionary and thus a requirement to change in line with market forces means the lifecycle of any product must be considered.

Life cycle

Whatever the industry or particular sector, trends dictate that both products and brands have a particular lifecycle. It was Theodore Levitt (1960), a Harvard lecturer, who wrote on the subject of 'management myopia'. Management myopia refers to the condition whereby firms are myopic, i.e. shortsighted in thinking that their products which are currently successful will continue to be successful and will sustain the company in the future. Levitt cited a number of examples of companies that soldiered on with their existing policies, oblivious to the fact that their markets were disappearing. He talked of the self-deceiving cycle whereby businessmen fall into the trap of believing that the conditions which ensure a demand for their product will continue indefinitely.

The product lifecycle is a marketing tool which is primarily used in considering the future shape of product categories within market sectors and only secondarily for assessment of the future of individual products (Ward, 1984). There are four phases in the product life cycle:

- Introduction
- Growth
- Maturity
- Decline

Wherever the product is positioned within the cycle determines the marketing action required. Food and beverage products require development due to menu fatigue and changing market requirements. In addition, a dislike of one particular meal experience can create a negative multiplier effect throughout the whole brand. Even with a well thought out total concept, failure can occur and constant reappraisal is required.

A product introduced into the marketplace should either be positioned to satisfy a customer need differently or satisfy a perceived new customer need. It presupposes that a degree of customer need is evidenced.

As soon as the caterer senses that the rate of expansion in market demand is beginning to wane, a new product improvement is required to push it back into growth. There is of course a limit to such a renewal process and alternative markets need to be investigated. An alternative, although this is obviously difficult in an established business, is to recreate customer expectations of that meal experience through re-theming and re-launching.

Clearly, the issue of lifecycle in product development is vitally important, coupled with the need to adapt to a changing environment.

Strategy

One of the central areas affecting development is the corporate strategy in place within the organization. Corporate strategy is a process which 'aims to direct the resource conversion process in such a way as to achieve the operation's objectives' (Ansoff, 1982, p. 23). The strategic decision-making process described by Ward (1984, p. 49) as 'ensuring that everyone is pushing in the right direction' will be superimposed upon new products considered within a market feasibility study. Equally, in order to pronounce a new product feasible, consideration should be given to its financial feasibility.

There is a need to manage the company's business and decide what needs to be built, maintained, phased down and closed. Therefore the requirement is for a plan to achieve stated objectives. In formulating a strategic plan, there is a need for both an external and internal analysis of the business environment.

Whatever the type of new product, there will always be a need for company commitment in its implementation and development. There are many industry examples where such commitment has not been in evidence, e.g. the sale of Pizzaland by both United Biscuits plc and Grand Metropolitan Group plc because it was a non-core business. Alternatively, the sale of Rank Restaurants to Bright Reasons is an example of not only lack of commitment by the Rank Organisation to this market sector but also a need to reduce debt. Another business strategy option related to product development can be seen by the growth of Harry Ramsden's Fish and Chip Restaurants. From a single outlet in Yorkshire with a national reputation and superior product, expansion has occurred in predetermined market locations, together with a franchise option both in this country and abroad. The company's subsequent flotation on the London Stock Market has financed this expansion.

An emerging trend for the 1990s is seen in the establishment of partnerships, such as the Criterion with its partnership between My Kinda Town and Forte (*Caterer and Hotelkeeper*, 1992a).

While the motivation for new product development is primarily increased levels of growth and profits, one method of achieving such a strategy in food and beverage provision may be through the acquisition of brands and the development of brand loyalty.

This route to expansion and growth is illustrated by Compass Services Group plc and its purchase of Travellers Fare (*Caterer and Hotelkeeper*, 1992b), and SAS Partnership (*Caterer and Hotelkeeper*, 1993), and will allow Compass to adapt recognized brands to their market-led operating companies. The recent acquisition by Compass of catering interests in Europe will extend this strategy on a European-wide basis.

Strategic development of this kind will impinge on managing its contract catering division and so have implications for: human resource management; marketing; quality assurance; merchandising; purchasing and supply.

A structured approach to new product development
(Feltenstein, 1990)

The main goal in developing a new product is to establish its potential market share, identify the sales volume and determine the customer mix. Following on from this approach, the individual elements of the marketing mix, e.g. product, price, promotion and place, would be tested and reappraised. Such research would determine the target market and age groups, along with their average spending power. It is important that this approach is taken in order to eliminate personal bias and subjective preferences.

An integral part of this process is to audit current concepts in development. Such an audit would relate back to established budgets and time schedules, and will help determine future resources. The company would at this stage withdraw obvious failures which would free up resources for further development.

Product testing

Food products

There are essentially three types of new food products:

1 An additional meal offering, e.g. a gourmet pizza, may expand, extend or enhance the menu without departing from the operation's basic concept. It maintains the menu's competitiveness and allows an opportunity to increase the average spend.
2 A side dish usually extends or enhances the current menu, increases average spend and may differentiate an operation from its direct competitors.
3 New category products are outside the scope of the current menu, but they address important consumer needs or expectations that the catering operation has not met. A new category product is a departure from the existing menu concept. The objective is to broaden the customer base and increase the frequency of visits from existing customers.

Total concept

Product testing is essentially a trial of the concept's appeal. It typically includes its intrinsic product performance and considers the various psychological factors influencing the consumer.

The development of a new concept can be considered at three levels;

1 As a unique product with no existing close competitors, e.g. Henry J Bean's, part of the My Kinda Town chain, or Ed's Diner, a 1950s style burger restaurant located in Soho in London.
2 As a similar product but superior to existing competitors, e.g. Travellers Fare, The Upper Crust or Café Select. The former offers an imaginative selection of baguettes with a wide variety of fillings. The latter provides a range of coffees, teas and pastries in an Italian-themed atmosphere.
3 As a product which matches existing competitors, e.g. Domino's and Little Caesar's alongside Perfect Pizza and Pizza Hut Delivery. Such a development implies that there are opportunities for growth within this particular segment of the pizza market and assumes that a market feasibility study has established the viability of adding an additional operation.

The development of an existing concept can be considered at four levels:

1 Substantial improvement, e.g., the major re-launch of the Rank Motorway Service Areas under the Pavillion name following their purchase by Bright Reasons. Menus, decor and service style have all undergone substantial change.
2 Marginal improvement which it is hoped will be noticed by some but not all customers, as demonstrated by the current changes within the Muswells chain. In this case, change has been limited to menu development following the purchase of the 28 outlets by Priorswood from Allied Lyons in November 1992 (EIU, 1993).
3 A defensive improvement, where for competitive reasons a company wishes to strengthen the appeal of a product, e.g. Bright Reasons' repositioning of the Pizzaland brand with the addition of new menu items and an improvement in decor and signage.
4 Rationalization of an existing brand, i.e. the development of a formulation which is equally acceptable as the current one, but is done so because of reasons of cost savings or raw material availability. This level of development is witnessed by the rationalization of the Calendars and Exchange brands into a single chain under the Exchange name (Harmer, 1993).

Multi-stage testing

Once the objectives have been defined, a totally new product or the full-scale re-launch of an existing product will go through a physical product and concept acceptance testing stage.

The marketing mix is thus tested. This checks the concept, product packaging, price and advertising and ensures that they are all complementary. Site selection is critical in the formulation of product testing and performance levels should be measured against control sites.

Testing of the product should be aimed at the target segment identified, but depending on company strategy it could be consumers of the existing major brand or some subset of the market that has been identified and whose needs are not being met.

Product testing is essentially a quantitative field, but in the research process there should be a qualitative element where focus groups are convened and attitudinal and taste preferences are evaluated.

It is important that the test product is considered against similar products within the market. If this is not possible, it is important to test against established norms within that particular product segment range.

Data collection from the test units should be measured in both quantitative and qualitative terms. In addition, a paired comparison on an existing product and a test product would provide additional information on which to base a decision. It is important to remember that a new product is one that is perceived as new by the majority of people within the target market. Once all data are collected and evaluated, objectives may need to be redefined and retested before product launch.

New products in food and beverage

In terms of new products introduced within the catering field, the failure rate can be particularly high. This can be attributed to the high proportion of single operators and because of the high fixed costs associated with a food and beverage operation. It is therefore sometimes regarded as an easy option to experiment with the menu. Single operators, through lack of finance or sufficient cash flow, are reluctant to test and tend to have a 'do or die' approach. They also believe that development is consumer led and are therefore reacting to known market requirements which in their opinion eliminates the need for a formalized product testing process.

New product development and creativity

While NPD can be treated as part of a structured process, the issue of creativity is just as important. Companies require a variety of team members possessing differing skills and attributes to achieve the optimum results. A common division of these abilities could be:

- Acumen – the ability to make quick and accurate judgements
- Creativity – the ability to generate new ideas

The reason why one needs the creative element is in order to change, to question existing principles and indicate new opportunities for development. The basic problem of 'respected authorities' at a senior level within a business is that whereas they are consistent, stable, dependable and make few mistakes, their behaviour offers few surprises and may develop some degree of tunnel vision or what may be called 'educated incapacity'. The need is therefore to challenge irrefutable truths and universal assumptions, a process which is difficult to do in any autocratic organization where deference is accorded to those in charge.

Different writers appear to come to the conclusion that creativity is about joining different concepts to make something new. The reason why a company needs such creative people is that they generate lots of new ideas which may or may not be valuable, and therefore this input is more often contracted externally and adapted, if necessary, for internal application.

Conclusions

It has been shown that the subject of NPD in food and beverage operations evolves from considering both the total concept and elements of that concept. Due to the lifecycle process, where decline occurs following maturity, both the total concept and elements of that concept require continual review and development in line with market forces. The decline of Berni Inns and the revitalization of Pizzaland International are examples which illustrate this point. A structured approach is therefore required which allows testing of the product's marketing mix within the company's business objectives and overall strategy. Creativity is central to this overall approach and must be applied to both the total concept and its elements in order to provide a unique experience.

References

Ansoff, H. I. (1987). *Corporate Strategy,* revised edn. London: Penguin,

Booz, Allen and Hamilton (1982). *New Products Management for the 1980's,* New York, USA.

Campbell-Smith, G. (1967). *Marketing of the Meal Experience,* Guildford: University of Surrey Press.

Caterer and Hotelkeeper (1992a). Criterion reopens. *Caterer and Hotelkeeper,* 10 September, p. 12.

Caterer and Hotelkeeper (1992b). Compass moves into the High Street. *Caterer and Hotelkeeper,* 12 November, p. 11.

Caterer and Hotelkeeper (1993) Compass sets new course. *Caterer and Hotelkeeper,* 27 May, p. 10.

Davis, B., and Stone, S. (1991). *Food and Beverage Management*, 2nd edn. London: Butterworth-Heinemann, Chap. 12.

EIU (1993). *The UK Consumer Catering Market*. London: Economist Intelligence Unit.

Feltenstein, T. (1989). New product development in food service. *Consultant*, **22**(1), 46–50.

Feltenstein, T. (1990). New product development in food service – a structured approach. *Consultant*, **23**(4), 45–50.

Gamble, P. R. (1980). 'Assessment of hotel projects'. In R. Kotas (ed.), *Managerial Economics for Hotel Operations*. Guildford: Surrey University Press.

Harmer, J. (1993). Winning exchanges. *Caterer and Hotelkeeper*, 16 September, pp. 32,34.

Kotler, P. (1991). *Marketing Management; Analysis, Planning, Implementation and Control*, 7th edn. Engelwood Cliffs, NJ: Prentice-Hall.

Levitt, T. (1960). Marketing myopia. *Harvard Business Review*, July–Aug., pp. 45–56.

Ward, J. (1984). *Profitable Product Management*. London: William Heinemann.

10 Catering systems

Peter L. M. Jones

Introduction

In order to understand catering systems it is essential to identify the extent to which all such systems are the same or different one from the other. The classification of systems into types is known as a 'taxonomy'. However, the analysis of catering systems is constrained by the lack of an internationally accepted taxonomy and the seemingly infinite variety of operations. This chapter discusses a proposed new taxonomy based on the 'process flow' of the operational activity. It reviews first the taxonomies of service operations in general and applies these to catering. It then reviews alternative classifications of catering systems proposed over the past fifteen years. The chapter discusses an existing taxonomy which proposes ten generic systems. The basis of this taxonomy is that each system has a unique combination of some or all of ten stages in the delivery process. Finally it reviews a revision of this taxonomy which takes into account fundamental dimensions of service operations in general. This new taxonomy proposes eleven catering systems subdivided into three main types: integrated systems, manufacturing systems, and delivery systems.

When people talk about 'catering systems' they are not necessarily talking about the same thing. Commonly used phrases are based on assumptions or common usage rather than clear definition. For instance, fast food as defined by Jones (1989) is quite different to that proposed by Ball (1992). The former bases his definition on operational characteristics such as technology and processes, the latter on economic and market criteria. The introduction of new concepts such as fast food, new configurations such as central production kitchens, new technologies such as cook-chill or sous-vide, new food products of 'convenience', and other innovations, have tended to result in an increasingly varied number of operations, each of which is slightly different. In attempting to classify these operations, assumptions are made that are not always supported by detailed examination of the facts. For instance, is cook-chill a new 'system' or a modification of an existing one?

Likewise it is implied that central production facilities are a specific system, whereas the reality may be that the physical separation of one stage of the production process from another has very limited impact on the actual processes involved or the management of the total system. This lack of clarity appears to arise from a failure to identify what criteria should be used to distinguish between one system and another.

Definition of catering systems

The concept of 'service delivery system' was first conceptualized by Sasser *et al.* (1976). Such service delivery systems are designed to carry out the basic function of converting inputs, through processes, into outputs. Ideally, a service delivery system has to behave like the 'ideal operation', that is to say 'as if the market will absorb a single kind of product (*sic*) at a continuous rate and as if the inputs flowed continuously at a steady rate and with specified quality' (Thompson, 1967). This goes back to the early days of manufacturing industry, when Henry Ford first mass-produced cars and customers 'could have any colour so long as it is black'. Continuous, processes producing a standard product, are the most cost efficient means of production.

The same is also likely to apply to services, even though services may have different characteristics to manufactured products. Sasser and colleagues identify that four characteristics of services – heterogeneity, simultaneity, perishability and intangibility – all conspire to prevent the achievement of the above ideal. As we shall see, it is for these reasons that there is an increasing interest in theories and paradigms that relate specifically to services.

Pickworth (1988), in a seminal article about foodservice operations, adopts the concept of the service delivery system and applies it to catering. Pickworth defines a service delivery system as an 'operation in which products/services are created and delivered to the customer almost simultaneously'. In some cases a service delivery system is 'dedicated', that is to say it is an 'SDS which is designed to produce a specific range of menu items'. Pickworth uses the example of fast food chains. However in other cases, an SDS can be 'multi-faceted', so that it is an 'SDS which is able to produce and serve a broad range of menu items'. Thus in a dedicated SDS the expectation is that there would be one specific catering system, whereas in a multi-faceted operation more than one specific system may operate together.

Catering systems are therefore designed to carry out the basic function of changing inputs (foodstuffs, labour, capital, etc.) through processes (mainly 'production' and 'service') into desirable outputs (meals, customer satisfaction, profit, etc.). A key feature of such transformations in the catering context is that production and consumption are usually regarded as almost simultaneous. However, as we shall see, some recent trends in the industry suggest that not all operations now have almost simultaneous production and consumption.

Taxonomies of service operations

Systems are generally analysed by 'mapping' or 'charting' the flow of some input through the relevant sequence of processes. This is well established (Morris and Johnston, 1987; Jones, 1988b). The conventional production management approach to understanding manufacturing is to map the flow of raw materials through the system. Such flow chart processing has been proposed for services (Shostack, 1984, 1987) as well as manufacturing-based operations. The challenge of services is the extent to which the participation of the consumer in the service 'event' can be accommodated in a model based solely on 'materials flow'. As we shall see, a number of taxonomies include both these aspects of the operation.

Before reviewing alternative approaches to foodservice classification, it is insightful to examine the nature of foodservice in the context of classifications of service operations in general. It is intended to review three such taxonomies here. Wemmerlov (1990) has provided a more comprehensive review already (with 50 different citations).

Morris and Johnston (1987) identify three main categories of service operation:

- People processing operations
- Information processing operations
- Materials processing operations

It is clear that the criteria they use for placing a service operation into each of these categories do not make it easy to categorize foodservice operations. To put it simply, back-of-house activities, i.e. food production, are materials processing, whereas front-of-house activities, i.e. foodservice, are essentially people processing operations. It may be that a taxonomy of foodservice has to recognize this fundamental difference if it is to be credible and meaningful.

Schmenner (1986) analysed service operations on a 'service process matrix' based on two key variables: the 'degree of interaction and customization', and the 'degree of labor intensity'. This results in four generic kinds of operation:

- Service shop
- Service factory
- Mass service
- Professional service.

It is interesting to note that while he places many different kinds of service operation on this matrix, he does not place foodservice or restaurants. However, in the text he does discuss how the 'traditional restaurant' has evolved into the fast food outlet. In this discussion, he concludes that foodservice 'today encompasses a wide diversity of operations', that apparently includes service shops, service factories and mass service.

Finally, Wemmerlov (1990) presents the most complex taxonomy of service operations, identifying potentially 24 different operational types. His classification system includes some of the criteria discussed previously. For instance, operations can be categorized on the basis of 'processing goods', 'processing information/images', or 'processing people'. Likewise the level of customer contact is important, ranging from 'no customer contact', through 'indirect', e,g. by telephone, to 'direct' of which there are two kinds – that involving no customer/service worker interaction, and that which has such interaction. In addition, these three different kinds of processing can be either 'rigid' or 'fluid'. In explaining this taxonomy, Wemmerlov uses three examples drawn from foodservice. 'Food serving in a restaurant' is a rigid processing of goods involving direct customer contact with service worker/customer interaction, whereas 'sampling food at a buffet dinner' is a fluid processing of goods involving direct customer contact with no service worker/customer interaction. Finally, a vending machine is the same as a buffet dinner, except it is a rigid process rather than fluid process.

Several interesting points emerge from this review of service operations taxonomies. First, consideration of catering is often avoided because it does not easily fit the model proposed. This may be due to inherent shortcomings of the model itself, or the fact that as Pickworth (1988) identified, many catering operations are 'multi-faceted' and hence difficult to categorize. Secondly, when it is considered, the analysis of catering does not always demonstrate a level of understanding that 'experts' in the field are happy with. And thirdly, in every case, catering operations obviously fit in more than one category as defined by these taxonomies.

Alternative taxonomies of catering systems

One of the first basic analyses of catering systems (Cutcliffe, 1971) was developed over twenty years ago. Following on from this, Jones (1982) developed four simple models of alternative systems which were called conventional, commissary, cook-freeze, and assembly serve. This model

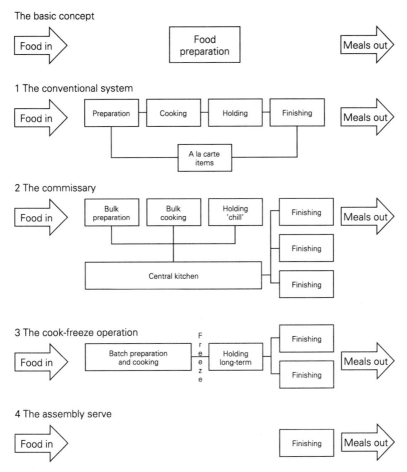

Figure 10.1 Food production systems (*Source*: Jones, 1982)

subdivided the operation into stages based on the flow of materials through the system, as illustrated in Figure 10.1.

Escueta *et al.* (1986) have proposed a taxonomy for use in relation to catering provision in hospitals. Their BMKPHD classification scheme subdivides the total service delivery system into six distinct stages. They use a capital letter to signify bulk operation, and lower case to signify individual mode. Since not all six stages are essential to the catering operation, there can be two-component, three-component, four-component, five-component and six-component systems, resulting in eighty-one different possible configurations of a hospital system.

Jones (1988a) developed an alternative view of foodservice systems based on an analysis of trends in service operations, namely production-lining,

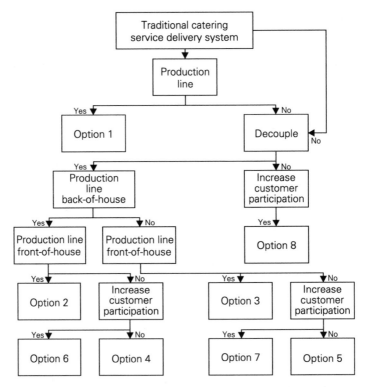

Figure 10.2 Hierarchy of operational types in the catering industry (*Source*: Jones, 1989)

decoupling and consumer participation. This 'hierarchy of operational types' identified nine different systems, as illustrated in Figure 10.2. These systems were as follows:

1 Fast food.
2 Decoupled system based on batch food production, chilled/frozen storage, regeneration in combination with cafeteria service.
3 Decoupled conventional kitchen with cafeteria service.
4 Decoupled system based on batch food production, chilled/frozen storage, regeneration in combination with traditional service.
5 Meals-on-wheels.
6 Decoupled system based on batch food production, chilled/frozen storage, regeneration in combination with some element of self-service.
7 Decoupled conventional system with some element of self-service.
8 Traditional kitchen with some element of self-service.
9 Traditional catering service delivery system.

A 'definitive' catering systems taxonomy

Arguably the most 'definitive' taxonomy of foodservice has been proposed by Huelin and Jones (1990). They identified that the 'traditional catering system' originated in large hotels in the late nineteenth century. Such operations were based on the processing of predominantly fresh raw materials by a large number of specialist personnel working in a production area located as near to the service point as possible. Using the flow of materials through the system as the criteria for classification, they proposed that this traditional operation comprises eight distinct stages, half of which occur back of house, as follows:

- Storage
- Preparation
- Production ('cooking')
- Holding
- Service
- Dining
- Clearing
- Dishwash

This model therefore extends the Escueta model of six stages. Huelin and Jones go on to suggest that this basic, traditional system has three alternative configurations, essentially in the production system:

> Food can be cooked with or without preparation, it can be held prepared or cooked, or it can be served immediately after cooking or after holding. Typically, à la carte menu items are served immediately after cooking. This is sometimes called the call order system, which we shall call (A). Likewise, the table d'hôte menu usually comprises dishes prepared in advance and held for a period of time before service (B). Where food is served without cooking, this is the buffet catering system (C).

A Storage   Preparation   Cooking   Service   Dining   Clearing   Dishwash
B Storage   Preparation   Cooking   Holding   Service   Dining
  Clearing   Dishwash
C Storage   Preparation   Holding   Service   Dining   Clearing   Dishwash

Such systems in reality are rare because, as Pickworth identified, there are very few 'dedicated' systems. Huelin and Jones therefore proposed that the Pareto principle should be applied to this analysis, i.e. that within each of these generic types, 'at least 80% of the raw materials should flow through the system in the sequence of stages specified. However, up to 20% of raw materials may well follow other routes, bypassing some stages, going through additional stages, or following a different sequence'.

In addition to these three systems, Huelin and Jones go on to analyse developments in the industry that have led to seven further systems emerging.

Over the last one hundred years, there have been innovations that have enabled this basic model of three systems to be modified in a number of significant ways. There have been major changes in the supply of raw materials both in terms of increased shelf life (freezing, canning, etc.) and state of preparation (semi-prepared, convenience products, fully finished products, and so on). This now enables the complete avoidance of preparation and cooking stages with the introduction of fully pre-prepared meals requiring a new stage called 'regeneration'. The second major innovation is at the holding stage. The introduction of cook-chill, cook-freeze and sous-vide have extended the period of time that food can be held between the production stages and the service stages. This has also made possible decoupling (Jones, 1988a) these two distinct areas, both in terms of time and place. Where these technologies are used, there is also the need for the additional stage of regeneration to be included, to make the food ready to eat. Where meals or dishes held in these ways are to be served in locations away from the point of production, there now also needs to be a transportation stage between holding and regeneration.

The impact of these developments is a ten-stage flow of raw materials through the system, modelled in Figure 10.3. The ten stages are as follows:

- Storage
- Preparation
- Production ('cooking')
- Holding
- Transportation
- Regeneration
- Service
- Dining
- Clearing
- Dishwash

This was similar to Cousins and Foskett (1989) who suggested five stages of production and Boella (1989) who proposed nine stages, without transport between holding and regeneration, along with alternatives within each stage. It differed from the BMKPHD classification in some significant ways. First, it considered the total system rather than concentrating on food production. It therefore included four stages within the 'distribution' stage of the Escueta et al (1986) taxonomy. Secondly, it applied to all foodservice operations, not just hospitals. For this reason it used different terminology for the different stages, for instance, regeneration rather than reheat because

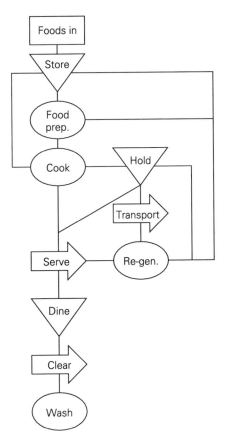

Figure 10.3 Flow diagram of modern catering systems (*Source*: Huelin and Jones, 1990)

the former is generic to that stage while reheat is a specific form of regeneration. It also recognized that there may be significant distribution of held foodstuffs, between the holding stage and regeneration stage. And finally, it considers inventory from a storage perspective, rather than a purchasing perspective due to the implications this has for the technology within the system.

On the assumption that there are no variations in how each stage is performed, this resulted in these 'ten generic dedicated service delivery systems':

A Storage Preparation Cooking Service Dining Clearing Dishwash
B Storage Preparation Cooking Holding Service Dining
  Clearing Dishwash
C Storage Preparation Holding Service Dining Clearing Dishwash
D Storage Preparation Cooking Holding Transport
  Regeneration Service Dining Clearing Dishwash

E Storage Cooking Holding Transport Regeneration
  Service Dining Clearing Dishwash
F Storage Cooking Holding Service Dining Clearing Dishwash
G Storage Preparation Cooking Holding Service Dining Clearing
H Storage Preparation Cooking Holding Transport
  Regeneration Service Dining Clearing
I Storage Regeneration Service Dining Clearing Dishwash
J Storage Preparation Cooking Dining Clearing Dishwash

Huelin and Jones related these ten to specific contexts, as follows:

A Conventional à la carte restaurant using fresh commodities cooked to order
B Conventional restaurant using fresh commodities cooked in advance
C Catering outlet serving only uncooked foods, e.g. buffet, sandwich bar
D Conventional à la carte restaurants using fresh commodities and sous-vide
E Conventional restaurants/cafeterias using convenience commodities and cook-chill
F Conventional restaurant or cafeteria using convenience commodities served to order
G Fast food outlet
H In flight catering
I Restaurant/cafeteria/store buying all fully prepared meals from supplier
J Benihana concept

A revised taxonomy

In reviewing this earlier work, this author proposed a revision to the 'definitive' taxonomy (Jones, 1993). The basis of the difference is to divide catering systems into three types, before classifying them further. These three main types are:

1 *Integrated foodservice systems*, i.e. where both food production and food service are carried out as part of a single operation. This reflects the 'traditional' restaurant concept and matches with Pickworth's view of simultaneous production and consumption.
2 *Food manufacturing systems*, i.e. where the operation focuses on the production of meals separate from the service of those meals. This accommodates the trend of decoupling and recognizes that in the modern foodservice industry, there is the large-scale production of meals often served by other operators, as with in-flight and on-rail catering.
3 *Food delivery systems*, i.e. where the operation has little or no food production and focuses on only the service of meals. This accommodates the concept of decoupling, as well as that of production-lining. In this

instance, little or no meal production takes place, meals are either 'assembled' and/or regenerated. The focus is on serving consumers.

The impact this has on the 'definitive' ten operational systems is to extend these to eleven systems and define them differently. This is because all those systems that had the 'transport' stage are now identified as two different systems.

Hence, *integrated foodservice systems* are:

A Storage Preparation Cooking Service Dining Clearing Dishwash
B Storage Preparation Cooking Holding Service Dining
  Clearing Dishwash
C Storage Preparation Holding Service Dining Clearing Dishwash
F Storage Cooking Holding Service Dining Clearing Dishwash
G Storage Preparation Cooking Holding Service Dining Clearing
J Storage Preparation Cooking Dining Clearing Dishwash

Food manufacturing systems are:

D/H Storage Preparation Cooking Holding Transport
E   Storage Cooking Holding Transport
    Storage Preparation Cooking Transport

Food delivery systems are:

D/E Transport Storage Regeneration Service Dining
    Clearing Dishwash
    Storage Regeneration Service Dining Clearing Dishwash

This revised taxonomy also enables the inclusion of a growing sector of the foodservice industry, namely home delivery. This leads to the identification of the following eleven operational types, using a revised coding:

Intregrated foodservice systems:

1A Conventional à la carte restaurant using fresh commodities cooked to order
1B Conventional restaurant using fresh commodities cooked in advance
1C Catering outlet serving only uncooked foods, e.g. buffet, sandwich bar
1D Conventional restaurant or cafeteria using convenience commodities served to order
1E Fast food outlet
1F Benihana concept

Food manufacturing systems:

  2A Production kitchens using fresh commodities and sous-vide or cook-chill
  2B Production kitchens using convenience commodities and sous-vide or cook-chill
  2C Home delivery

Food delivery systems are:

  3A In-flight/some hospital tray service/on-rail
  3B Restaurant/cafeteria/store buying all fully prepared meals from supplier

Conclusions

Huelin and Jones (1990) proposed that a test of the generic nature of each of their systems would be to identify objective criteria for distinguishing the key features of the catering system. Such criteria should include type of raw materials, inventory size, product range width and depth, capacity, production batch sizes, and flexibility. This would have to be applied to 'dedicated' systems, in the first instance. Table 10.1 demonstrates their hypotheses about their 10 generic systems.

  Research is currently being conducted into catering systems, in order to substantiate or modify the taxonomy proposed here. This operations

Table 10.1 Comparison of characteristics of generic catering systems (Based on Huelin and Jones, 1990)

	Raw materials type	Inventory size	Product range		Capacity	Batch size	Flexibility
			Depth	Width			
A	Fresh	High	High	High	Low	Low	High
B	Fresh	High	High	High	High	High	High
C	Fresh	High	High	Low	Low	Low	High
D	Fresh	High	High	High	Low	High	High
E	Convenience	High	High	High	High	High	High
F	Convenience	High	High	High	High	Low	High
G	Convenience	High	Low	Low	High	Low	Low
H	Fresh	High	Low	High	High	High	High
I	Convenience	Low	Low	Low	High	Low	Low
J	Fresh	Low	Low	Low	Low	Low	Low

analysis involves on-site examination of detailed criteria to enable direct comparisons between one operation and another. Once the extent of similarities and differences between systems is more fully understood, the next stage will be to explore the extent to which management behaviour and action varies from one kind of system to another.

References

Ball, S. (1992). *Fast Food*. London: Stanley Thornes.

Boella, M. J. (1989). Foodservice systems. *Croners Catering*, Sept.

Cousins, J. and Foskett, D. (1989). Curriculum development for food production operations teaching for the hospitality industry: a systems framework. *International Journal of Operations and Production Management*, **9**(5), 77–87.

Cutcliffe, G. (1971). *Analysing Catering Operations*. London: Edward Arnold.

Escueta, E. S., Fielder, K. M. and Reisman, A. (1986). A new hospital foodservice classification system. *Foodservice Systems*, No. 4, pp. 107–116.

Huelin, A. and Jones, P. (1990). Thinking about catering systems. *International Journal of Operations and Production Management*, **10**(8), 42–52.

Jones, P. (1982). *Foodservice Operations*. London: Holt Rinehart Winston.

Jones, P. (1988a). The impact of trends in service operations on food service delivery systems. *International Journal of Operations and Production Management*, **8**(7), 23–30.

Jones, P. (1988b). Quality, capacity and productivity in service industries. *International Journal of Hospitality Management*, **7**(2), 104–112.

Jones, P. (1989). *Foodservice Operations*, 2nd edn. London: Cassell.

Jones, P. (1993). A Taxonomy of Foodservice Operations, 2nd Annual CHME Research Conference, Manchester, April.

Morris, B. and Johnston, R. (1987). Dealing with inherent variability: the difference between manufacturing and service? *International Journal of Operations and Production Management*, **7**(4), 13–22.

Pickworth, J. R. (1988). Service delivery systems in the foodservice industry. *International Journal of Hospitality Management*, **7**(1), 43–62.

Sasser, W. E., Wyckoff, D. D. and Olsen, R. P. (1976). *The Management of Service Operations*. Boston: Allyn and Bacon.

Schmenner, R. (1986). How can service businesses survive and prosper? *Sloan Management Review*, Spring, pp. 21–32.

Shostack, G. L. (1984). Designing services that deliver. *Harvard Business Review*, Jan./Feb.

Shostack, G. L. (1987). Service positioning through structural change. *Journal of Marketing*, **51**, 34–43.

Thompson, J. D. (1967). *Organisations in Action*. Maidenhead: McGraw-Hill.

Wemmerlov, U. (1990). A taxonomy for service process and its implications for systems design. *International Journal of Service Industries Management*, **1**(3) 20–40.

11 Design and layout

David Kirk

Overview

Whether it be the replanning of an existing kitchen in a small restaurant or the development of a multi-million pound food court in a shopping centre, the design and layout of food production and service areas play a key role in terms of converting a planned food and beverage concept into a functioning system. The design must ensure that the system can deliver food and beverages to the customer at the time that the customer wants them, to a defined level of quality and safety and in such a way as to meet financial and other policy goals of the organization. This inevitably involves trade-offs between capital costs and operational costs, but the objective must be to develop a design, within the budget available, which is efficient and which creates a pleasant and safe working/dining environment.

The planning process

The design team

The composition of the design team varies, depending upon the complexity of the project, but typically consists of an architect, a mechanical and electrical consultant(s), a foodservice consultant and an interior designer, together with representatives of the client. This team, supplemented by the building contractor, the equipment supplier(s) and the equipment installer (once these have been appointed) will liaise throughout the period of planning, to ensure that a number of separate activities are controlled, particularly in terms of cost and co-ordination to ensure that the project is completed within financial budgets and time deadlines. In the case of complex projects, critical path analysis can be a useful technique (French *et al.*, 1986). Other experts will be consulted during the design process to ensure that the building conforms to requirements for building codes, fire safety, food safety, health and safety and other mandatory and voluntary standards.

Involvement of the client and particularly those staff with a knowledge of the detailed operational requirements is essential, and the catering manager and head chef are increasingly involved in the design process. This development has been accentuated through the use of computer assisted design (CAD). Because this approach allows the design to be manipulated on a computer screen during discussions with representatives of the client, it is possible to have a greater level of interaction (Mascord, 1993). Increasingly, equipment manufacturers and foodservice design consultants are using CAD (Kirk, 1991).

Stages in the development of a design

Before commencing any design studies it is imperative that there are clear objectives (Birchfield,1988; Mill, 1989) and a fully developed food service concept which defines key parameters such as:

- Customer requirements in terms of food and beverage products and service style.
- Projected numbers of customers, with an indication of the variation in demand throughout the day, week and year.
- Menu type (fixed, cyclic, market, etc.).
- Menu format, structure and content.
- Projected sales volume for each menu item.
- Method of production and service for each menu item to customer's order, assembled to customer's order from pre-prepared components or prepared in advance in batches to production schedule.
- Quantity of food to be produced at a time.
- Preparation area and equipment required to produce the menu item.
- Storage required before and during preparation and prior to service – volume of food and storage conditions.
- Foodservice concept – the form of delivery of the food/beverage product to the customer, ambience of restaurant, etc.
- Method of service delivery and the nature of the interaction between the customer and the operation: waiter/waitress, silver, banquet, cafeteria, self-serve, self-help, buffet, vending, etc.
- Type of crockery and utensils, harmony with decor and menu, reusable or disposable.
- Purchasing policy for food, beverages and other consumables.

This information will then lead to an outline plan, allowing the requirements for storage, production facilities, service facilities, dining area, dishwash and other key elements of the system to be mapped onto the available building envelope. If this mapping cannot be done, either because of a lack of space or an unsuitable building envelope, there may be a need to either negotiate a change in the building envelope or to modify the foodservice concept. Guidelines are available which give an indication of the relationship between sales volume, production and service methods and floor area requirements (Lawson,1979).

Once the outline plan has been agreed, detailed planning of work areas can commence. At this stage, the interrelationships between staff, equipment and customers must be given detailed consideration. Another important factor is to control the flow of food products to avoid food safety risks, particularly the risk of cross-contamination from raw food and refuse to prepared food.

Production planning techniques are available for determining the optimum relationship between a number of activities or departments, including the use of relationship charts (Murdick *et al.*, 1990). These techniques are useful in large complex designs, for example a kitchen which must serve multiple outlets. They are also useful in terms of integrating a kitchen and restaurant into a complex organization such as a hotel or hospital. Work design techniques can be used to optimize individual work centres (Avery, 1989a).

The relationships between food production and service equipment and the building services (gas, electricity, water, drainage, ventilation and air conditioning) require detailed negotiation between specialist members of the planning team. The detailing of the building services is often fixed at an early stage in the design process, which can limit the freedom of the foodservice consultant. Additionally, the mechanical and electrical consultants will need specific detail of equipment service requirements, often before the detailed foodservice layout has been completed. As with all other elements of design, the building services should be designed in such a way as to be hygienic, allow for easy maintenance, be adaptable to suit future building changes and be aesthetically pleasing.

Detailed consideration needs to be given to the method which is to be used to connect equipment to the building services. There has been considerable progress in developing designs for service ducting systems which are hygienic, easy to maintain and easy to modify for future needs. Another development has been the use of flexible service connections to allow adaptability within kitchen and servery areas (DES,1986).

A detailed equipment specification can then be developed (Scriven and Stevens, 1989), which can be used to select a supplier and/or installer. This specification will contain details of materials of construction, equipment capacity, service requirements and compliance with legal and voluntary standards. Drawings will be required for any one-off fabrications, such as customized service counters.

Once building work and equipment installation have been completed, the design team will inspect the building for aspects of the work which do not conform to specifications. Additionally, all equipment must be commissioned to ensure its correct functioning. Once these activities have been completed, the building can be handed over to the operating staff for induction and staff training.

The function of design and layout

General principles

It is useful at this stage to consider the system which is to be used for the production and service of food and beverages in terms of generalized processes (Wild, 1990a). For each menu item, it is possible to analyse the stages in its production and service in terms of unit operations, as shown in Figure 11.1.

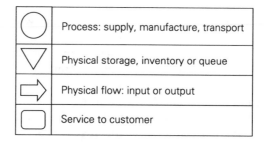

Figure 11.1 Symbolic representation of stages in production and service

Using this convention, it is possible to identify the stages involved (and hence the design requirements) of a number of catering systems, as shown in Figure 11.2. A number of researchers have investigated the possibility of classifying catering systems in similar terms (Escueta *et al.*, 1986; Huelin and Jones, 1990). By using diagrams such as these, it is possible to identify a number of interrelated operational issues which impact on the design. For example, for each item on the menu we need to know:

1 *Make or buy.* If we prepare menu items from raw materials or buy partially or fully pre-prepared items.
2 *Inventory.* How much we buy at a time, the frequency of delivery and the required storage conditions for that item. We also need to know of any storage requirements for partially and fully prepared menu items and for items waiting for service.

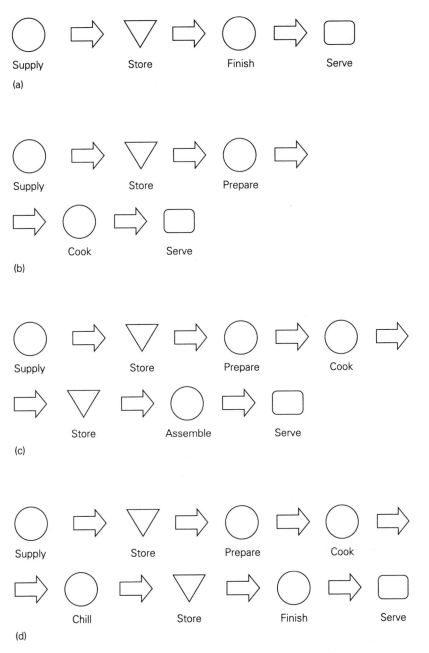

Figure 11.2 Representation of production/service systems: (a) purchase materials in ready to finish form; (b) cook to customer order from raw materials; (c) prepare components ready to assemble to customer order; (d) cook to chilled buffer stock and finish to customer order

3 *Scheduling.* How is production to be scheduled? Is it based on customer orders or a planning schedule based on projected demand? For production, which items are to be prepared in advance and what batch size is required? What is the relationship between batch size, stock-holding of finished items and quality?

4 *Production method.* What processes are required to convert purchased material into a ready-to-serve product? What alternative types of equipment can be used for this conversion?

5 *Capacity management.* What is the volume of material which has to be processed at any one time? What is the interrelationship between batch size of material which is the output of one process and the input to another? Can items of equipment be used for more than one menu item or is it required for exclusive use of a single item?

The relationship between these factors and their impact on design allows a trade-off between space allocation, staffing levels, capital costs and running costs. It is in this area that there is a need for clear communication between the planning team and operational staff. For example, the relationship between make–buy decisions impacts on an assessment of storage needs, preparation areas and equipment requirements. A lack of communication at the design stage can materially affect labour, space and capital productivity.

Capacity planning is a key factor in the design. Excess capacity results in a low resource productivity, since capital and space are tied up in an under-utilized resource. On the other hand, insufficient capacity can lead to excessive queues, poor customer service and a possible lost sale because of the volatility of service (Sill,1991). The balancing of capacity between stages of the process is also a key design factor. For example, in a bakery the batch size needs to be related to mixing, dividing, proving and baking equipment.

Layout of production areas

In general, manufacturing (Harris, 1989) methods of production may be classified as:

1 *Jobbing.* One-off items made to a customer's order, such as in an à la carte restaurant.

2 *Batch production.* The plant is organized to produce one type of product for a period of time, as in hospital catering; following the production of a number of batches, the production set-up may be changed to that required for an alternative product.

3 *Mass production (production line).* Items being manufactured move along a production line, from one process to another, as in a cook-chill system where all products pass through packing and chilling processes.

4 *Continuous production.* As with mass production, except that the products are moved on a conveyor belt: there are few foodservice examples of continuous production, but continuous equipment is used in cooking processes and utensil-cleaning systems.

Most food service applications use either jobbing or batch production. Within both of these two forms of manufacture, two alternative forms of layout can be used (Murdick *et al.*, 1990):

1 *Product layout.* Specialized areas within the layout are designed to manufacture a single product, or group of closely related products. For example, a bakery area will have all of the necessary equipment, space and staff to produce bakery products. In terms of service industries we may interpret this as, for example, a beverage section on a cafeteria service line.
2 *Process layout.* Specialised areas within the layout are designed to perform a single process. For example, in a kitchen we may have all frying equipment concentrated at the same location in the kitchen and any product which needs frying must be transported to and from this area.

A product layout is inflexible but minimizes movement of the product. It is most frequently used where there are specialized requirements for a limited number of products which do not change. A process layout can be more economical in terms of space and equipment, but can increase the amount of movement of products.

The traditional catering layout uses a combination of both of these: the work of the kitchen is divided into a number of self-contained areas, each of which operates independently on menu items or processes, but synchronized so that all the food for a table/course is ready simultaneously. For example, a bakery or larder area can be seen as a form of product layout, since their design is focused on the production of a limited range of similar products. On the other hand, many traditional kitchens have a centralized cooking area, where all products which require the cooking process must be taken for processing – a form of process layout.

The relationship between design and productivity

Design plays an important part in determining the productivity of an operation. Traditionally, productivity has been defined as the ratio of output to input; however, it is normal now to use a broader definition of productivity which covers not only the consideration of ratios of outputs against inputs, but also takes in other aspects such as quality, customer satisfaction and employee satisfaction (Ball and Johnson, 1989) as well as the reduction of cost and wastage (Heap,1992a).

Jones (1990) points to the importance of improving total productivity in developing strategies for foodservice organizations in the next few years. Some of the strategies which he proposes have implications for foodservice design, including work simplification, task scheduling, ergonomic analysis and time and motion study.

Catering employment can be tiring because of a poor environment and because staff must walk long distances. Staff who are tired work inefficiently and are more prone to making mistakes. Because of this, attention must be given to the design of the individual workstation. This involves the use of anthropometric data (Goldsmith,1979), principles of work design (Wild,1990b), to provide staff with a work area which is comfortable and which has all of the necessary equipment and utensils located in a convenient position. Another aspect of design which can influence labour flexibility is the consideration of the methods used for the movement of materials and products. Systematized product handling systems such as trolleys and standardized containers can greatly reduce the cost of materials handling. In relation to comfort and control of costs, the design of air-conditioning and/or heating and ventilation systems is a key part of the design (Redlin and Stipanuk, 1987).

Productivity may be affected by the use of technology within the design (Kirk, 1989; Haywood,1990). Modern processing equipment can have a much higher space and energy productivity than its more traditional counterpart. Similarly, computerized controls can increase labour productivity. However, investment in technology has not always resulted in the expected productivity gains. Additionally, technology may pose a threat to employees and to product (Heap, 1992b). This is one reason for the involvement of staff at the design stage and for the inclusion of training as part of the design process (Pine,1989). Avery (1989b) proposes a number of techniques for improving productivity, all of which relate to the design stage. These include human engineering (ergonomics), the use of labour saving equipment and the concentration of labour through the use of centralized preparation areas.

Flexibility in the use of labour is another aspect of productivity which is related to design (Kelliher,1989). Within the catering industry, this is most commonly associated with the use of technological systems such as cook-chill.

The relationship between production and service

The design and layout of a foodservice area play a key role in terms of translating the foodservice concept into an operational system. Because a foodservice operation is a complex mix of production and service activities, it has specialized requirements as a delivery system of both a product and a service. This poses specific problems in terms of design and layout.

Techniques of production and service smoothing should be considered at the design stage. Production and service systems both work best when there is an even demand While it is possible to control the flow of customers and to design queuing areas to make them less objectionable, the extent to which this can be done is limited.

An important variable is the extent to which peaks and troughs of demand impact on the production and service delivery system (Harris,1989). This largely determines the relationship of supply (production) and demand (service). One of the characteristics of a service is that it cannot readily be stored; therefore, any storage must relate to the production aspects of the operation. In some foodservice situations, sales forecasting techniques can be used to determine food production levels (Miller *et al.*,1991a, 1991b) which is valuable information at the design stage.

In terms of design elements, demand for service can be smoothed using methods such as separating aspects of the service (separate coffee lounge to take pressure of the dining room) and use of a reception area or bar in a restaurant. But the main design aspects of controlling the relationship between supply and demand involve techniques such as those identified by Jones (1988):

1 The development of production lines – conversion from a traditional job-shop approach to batch or mass production systems resulting in a high-volume, low-variety system as in fast food operations.
2 Increase customer participation in the service element of the operation through the use of self-service, self-selection and self-cooking elements of the catering system.
3 Decoupling of production and service so that productivity gains can be made in the production aspects of the business without diminishing the value of the 'high contact' service aspect, as in cook-chill and cook-freeze systems.

The logical extension of the last point has resulted in the development of systems such as cook-freeze, cook-chill and sous-vide (Johns *et.al.*, 1992). These systems introduce a shelf-stable intermediary stage into the production system so that products can be stored to balance variable demand for service. The introduction of buffer stock into the process introduces new elements to the design process. The buffer stock may be short term or long term depending on the nature of the fluctuation. For example, if there is a change from minute to minute, a short-term buffer stock will suffice. The design of suitable hot and cold food display counters may allow this to be done with negligible loss of quality. On the other hand, weekly or seasonal variations in demand can only be smoothed using a long-term buffer stock (Fuller and Kirk,1991a). Consideration must be given to the design of storage areas for buffer stocks to ensure that there is minimal loss of quality and no risk of food poisoning.

Developments in the service delivery system, as implemented in fast food operations, have placed additional demands on foodservice equipment and layouts (Pickworth,1988). For example, the degree of product customization can be a major factor. This can be balanced by the extent to which preparation is done off site in either a central production kitchen or by a food manufacturer.

Foodservice area layouts must be designed in relation to the foodservice concept and to the requirements of the customer (Nevett, 1985). This part of the system is often in view of the customers, in which case merchandising plays an important part. The service area acts as the primary interface between the customer and the service delivery system (Normann, 1991); therefore considerable thought must be give to: the control of queues (Hollins and Hollins,1991); to the display of food and beverages products; to point of sale information; and to the management of quality. Modlin (1989) discusses various arrangements of food service areas.

Constraints on the planning process

Hygiene and food safety

Snyder (1991) identifies a number of food safety risks within the foodservice industries. A number of the greatest hazards (improper cooling, improper hot holding, inadequate cooking and cross-contamination) are related to design and equipment selection. Flow diagrams help to identify progress from raw material to finished product and opportunities for cross-contamination. Systems for temperature control and temperature monitoring are key aspects of current design for all storage areas. The procedure of 'hazard analysis and critical control points' can be useful at the design stage.

Health and safety

International and EC legislation is having an increasing impact on the design of food production and service facilities. This covers areas such as the mechanical safety of machines, electrical safety, VDU emissions, the handling and storage of hazardous chemicals and the provision of a safe environment for employees.

Environmental issues

There is now considerable interest in the impact of a business on the environment. For example, the International Hotels Environment Initiative has seen a number of international hotel companies working together in this area (IHEI, 1993). This initiative covers waste management, water and energy conservation, water quality, purchasing policy, air quality, external emissions, noise and chemical hazards. A number of these areas will impact on design.

One example is the use of plastics and disposables and the collection of waste materials for recycling. This will have a bearing on the design of refuse areas, if waste is to be segregated for recycling purposes. Where possible, the design implications of recycling should be incorporated at an early stage in the process. Storage should be allocated to allow the separation of paper, cardboard, plastic, metal and food waste. A decision should be made, not just on the capital and running cost implications, but also based on environmental issues (Jafee *et al.*,1993).

Consideration should be given to energy conservation at an early stage in the design process (Fuller and Kirk, 1991b). This includes a number of factors:

- Not siting refrigeration equipment in warm environments
- Minimizing the lengths of hot water piping
- Using energy efficient appliances and property management systems (Kirk, 1987)
- Energy efficient heating, ventilation and air-conditioning systems (HVAC)
- Recovery and recycling waste heat from cooking canopies and dishwashing areas

In order to control the consumption of energy, accurate information is needed by management on actual consumption. Metering of the major utilities should be built in to the design to allow departments or sections to operate as energy cost centres. Information on consumption by cost centres then allows for the monitoring of consumption and the targeting of improvements (Dale and Kluga,1992). Closely related to energy management is water management. As with energy, water should be metered at a local level to allow monitoring and target setting (Borsenik,1979).

Controls on chlorofluorocarbons (CFCs) will affect refrigeration equipment. Those CFCs which cause the greatest harm to the ozone layer are not to be used in new equipment after 1993. Any redesign of foodservice facilities should take into account that existing plant may utilize harmful CFCs, which may need to be replaced. Advice is available from professional refrigeration organizations on their safe disposal.

Other aspects of environmental pollution which can be controlled at the design stage are noise, smells, and visual/aesthetic factors.

Conclusions

This chapter has been concerned with giving an overview of foodservice design and to provide a discussion of some of the current issues related to the design process, rather than providing detailed design data. Foodservice design is becoming increasingly more sophisticated, given the need to control factors such as productivity and service quality. Each situation is unique and requires a detailed analysis of the operational requirements before the design process can commence. This design process should be fully integrated into production and operational management activities in order to avoid expensive mistakes which can affect operational factors for the whole lifetime of the installation.

References

Avery, A. C. (1989a). Principles of kitchen design. In R. A. Modlin (ed.), *Commercial Kitchens*. Arlington, Virginia: American Gas Association, pp. 101–122.

Avery, A. C. (1989b). Up the productivity. In R. A. Modlin (ed.), *Commercial Kitchens*. Arlington, Virginia: American Gas Association, pp. 205–214.

Ball, S. D. and Johnson, K. (1989). Productivity management within fast food chains – a case study of Wimpy International. *International Journal of Hospitality Management*, **8**(4), 265–270.

Birchfield, J. C. (1988). *Design and Layout of Foodservice Facilities*. New York: Van Nostrand Reinhold, pp. 1–21.

Borsenik, F. D. (1979). *The Management of Maintenance and Engineering Systems in Hospitality Industries*. New York: Wiley, pp. 292–351.

Dale, J. C. and Kluga, T. (1992). Energy conservation. *Cornell HRA Quarterly*, **33**(6), pp. 30–35.

DES (1986). *Adaptable Teaching Kitchens in Further Education*. London: HMSO.

Escueta, E. S., Fielder, K. M. and Reisman, A. (1986). A new hospital foodservice classification system. *Journal of Foodservice Systems*, **4**, 107–116.

French, S., Hartley, R., Thomas, L. C. and White, D. J. (1986). *Operational Research Techniques*. London: Arnold, pp. 93–114.

Fuller, J. and Kirk, D. (1991a). *Kitchen Planning and Management*. Oxford: Butterworth-Heinemann, pp. 37–57.

Fuller, J. and Kirk, D. (1991b). *Kitchen Planning and Management*. Oxford: Butterworth-Heinemann, pp. 214–224.

Goldsmith, S. (1979). Anthropometric data. In P. Tutt and D. Adler (eds.), *New Metric Handbook Planning and Design Data*. London: Architectural Press, pp. 23–28.

Harris, N. D. (1989). *Service Operations Management*. London: Cassell, pp. 7–15.

Haywood, K. M. (1990). A strategic approach to managing technology. *Cornell HRA Quarterly*, **31**(1), pp. 39–45.

Heap, J. (1992a). *Productivity Management: a Fresh Approach*. London: Cassell, pp. 3–28.

Heap, J. (1992b). *Productivity Management: a Fresh Approach*. London: Cassell, pp. 75–80.

Hollins, G. and Hollins, B. (1991). *Total Design: Managing the Design Process in the Service Sector*. London: Pitman, pp. 157–167.

Huelin, A. and Jones, P. (1990), Thinking about catering systems. *International Journal of Operations and Production Management*, **10**(8), pp.42–52.

IHEI (1993). *Environmental Management for Hotels*. Oxford: Butterworth-Heinemann.

Jafee, W. F., Almanza, B. A. and Chen-Hua, J. M. (1993). Solid waste disposal: independent foodservice practices, *FIU Hospitality Review*, **11**(1), pp. 69–77.

Johns, N., Wheeler, K. and Cowe, P. (1992). Productivity angles on sous vide production. In R. Teare (ed.), *Managing Projects in Hospitality Organisations*. London: Cassell, pp. 146–168.

Jones, P. (1988). The impact of trends in service operations on food service delivery systems. *International Journal of Operations and Production Management*, **8**, 23–30.

Jones, P. (1990). Managing foodservice productivity in the long-term: strategy, structure and performance. *International Journal of Hospitality Management*, **9**(2), 143–154.

Kelliher, C. (1989). Flexibility in employment: developments in the hospitality industry. *International Journal of Hospitality Management*, **8**(2), 157–166.

Kirk, D (1987). Computer systems for energy management. *International Journal of Hospitality Management*, **6**(4), pp. 237–242.

Kirk, D. (1989). Advances in catering technology. In C. P. Cooper (ed.), *Progress in Tourism, Recreation and Hospitality Management*, Vol. 1. London: Belhaven, pp. 232–241.

Kirk, D. (1991). The use of computer assisted design of kitchens. In R. Collison (ed.), *Advances in Catering Technology 4*, Bradford, UK: Horton, pp. 7.1–7.11.

Lawson, F. (1979). Catering design. In P. Tutt and D. Adler (eds.), *New Metric Handbook Planning and Design Data*. London: Architectural Press, pp. 164–173.

Mascord, D. (1993). Kitchens to be proud of. *Hotel and Restaurant*, **2**(1), pp. 33,34,37.

Mill, R. C. (1989). *Managing for Productivity in the Hospitality Industry*. New York: Van Nostrand Reinhold, pp. 40–52.

Miller, J. L., McCahon, C. S. and Bloss, B. K. (1991a). Food production forecasting with simple time series models. *Hospitality Research Journal*, **14**(3), pp. 9–21.

Miller, J. L., McCahon, C. S. and Bloss, B. K. (1991b). Foodservice forecasting using simple mathematical models. *Hospitality Research Journal*, **15**(1), pp. 43–58.

Modlin, R. A. (1989). *Commercial Kitchens*. Arlington: American Gas Association, pp. 123–158.

Murdick, R. G., Render, B. and Russell, R. S. (1990). *Service Operations Management*. Boston: Allyn and Bacon, pp. 171–205.

Nevett, W. (1985). Operations management perspectives and the hospitality industry. *International Journal of Hospitality Management*, 4(4), 173–178.

Normann, R. (1991). *Service Management: Strategy and Leadership in Service Business*, 2nd edn. Chichester, UK: Wiley, pp. 35–48.

Pickworth, J. R. (1988). Service delivery systems in the food service industry. *International Journal of Hospitality Management*, 7(1), pp. 43–62.

Pine, R. (1989). *Catering Equipment Management*. London: Hutchinson, pp. 99–105.

Redlin, M. H. and Stipanuk, D. M. (1987). *Managing Hospitality Engineering Systems*. East Lansing, Michigan: American Hotel and Motel Association, pp. 148–197.

Scriven, C. R. and Stevens, J. W. (1989). *Manual of Design for the Foodservice Industry*. New York: Van Nostrand Reinhold, pp. 5–11.

Sill, B. T. (1991). Capacity management: making your service deliver more productivity. *Cornell HRA Quarterly*, 31(4), pp. 76–87.

Snyder, O. P. (1991). Food safety. Technical Standards Workshop Report. *Journal of Foodservice Systems*, 6(2), pp. 107–139.

Wild, R. (1990a). *Essentials of Production and Operations Management*, 3rd edn. London: Cassell, pp. 6–21.

Wild, R. (1990b). *Essentials of Production and Operations Management*, 3rd edn. London: Cassell, pp. 109–145.

Part Three

Managing Operations

12 Managing human resources in restaurants and catering outlets

Yvonne Guerrier and Geoffrey Pye

Introduction

In many respects the issues to do with managing human resources in restaurants and catering outlets are no different from the issues of managing human resources in any organization. The fundamental problems are those of how to design appropriate jobs and link these jobs together into appropriate organizational structures; how to recruit and select staff, allocate them to jobs and ensure they have the right skills to do those jobs; and how to control, motivate and reward performance. However, there are a number of factors that, if not unique to the restaurant and catering sector, pose special people management problems. It is on some of these issues that this chapter will focus.

As has been discussed elsewhere in this book, there are a wide range of ways in which food can be prepared and served to customers. Customers do not expect (or get) the same from a branch of McDonald's, as from a TGI Friday's, as from their local Italian restaurant, as from the Savoy Grill Room. Similarly, methods of managing human resources that may be appropriate in a fast food outlet would be inappropriate in the best restaurant of a five star hotel. This implies that any strategy for the management of human resources within a specific restaurant or restaurant brand has to take as its starting point the marketing strategy. Without a clear understanding of the customers to whom the restaurant is designed to appeal, their needs and expectations, the product and pricing structure, it is impossible to plan ways of staffing. This is not to suggest that the human resource function is subservient to the marketing function. There may be occasions when it is not possible to find people with the appropriate skills at a price which would match a given marketing specification and the marketing strategy needs to be re-examined.

The growth of branded restaurants poses particular human resource issues which will be considered here. Human resources may be regarded as the 'Achilles' heel' of branded restaurants. The less room for local discretion, the easier it is to manage standardized products and services. But to what extent can people be standardized and indeed does the customer actually want standardized treatment? Branding has implications for the role of the restaurant manager as well of operative staff. Is the manager being de-skilled by being required to conform to brand standards or given more space to focus on the important functions of monitoring customer satisfaction, motivating staff and responding to problems?

A restaurant consists of a service operation and a production unit (the kitchen) sharing the same site. This combination of service and production distinguishes restaurants from other types of retail operation. The trend is to simplify the production process through the use of technology and through buying in more part-processed product, but it is not yet possible to remove production totally. (The process of separating meal production from meal service is most fully developed in operations like in-flight airline catering, but even then the product needs to be 'finished' as it is served, if only by heating it up and removing lids.) This chapter will examine the main issues connected with managing foodservice staff first, then look at human resource management in the food production area and finally examine the issues of integrating these two operations and managing the whole unit and indeed the brand in a multi-unit operation. The last section of the chapter will give a checklist of the human resource issues which need to be taken into account in the management of a restaurant or catering operation. Each point in the list would be worthy of a chapter in its own right and it is beyond the scope of this chapter to discuss them in detail, but the authors wish to flag their importance.

Managing foodservice staff

Foodservice staff are crucial to the success of an operation but often they are the lowest paid, least skilled employees in the operation and those with the highest labour turnover. The problems associated with this role are well documented; such staff have variously been described as filling 'boundary-spanning roles' (Bowen and Schneider, 1988) and 'subordinate service roles' (Shamir, 1980) and as requiring 'emotional labour' (Hochschild, 1983) for their work. In simple terms this means that such staff are the organization's most immediate interface with the customer – they are as close to the customer as they are to other employees – but, unlike professional service workers like doctors or lawyers, they are not perceived as experts or high status individuals. The status of a waiter is lower than that of his client; he is expected to 'build up the client's ego' and conform to the motto that 'the customer is always right even when he is wrong' (Shamir, 1980). This has several implications. First, it requires no small skill to control a client's behaviour while creating the illusion that he or she is in charge and it has long been recognized that a good waiter or waitress even in a modest restaurant possesses these subtle interpersonal skills. For example, Whyte (1946) comments that ' . . . the waitress who bears up under pressure does not simply respond to customers. She acts with some skill to control their behaviour' (p. 132). Secondly, there may be psychological costs and discomfort in fulfilling this type of role. Hochschild (1983) highlights the emotional dissonance and self-alienation which can be created by working in a role where one is continually required to feign emotions one does not feel; keeping smiling and being pleasant to customers one would cheerfully pour the soup over.

Bowen and Schneider (1988) identify three approaches towards controlling the work of the service provider:

- Through careful selection of people with a predisposition and a motivation to play the role in an appropriate way
- Through the training, development and socialization of employees
- Through designing the work in such a way as to minimize and simplify the encounter between the customer and employee.

This last approach was advocated by Levitt (1972) in an article extolling the ways in which the service sector could learn from manufacturing and 'instead of thinking about better and more training of their customer-service representatives . . . (thinking) how to eliminate or supplement them (with technology)' (p. 52).

It is the approach taken by most fast food restaurants and pioneered by McDonald's. Here food is produced and served in a highly controlled way and communications between the food server and the customer are relatively short, simple and predominantly task-related (Buergermeister, 1988; Czepiel *et al.*, 1988). This means that the operation can be staffed with unskilled people who may have little long-term commitment to the work and may leave relatively quickly. Fast food has traditionally provided first job opportunities to young people; indeed 7 per cent of the entire US workforce has worked for McDonald's at one time or another (Love, 1986, quoted in Buergermeister, 1988). Because of the nature of the work in this type of operation, with relatively little task variability and limited task difficulty for the majority of employees, boredom sets in relatively quickly (Buergermeister, 1988; Gabriel, 1988) and relatively high labour turnover might even improve performance.

Compare this with a restaurant in which explicit theatricality is an important part of the operation (e.g. TGI Fridays). In this case the nature of the service provided is what transforms the meal experience – the waiting staff have a key role in ensuring that the customer enjoys him or herself. Here the emphasis is on the selection of appropriate people and their training and socialization. Staff need to be highly technically skilled, although not necessarily with the skills one would normally associate with food and beverage service, but additional skills such as the ability to juggle glasses. They also require the interpersonal skills necessary to create a fun atmosphere for the customers.

Gardner and Wood (1991) describe the way in which new staff are selected in a chain of restaurants using this theatrical style:

> Staff are hired for their personalities not their basic culinary or service skills. . . . The personality of a member of staff is so central to (the company's) ethos that many of the waiting staff in the unit studied were also actors, singers and models, the shiftwork system allowing them to actively pursue theatrical careers outside the workplace. ... For a new store a theatre is hired and potential staff are auditioned.. Personality tests are also employed. (Gardner and Wood, 1991, pp. 271–272).

These two examples represent the two poles of a scale going between simple, structured and low-skill service to complex, high-skill service giving considerable discretion to the service provider. That is not to suggest that the waiters in the theatrical style of restaurant can do exactly what they want. Gardner and Wood (1991) comment on the extent to which the rituals of service in such an operation are stage-managed. For example, 'the end of a "performance" (is) clearly signalled not only by the presentation of the bill ... but by the use of small devices to encourage the customer to leave. ...' (p. 276). This last point also highlights the way in which in both types of operation the customer service staff are supported by systems that make it easier for them to do their work. TGI Fridays, for example, makes use of quite sophisticated information technology to ensure a match between workload and employees to handle it and to ensure employees enjoy 'quality shifts' (NEDC, 1992). They also place a premium on the training of their staff. Compare this with McDonald's who claim that 'effective scheduling and training are ... the major contributors to store profitability' (NEDC, 1992). In both cases there is a recognition that employees perform better if they know what is expected of them, are confident in their skills to meet those expectations and are given the support they need to work effectively.

In some ways, the human resource issues at both McDonald's and TGI Fridays are relatively straightforward. In the former case, the product and service style is simple enough to allow a production line approach to service. In the latter case, the operation is sufficiently unusual and glamorous to allow roles to be presented almost as a branch of show business rather than a job in catering, making it easier to attract people with appropriate attitudes and skills. Most branded restaurants fall somewhere between those two extremes in their requirements from staff. Restaurants like the Harvester chain in the UK are, on the one hand, highly standardized. Staff are expected to serve a meal in exactly the way they have been trained and to provide condiments, etc., again according to the standard procedures. However, should a customer ask for milk rather than the normal cream with her coffee, the waiter is expected to use his or her discretion and initiative to try to meet that request. The standard part of the service can be handled through systematic training and the use of manuals, but it is harder to encourage this appropriate use of discretion in a predominantly standard operation. In Harvester, the attempt is to achieve this through developing a strong organizational culture with a common values system and shared mission. Authority is devolved down the organization but within clear boundaries; the cultural values emphasize that each individual is ultimately responsible for the success of his or her part of the operation. Harvester is a relatively small chain and it must be questionable whether this type of approach would be equally effective in a larger organization. There would also be problems using this approach in an operation which experienced very high levels of labour turnover (although the development of a strong culture might encourage more stability among the workforce).

Another type of food service operation which poses particular human resource management problems is event catering. It is not possible to totally standardize and systematize such an operation because customer needs and expectations can vary even between two apparently similar events. There is also a need to rely on large numbers of casual staff. The more successful companies seem to cope with these problems by recruiting casual staff who are resilient and capable of coping with a range of demands and by ensuring that they are carefully and clearly briefed about what is expected of them before each event. They also seem to employ a relatively high number of 'core' staff as supervisors to handle problems should they occur. Again the issue is that of matching the design of jobs and the selection and training of staff to the nature of the product and the expectations of customers.

Managing kitchen staff

If the restaurant is essentially a service operation, the kitchen is essentially a manufacturing operation. As with other types of manufacturing, one of the key issues in recent years has been the extent to which technology can be used to change the production process and to simplify it, ensuring a product of consistent quality at a cheaper price. The pressures to look at new methods of food production are highest in popular branded restaurants and the trends are to move towards a system of buying in part-prepared products so that the role of the restaurant kitchen becomes that of finishing the product. What needs to be done to finish the meal can be tightly specified, so the operation can be taught to someone with few or no traditional catering skills and the risk of failure is minimized.

The above description of the new type of kitchen job would seem to conform to Braverman's hypothesis about the link between technology and the de-skilling of jobs (Braverman, 1974). Braverman argued that top management are motivated to increase their control over the production process and that a main motive for introducing new technology is that it allows them to do just that by moving towards more fragmented and simplified jobs and ultimately by automating these jobs completely (with the advantage that 'robots don't strike').

Gabriel (1988) studied the experience of catering workers in the least glamorous sectors of the industry – in fast food, hospital catering, club catering, etc. – and concluded that:

> ... there is no iron law stipulating that technology 'determines' the worker's experience at work or that it 'causes' worker alienation. ... Technology does not have the last word on how much people talk to each other, nor does it dictate the degree of formality in interpersonal relations, the quality of the product, or even the speed of the work. .. In all the establishments I visited workers tried actively to influence their work environment, to stamp their own identity on it and humanize it. (p. 163)

New catering jobs may not be intrinsically interesting to someone who has trained as a chef, but that does not mean that managers cannot think of ways of organizing work to produce reasonably rewarding jobs for people. As Gabriel points out, there is also a need to consider how people can be given some degree of control over their work and work environment even while performing a routine and standardized task. Although new technology and systems of food production have meant that good meals can be produced by relatively low-skilled staff, it is also worth remembering that technology has removed the need for some of the least skilled and most repetitive jobs, e.g. peeling potatoes.

There will always be a need for some high-class restaurants producing a wide range of quality dishes to order and staffed in relatively traditional ways. We suggested above that middle range restaurants that provide mainly standardized service but give some discretion to the service provider are hard to manage effectively. Similarly, those establishments that attempt to mix a batch method of production with some one-off à la carte dishes pose a particular problem for the human resource specialist because the price structure of these establishments does not normally allow them to be staffed as one would an à la carte operation.

Managing the whole operation

The potential problems in handling the relationship between foodservice staff and food production staff were highlighted in one of the earliest studies of restaurant work, that by Whyte (1948). In his study of a large popular restaurant, Whyte argued that friction between the waitresses and the cooks was not merely a reflection of their different roles but also a reflection of different values (quick service in the right order for the waitresses against quality of the meal and its presentation for the chefs). This friction was compounded because most of the serving staff were female and most of the chefs were male and the men disliked being 'given orders' by women. A simple piece of technology, a spindle, could be used to reduce direct contact between waiters and cooks, give the cooks more feeling of control over how they manage orders and reduce the impression that their work is being managed by the waiters (see Porter in Handy, 1976). Computerized systems can perform the same function in modern restaurants.

One of the trends in the newer styles of restaurant is to reduce the boundary between back of house and front of house. In the traditional high-class restaurant moving from back of house to front of house is akin to coming on stage and the change of role that this involves is well illustrated in the following passage from George Orwell about Paris waiters seen from the viewpoint of a *plongeur* (dish-washer) who has experienced their swearing and cursing in the kitchen:

> It is an instructive sight to see a waiter go into a hotel dining room. As he passes the door a sudden change comes over him. The set of his shoulders alters; all the dirt and hurry and irritation have dropped off in an instant. He glides over the carpet with a solemn priest-like air. (Orwell, 1940, p. 68. See also Goffman, 1959, for a discussion of this type of role-playing)

With carvery systems of service, chefs are now also on stage in the restaurant. In other types of restaurant the kitchen area may be visible from the restaurant. Also, because of the changes in staffing practices discussed above, kitchen staff are now often very similar in their backgrounds and orientations to work to the foodservice staff. This similarity may be exploited in multi-skilling strategies which encourage a systematic progression between back-of-house and front-of-house jobs and decrease inter-departmental conflict. In TGI Fridays, for example, the progression is normally from kitchen to restaurant to bar. In Little Chef (a roadside restaurant chain) the progression would be from waiter or waitress to grill chef as a preparation for a supervisory role. In both cases, the move is from what are perceived as less important roles towards the roles that are perceived as the crucial ones for the success of the operation although, as these examples illustrate, the key role in the operation will vary according to the nature of the product. These examples also demonstrate the importance of ensuring that the reward and progression system encourage the development of a local culture that supports rather than contradicts the marketing strategy for an operation. Woods (1991) describes how the dominant culture of one chain of restaurants actually rewarded back-of-house competence, although the current goal of the organization was to achieve customer service excellence.

Dann and Hornsey (1986) identify stress as a major source of inter-departmental conflict. Ensuring that appropriate staff are recruited, that they know what is expected of them and that they are supported by sufficient resources and good systems might then be expected to reduce this type of conflict. Indeed, Gardner and Wood (1991) suggest that the lack of this type of conflict in the 'theatrical' restaurants they studied may be due to good systems and generous resourcing rather a product of team building and co-operation. (In a similar vein, Galbraith, 1977, reinterpreted Whyte's classic restaurant study and argued that the problems between cooks and waiters were due to failures in organizational design and lack of slack in the system rather than about poor interpersonal relationships and differences in values.)

Whatever systems do exist, they are stretched in restaurant and catering operations that have to cope with major peaks and troughs in demand. While, as has been discussed above, some restaurant chains are becoming quite sophisticated in their procedures for forecasting demand and scheduling staff to match that demand, most still use relatively simple approaches to adjusting supply and demand. A survey of the English hotel food and beverage sector, for example, suggested that the most favoured ways of increasing the labour supply at short notice were to rearrange the rota quickly, bring in casuals or for the manager to stand in (NEDC, 1992). Restaurants that are open for long hours each day also pose problems in the scheduling of staff. Forte's motorway service areas are experimenting with a system of scheduling staff in teams each with their own supervisor; the analogy can be made with organizations like the fire-service where as 'red watch' comes off duty so 'blue watch' goes on duty.

This raises the issue of the role of the unit manager. To what extent is the unit manager expected to be a hands-on manager, on duty when the unit is open, ready to help out if the unit is short staffed – little more than a senior supervisor. Or is something more or different expected of him or her? In a branded restaurant, as discretion is removed from operative staff so it is also removed from the unit manager. There is no discretion over the menu or pricing; staffing, reward systems and training will be tightly controlled. The manager remains responsible for the motivation and control of staff, for monitoring the quality of the product and service to the customer and for resolving problems, and this may be sufficient for a demanding and rewarding role. However, some companies may look to provide some area of local discretion, perhaps the opportunity to develop local marketing initiatives, as a way of further motivating and developing their unit managers.

With chain restaurants, there is also the need to consider the management structure at the multi-unit level. The trend currently is towards flatter organizations with fewer levels in the hierarchy and many companies are carefully considering the need for area or regional managers. However, in a chain of, for example, 400 relatively small restaurants it is difficult to envisage any way of managing without some intermediate level between the unit and head office. The role of the area manager can be ambiguous; is he or she a controller, a coach and developer of the unit manager or akin to a small business adviser? The appropriate role will vary from operation to operation. What is important is that the division between the responsibilities of the unit manager and those of the area manager is absolutely clear.

A checklist of current issues

It has not been possible, within this chapter, to explore all the issues that need to be addressed when managing human resources within restaurant and catering operations. The checklist below, therefore, flags up a number of issues which are of particular current relevance in this sector and which we have not been able to address above.

Recruitment/selection

- Generating candidates. Should advertising be centralized or devolved locally? How should internal transfers be handled?
- Selection of candidates with a service orientation. What does this mean and how can it be done?
- Image versus reality in restaurant and catering jobs. How can one help candidates and potential candidates to develop realistic expectations?

Training and development

- Delivering standard training and monitoring it in chain operations.
- Training in customer service skills. How can this best be done?
- Ensuring 'due diligence' on statutory training (e.g. food hygiene training in the UK).
- Simplifying training tasks through the development of simpler procedures and good training materials.
- Developing and accrediting the skills in jobs not traditionally recognized as needing skills (e.g. through the National Vocational Qualification, NVQ, system in the UK).

- Developing the skills and careers of those who start with few qualifications. (Many managers in this sector start their careers as waiters or cooks.)

Compensation/benefits/working conditions

- Low pay. How is pay in this sector affected by the legal and institutional framework in a country? (For example, what will be the impact of the abolition of the Wages Council in the UK?)
- Tipping. What impact does tipping have on the behaviour of customer service staff? The distortion of pay scales and issue of fairness towards staff who do not receive tips.
- The management of flexible working. Rewarding irregular hour working. Managing 'casual' workers. Matching hours with business needs (e.g. annualized hours, nil hour contracts, part-time contracts and key-time workers). (See, e.g., Guerrier and Lockwood, 1989, and NEDC, 1992, for a discussion of some of these issues in relation to hotel work.)
- Maternity policy (given a high percentage of female staff, many working part-time).

Employee relations

- Applying consistent disciplinary/grievance procedures.
- Balancing equal opportunities legislation with the image critical to the offer (e.g. in ethnic restaurants).
- 'Hearing' the grass-roots views in a large multi-unit organization.
- Uniforms. These help to create the image of the product but need to be balanced against employee opinions and variety of sizes and shapes.
- Managing a high proportion of part-time workers.
- Managing in a sector that traditionally experiences high turnover.
- Managing security. Cash and consumable products always carry a risk.

Structure

- Appropriate spans of control for area management.
- Making the most of rare skills (e.g. culinary skills, interpersonal skills).
- The impact of shift working on structure.

References

Bowen, D. and Schneider, B. (1988). Boundary-spanning role employees and the service encounter: some guidelines for management and research. In J. Czepiel (ed.), *The Service Encounter: Managing Employee/Customer Interaction in Service Businesses*. Lexington, MA: Lexington Books.

Braverman, H. (1974). *Labor and Monopoly Capital*. New York: Monthly Review Press.

Buergermeister, J. (1988). Communication in fast food organizations. *Hospitality Education and Research Journal*, **12**, 53–65.

Czepiel, J., Solomon, M., Suprenant, C. and Gutman, E. (1988). Service encounters: an overview. In J. Czepiel (ed.), *The Service Encounter: Managing Employee/Customer Interaction in Service Businesses*. Lexington, MA: Lexington Books.

Dann, D. and Hornsey, T. (1986). Towards a theory of interdepartmental conflict. *International Journal of Hospitality Management*, **5**(1), pp. 23–28.

Gabriel, Y. (1988). *Working Lives in Catering*. London: Routledge and Kegan Paul.

Galbraith, J. R. (1977). *Organizational Design*. Reading, MA: Addison-Wesley.

Gardner, K. and Wood, R. C. (1991). Theatricality in food service work. *International Journal of Hospitality Management*, **10**(3) pp. 267–278.

Goffman, E. (1959). *The Presentation of Self in Everyday Life*. New York: Doubleday.

Guerrier, Y. and Lockwood, A. (1989). Managing flexible working in hotels. *Service Industries Journal*, **9**(3) pp. 406–419.

Handy, C. (1976). *Understanding Organizations*. Harmondsworth, UK: Penguin.

Hochschild, A. R. (1983). *The Managed Heart: the Commercialization of Human Feeling*. Berkeley, CA: University of California Press.

Levitt, T. (1972). Production-line approach to service. *Harvard Business Review*, Sept.–Oct., pp. 41–52.

NEDC (1992). *Costs and Manpower Productivity in UK Hotels*. London: NEDC.

Orwell, G. (1940). *Down and Out in Paris and London*. Harmondsworth, UK: Penguin.

Shamir, B. (1980). Between service and servility: role conflict in subordinate service roles. *Human Relations*, **33**(10), 741–756.

Whyte, W. F. (1946). When workers and customers meet. In W. F. Whyte (ed.), *Industry and Society*. New York: McGraw-Hill.

Whyte, W. F. (1948). *Human Relations in the Restaurant Industry*. New York: McGraw-Hill.

Woods, R. H. (1991) Surfacing culture: the 'Northeast Restaurants' case. *International Journal of Hospitality Management*, **10**(4) 339–356.

13 Managing quality in food and beverage operations

Andrew Lockwood

Introduction

Attending a conference in France recently, the fifty or so delegates were entertained to lunch in the upstairs room of an American-style restaurant. The restaurant was newly opened, with excellent decor and expensively appointed. It was late November and the upstairs room had been closed down for the winter season. The bar had been cleared of all bottles and glasses and there was an air of emptiness about the place. Fifty people on long tables of ten soon livened the place up – but in fact despite the emptiness, we were crammed into one side of the room so tightly that the service staff could not get between the tables easily to serve food or drinks. It had been a long morning and we were hungry. The restaurant was warned by two-way radio of our arrival, but it still took nearly half an hour for our starter to be served – a plated salad. The salad and dressing were crisp and piquant, respectively. The plates were cleared and we looked forward to our main course. Meanwhile the jugs of water that had been ready on the table for our arrival were removed and refilled – but left on the bar and only returned to the table on request. There were no wines or drinks included in the menu price. Not only was the upstairs restaurant closed for the winter but the upstairs kitchen was closed too. All the food had to be brought upstairs from the kitchen below, some by service staff carrying two plates, some on trays of four. The plates were cold. Fortunately, the food was hot. The main course was two large shallow fried breasts of chicken with a garnish of vegetables. The chicken was of an excellent standard – plump, juicy, tasty and much too large – one would have been generous, two was overkill. Clearing the main course plates was difficult. The space between the tables was too narrow, the staff not skilled nor experienced at clearing plates from large tables. One waiter managed to drop three half-full glasses of wine down one customer's back. The waiter was too embarrassed to apologize, but quickly got on with clearing away the broken glass and wiping the floor. The sweet was a dense white chocolate mousse on a biscuit base. The coffee was black and strong, but by now there were only a few minutes left before we were expected at the next session.

This restaurant is owned by a company that has one of the best reputations for their attention to quality in the hospitality business.

What is quality?

Quality, as defined by the British Standard 4778 (1987) is 'the totality of features and characteristics of a product or service that bear on its ability to satisfy a stated or implied need'. The stated or implied need is obviously that of the customer – the arbiter of quality. The customer translates these needs into a series of expectations of the service or product to be experienced. If these expectations are met or exceeded, then the customer will be satisfied and it will have been a 'quality' experience. If the expectations are not met – there is a gap between customer expectations and the perceived characteristics of the service or product delivered to them (Parasuraman *et al.*, 1985) – quality will not have been provided.

The range of features and characteristics that go to make up a meal experience are many and varied and can be identified in the scenario described above. They are made up partly of the food on the plate, partly the service received and partly the atmosphere or ambience created by the decor and fittings. One revealing way of looking at these characteristics is shown in Figure 13.1.

The matrix identifies that the food and beverage product consists of a combination of tangible and intangible elements. These relate both to the physical characteristics of the provision (the product) and the interpersonal contact that occurs during the meal experience (the service).

The product tangible elements consist of the food presented to the customer and the facilitating goods used to serve the food on or with. The style and nature of the crockery, cutlery and glassware as well as the linen and napkins are also part of the total experience. The menu also provides tangible evidence of the meal experience by displaying information, through verbal description or pictures, about the dishes available. The final element of this quadrant consists of the machine processes that a customer may come across in a food and beverage outlet. These may range from the effectiveness of the EFTPOS terminal to the way the vending machine dispenses a cup of coffee.

The product intangible quadrant includes the overall atmosphere of the establishment and the aesthetic appeal of the decor, furniture and fittings. Every restaurant and bar has its own feel – some are immediately warm and friendly but others are cold or clinical. Establishing the appropriate decor to engender the right feelings in the customer is obviously important. Compare the clean bright businesslike atmosphere of fast food operations such as Burger King or McDonalds with the warmer, darker, cluttered feel of a TGI Fridays or an Exchange. The product/intangibles help to provide that feeling of comfort, of being at ease or at home that is such an important part of the hospitality concept (Cassee and Reuland, 1983).

Although service is often thought of as intangible, there are still elements that can be seen as tangible. The actions the service staff carry out during service are tangible, as is the way the service process is organized. The speed of service is easily measured and the words service staff use – their 'script'

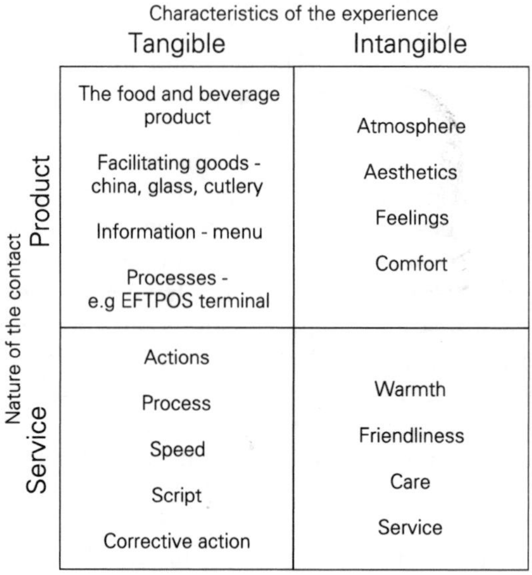

Characteristics of the experience

	Tangible	Intangible
Product	The food and beverage product Facilitating goods - china, glass, cutlery Information - menu Processes - e.g EFTPOS terminal	Atmosphere Aesthetics Feelings Comfort
Service	Actions Process Speed Script Corrective action	Warmth Friendliness Care Service

(Nature of the contact)

Figure 13.1 The quality characteristics matrix

– also provide hard evidence. Another example of tangible service is the action taken to put something right after it has gone wrong – the corrective action. In the scenario described in the Introduction, the action taken showed more consideration for the floor than it did for the customer!

The service/intangible quadrant is very hard to tie down but undeniably exists. The warmth and friendliness shown through a genuine smile is almost tangible. In some restaurants, customers know implicitly that the staff care about their meal, while in others, customers know that the staff care about very little. All these elements add up to a feeling of service.

It looks from the diagram as though each quadrant is of equal importance, but this is not necessarily so and may change from establishment to establishment and from occasion to occasion. The relative importance of each quadrant is difficult to measure, but evidence suggests (Parasuraman *et al.*, 1985; Nightingale, 1985) that the product/tangible component is more significant than the product/intangible component. From the food and beverage provider's point of view, it is, of course, also a lot easier to control. On the other hand, the service/intangible component is probably more significant than the service/tangible and this is very difficult for any manager to influence.

Quality as the satisfaction of customer needs and expectations accords very well with the definition used by Crosby (1984) as one of his quality absolutes, that is 'conformance to requirements'. These requirements are based solely on customers' needs, wants, desires and expectations. Any product or service that does not meet the customers' requirements is described as non-conforming. It is, however, of no use to the customers if they receive exactly what they require on one day but, because for example the chef has a day off, their next visit is a disaster. Quality must also include a strong element of reliability – what Crosby (1984) calls zero defects. He stresses that this is the only acceptable quality standard. Everyone in the organization should be striving to do their job right first time every time.

Increasingly, however, many organizations are moving away from simply satisfying the customer and striving to delight the customer. Deming (1986) suggests that while an unhappy customer will go to another supplier, a customer who is simply satisfied may also switch because there is not a lot to lose and there might be a gain. He argues that profit comes from repeat customers, customers who boast about the product and service they receive and bring their friends with them next time. Delighting the customer means exceeding the customer's expectations, but there are inherent dangers evident in this practice. Tenner and DeToro (1992) suggest that delight arises as a result of the value added characteristics and features that customers did not expect – arousing their latent expectations. Until a few years ago nobody expected their children to be given a helium-filled balloon when they visited a restaurant. Now, however, it is commonplace and this highlights the problem of escalating expectations. Over time, the little extras will become the expected norm and new 'delights' will have to be found.

To summarize, quality for food and beverage operations involves reliably providing the food, service and environment that meets customers' expectations and creating opportunities for adding value that exceeds expectations and results in delight.

Why is quality important?

The pressure on all businesses to pay attention to quality seems to come from three main sources (Lewis, 1989). First, customers are becoming increasingly demanding of the products and services they buy, as well as the way in which those products and services are delivered. Customers are no longer intimidated about complaining in restaurants, and the trend to instruct service staff to check that all is well part way through the meal is only asking for trouble. Secondly, the development of more sophisticated technology, both hard and soft, allows managers to provide a wealth of potential additional and convenience services, although personal contact is still seen as highly valued. The effectiveness of such preparation methods as sous-vide means that a high standard of dishes is available round the clock from a vending machine and a microwave oven. Lastly, in an increasingly competitive and international marketplace, quality is seen as providing an edge of competitive advantage.

Despite these pressures, many managers would argue that providing quality is too expensive or too much trouble to be of any real value. However, Zeithaml *et al.* (1990) suggest that there are three areas of benefit that result from an emphasis on quality:

1 *The payoff of quality.* The positive impact of quality on profitability is illustrated by the Profit Impact of Market Strategy (PIMS) study (Buzzell and Gale, 1987). According to this study, the most important single factor affecting a business unit's performance is the quality of its products and services, in comparison to its competitors. In the hospitality industry, Walker and Salameh (1990) have shown similar results. In the short term, a food and beverage operation that is perceived to have the quality edge over its competitors is able to boost profitability through charging premium prices. Quality provides leverage on the price/value relationship. For example, the prices charged by TGI Fridays or Planet Hollywood are above the market average, but the high perceived quality of these experiences maintains their value to the customer. In the long term, a quality advantage will result in business growth. This growth in volume will result in economies of scale and superior profit margins.
2 *Quality creates true customers.* The high perceived value identified above will result in loyal customers who will use the operation consistently over a long period and will recommend the unit to their friends. The value of long-term relationships in services marketing has only recently been realized (see Chapter 15), but good restaurateurs have always recognized the importance of repeat customers.
3 *Quality leads to efficiencies.* Quality improvement rather than increasing the costs of an operation can result in operational efficiencies which more than recoup the investment in quality. Quality costs can be divided into two types – the costs of conformance and the costs of non-conformance. The costs of conformance are the costs of assuring that everything comes out right and includes all prevention efforts and quality education. The costs of non-conformance can again be divided into appraisal or inspection costs and failure costs. Appraisal costs are the costs of inspection to make sure that mistakes are kept down and to ensure that

any mistakes that are made are identified before reaching the customer. Failure costs are the costs of having made mistakes. They can be split into internal and external failure costs. Internal costs are those incurred where mistakes are found before they reach the customer or cross the line of visibility. They include scrap, rework, down-grading and excess inventory. External failure costs are those incurred when mistakes are not found before they reach the customer. They include such things as repair and warranty claims, providing replacement goods or services and the potential loss of future business. Crosby (1984) suggests that a service firm can waste as much as 35 per cent of its costs on producing non-quality. He estimates that appraisal and failure costs account for approximately 95 per cent of this total, whereas prevention costs account for the other 5 per cent. Turning this ratio around by allocating a much higher share to prevention costs should provide a massive potential for reducing total cost in any service business.

While the internal failure costs of excess inventory and waste might be high, the real danger of poor quality for a food and beverage operation lies in those errors that are not discovered until they reach the customer, as the following example illustrates.

Imagine a party of four people who visit a restaurant for dinner and have a disaster of an evening. They are so disappointed with their meal that they complain there and then directly to the manager. He explains that a new chef has just been appointed who has not quite got used to the systems and equipment yet. He apologizes profusely and immediately cancels the bill for the meal to show his commitment to putting things right. The four customers are appeased by the manager, but avow that they will never visit the restaurant again.

If the average spend in the restaurant is around £15 per head for food and £5 per head for drink, then the 'disaster' has only cost the restaurant £80 in lost sales revenue and the manager convinces himself that the party will come back.

However, if the meal had gone well, then these customers would have expected to use the restaurant at least six times a year over the next five years. The lost sales revenue, at a conservative estimate, would have been an additional $80 \times 6 \times 5 = £2,400$.

An established rule of thumb suggests that every dissatisfied customer will tell another seven people, whereas every satisfied customer will tell another three people. Our party of four customers is therefore likely to tell $4 \times 7 = 28$ potential customers who are now lost to the business. Each of these customers is worth the same as the initial loss, i.e. £2,400 each or £67,200 in total. Also the business will not now welcome the three customers each of the party would have recommended to come and will have lost an extra £28,800.

The total loss so far is now therefore:

Cancelled bill	80
Lost potential from initial party	2,400
Loss from dissatisfied word of mouth	67,200
Loss of potential recommendations	28,800
Total loss	£98,480

In total, one dissatisfied table of four has cost the business nearly £100,000. Unfortunately it doesn't end there!

It is now well established that it costs between two and three times more in marketing costs to attract a new customer than it does to retain an existing one. The marketing cost to replace the 44 lost customers (4 + 28 + 12) will be large.

We may also assume that if one party of four had a disastrous evening, then there are likely to be more dissatisfied customers who did not want to make a fuss and did not complain, but will still never come again and will still tell their friends about how awful it was. The nightmare continues....

Quality therefore provides an opportunity for food and beverage operations to claim a winning edge over their competitors, to ensure the long-term loyalty of their customers and to improve both short-term and long-term profitability through cost savings and higher margins. If the benefits are so great, then why is it that so few food and beverage companies seem to have made much progress in this area?

Special features of food and beverage operations

The best known approaches to managing quality, propounded by the quality gurus such as Deming, Crosby, Juran, Ishikawa, Shingo, Taguchi and others (see, e.g., Flood, 1993), have grown up in the manufacturing sector. The tools and techniques used in manufacturing are well proven to be effective in these environments. Increasingly, attention has been drawn to the service sector and the particular challenges faced by companies wishing to pursue service quality (see Lewis, 1989; Zeithaml et al., 1990; Gummesson, 1992). Tools and techniques have been adopted and adapted from manufacturing to cope with these challenges and, where necessary, new approaches have been developed.

The quality matrix described earlier in Figure 13.1 illustrates the problem facing food and beverage operations. Not only must these operations deal with the manufacturing problems of meal or drink production, but they also have to act as a service operation. It is not surprising that the resulting complexity makes managing quality in food and beverage operations difficult but not impossible.

The issues that need to be tackled can be identified as follows. Looking at the characteristics of service operations that are seen to distinguish them from manufacturing (Fitzgerald *et al.*, 1991) provides some interesting insights for food and beverage operations:

1 *Intangibility.* Unlike a 'pure' service operation, food and beverage operations services do not simply consist of the service performance and the intangible factors that affect this interaction. A large part of their hospitality consists of the very tangible product elements of food and drink. On the product side there are the tangible elements of the food or drink itself – how hot is the food, what does it look like, how cold is the beer, how large is the glass, etc.? – but there are also the intangible elements of the atmosphere created – does the customer feel comfortable, 'at home', secure? On the service side there are the intangible elements of the friendliness or care offered by the hospitality provider. At the same time it is possible to identify tangible service elements such as the time taken to deliver the service or the effectiveness of the service performed – did the waiter spill the soup, how long between the order and delivery of breakfast?

2 *Heterogeneity.* As service outputs are heterogeneous, the standard of performance may vary, especially where there is a high labour content. It is therefore hard to ensure consistent quality from the same employee from day to day, and harder still to get comparability between employees, yet this will crucially affect what the customer receives. While a customer may expect some variability in the service received, the same cannot be true of the product dimension. A hamburger served by one unit of a restaurant chain at one end of the country must be consistent with every other hamburger served in every other unit of the same chain. The range of tolerance on the product side seems much lower than on the service side.

3 *Simultaneity.* The production and consumption of many services are simultaneous, for example having a hair cut or taking a plane flight. Most services then cannot be counted, measured, inspected, tested or verified before sale for subsequent delivery to the customer. The product element of hospitality ranges from simultaneous production – for gueridon service, where cooking is done in the restaurant at the table – to decoupled production – for cook-chill or cook-freeze, where food is batch produced at a central location, cooled, and then distributed for later consumption – with many other possible systems in between (Huelin and Jones, 1990).

4 *Perishability.* Services cannot be stored, so removing the buffer of an inventory that can be used to cope with fluctuations in customer demand. Even a restaurant seat is a perishable product. Empty places cannot be stockpiled for a busy day sometime in the future. Once a restaurant seat

has been left empty, the potential revenue from the occupation of that space is lost. From the product perspective, raw ingredients or a complete meal can be stored for a period depending on the method of storage. Normally, however, the period will be a matter of days rather than years.

Food and beverage operations display many of the characteristics of service industries in general, but with the added complication of a production element. However, even the production side of food and beverage is far from straightforward.

1 *The cost structure.* The need to provide the appropriate environment within which food and beverages can be delivered means that most businesses need a substantial investment in premises and plant and associated fixed costs. On the other hand, variable costs are low. This high fixed cost/low variable cost structure creates an unusual cost–profit–volume relationship. Generally the breakeven volume will be quite high. Exceeding this level will result in high profits, but low volumes will result in substantial losses. The number of hotel and restaurant operations in the hands of the receiver following the trials of recession bears forceful witness to this fact.

2 *The unpredictability of demand.* This would not be too difficult a problem to deal with if it were possible to predict with confidence the levels of demand for the operation. Unfortunately, food and beverage suffer from complex fluctuations in demand. Demand will fluctuate over time – hourly, daily, weekly, monthly, annually and cyclically – by type of customer – group or individual, business or leisure – and by menu item. The result is a mixture of patterns that makes forecasting and subsequent resource scheduling very difficult indeed.

3 *The short cycle of production.* The length of the food and beverage production cycle is short, giving little time for monitoring or for the correction of errors. A restaurant operation may well buy in fresh produce in the morning that is prepared during the morning, offered for lunch and consumed by early afternoon.

4 *The risk.* The food production process deals with raw ingredients that have a limited shelf life and that, if contaminated, can result in serious illness and death. Customers entering a food and beverage operation are placing themselves in the care of that host and the operation must employ all due diligence to ensure their safety. Customers must place their trust in the operation based on limited available evidence.

5 *The technology.* The food and beverage production system is labour intensive, but technological substitution is still possible in back-of-house operations. Recent developments in catering technology have allowed the decoupling of production and service through the use of cook-chill, cook-

freeze or sous-vide methods. The McDonald's industrialized service delivery system ensures high speed, high volume with high consistency over a limited product range and limited human intervention.

6 *The presence of the customer.* Throughout the complexity of the operations described above, the food and beverage operation is pressured by the physical presence of the customer, monitoring progress with the expert eye of someone who has eaten many meals before. Even in home delivery operations, the pressure of meeting the delivery time standard, usually 30 minutes, represents the customer's presence.

The quality management cycle

To deliver quality to the customer in the face of the complexities identified above, the food and beverage operation must adopt some form of systematic

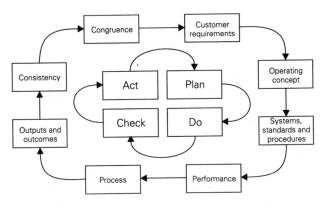

Figure 13.2 The quality management cycle

approach. The quality management cycle shown in Figure 13.2 has been developed from the basis of the Deming (1982) cycle.

PDCA (plan-do-check-act)

This approach has been developed to help identify and correct any errors that occur during production or service and lead to lasting quality improvement. The foundation of the cycle is one of continual improvement to reduce the gap between customer requirements and the actual performance of the operation. The cycle starts by planning what improvement to make, based on a clarification of the problem and the development of hypotheses about the underlying causes. The 'do' phase implements a small-scale experiment to correct the situation that is then 'checked' through measurement. The final step 'acts' to implement these quality improvements. The cycle is essentially a learning process and after one cycle is completed another one starts. It is, however, useful to extend this four step approach to the systematic management of quality throughout an organization, while maintaining the elements of learning and continual improvement.

Planning

The starting point for any quality initiative should be to establish the specific requirements of customers in each of the market segments that the food and beverage operation intends to serve. For example, what does a business traveller expect from a hotel breakfast and in what ways is that different from the weekend leisure visitor? In reality, it is more likely that there is already a fairly good idea of what the operation will be like, based on previous experience or an existing brand. Market research can still help to identify the most important characteristics of the operation so that they can be built into systems and procedures from the beginning.

From this customer base, management needs to prepare a detailed operating concept. This should start from an idea of the corporate mission to develop into a series of core-product values and then be translated into a practical service delivery system. For example, the mission statement for EuroDisney Resort Hotels is quite simply 'to be the highest quality service and hospitality organization in the world by creating an environment where all cast members and guests are happy'. This mission is then expanded into ten 'standards of excellence'. These are not strictly operating standards – these are laid out in detail elsewhere – but more a series of statements about the core values that the company feels are important. Heskett et al. (1990) have developed a detailed model that describes the integration of the target market segments with the service concept, operating strategy and the design of the service delivery system through positioning, value-cost leveraging and system-strategy integration. This strategic service vision forms the foundations upon which quality can be built throughout the organization. Translating these ideas into a concrete design is a complex challenge that is fundamental to the future success of the operation. Lockwood et al. (1992) discuss this process and particularly the use of flowcharting or service blueprinting developed by Shostack (1981,1987) and extended into the hospitality field by Senior and Randall (1991) as perceptual blueprinting.

Doing

Once the design of the food and beverage operation has been decided, it is then necessary to fill in the details of the systems, standards and procedures to be adopted. BS 5750/ISO 9000 provides an established framework within which systems can be developed (Lockwood and Brunner, 1991; Pearce, 1992), but the detail of operating standards and procedures must be related to customer needs and the specific characteristics of the operation. Jan Hubrecht (Lockwood *et al.*, 1992) describes standard setting as a fundamental part of the Scott's Hotels TQM Health Check. Scott's Hotels standards were reintroduced and all employees in the organization were retrained over a twelve-month period and signed off as competent to meet these new standards by their hotel general manager. British Airways Route Catering have designed, as part of their quality assurance and control procedures, a series of flow charts that illustrate their procedures, for example, for accepting and rejecting goods delivered or ensuring hygiene.

With all the design and planning done and all systems, standards and procedures in place, the next stage is to activate the operation and perform on a day-to-day basis.

Checking

Checking that the operation has performed according to the plan can take place at two levels. First, checks can be made that the process has been carried out correctly and then the outputs or outcomes of the operation can be checked.

Checking the process can be done either as part of the daily operations or as a periodic inspection. Statistical process control (SPC) is the term used in manufacturing for the collection of process data that can then be monitored against performance norms to identify when processes have or are likely to deviate from established tolerance levels (Oakland and Followell, 1990). There are, however, very few examples of the application of SPC to food and beverage operations. A similar approach that the industry does use is hazard analysis critical control point (HACCP). This technique, originally developed in food manufacturing to control hygiene risk, identifies the critical points in the production process and puts into place control measures to monitor performance at these points. As long as these measures stay in control, the quality of the whole process should be assured. (See Chapter 22 for a detailed discussion of this technique.)

Periodic inspection, although not controlling the process as it happens, will check whether all procedures are being followed. The method used here is some form of operational audit, whereby a detailed checklist is developed to cover all aspects of the operation. Harvester Restaurants have separate checklists for bar/cellar, hygiene, kitchen, restaurant and administration. Each area is then further divided into headings. For example, the restaurant quality assurance evaluation is broken down into cleanliness and hygiene, preparation, presentation/moments of truth, service, timing and guest reaction. Each heading then has a series of items to be looked for. For example, under the preparation heading you might check whether all tables are laid up, cruets and sugar containers are filled, promotional material is displayed, and ashtrays are available on smoking tables. Each correct item is awarded a number of points and totals can be calculated to compare with acceptable levels, previous performance or other restaurants in the chain.

South West Thames Regional Health Authority have a similar catering management quality assurance review that covers the hospital profile, performance indicators, hygiene and food handling, control at kitchen level, food volume control, financial control of food and staff, control of meal service at ward level, menu content for staff and patients, flexibility and customer awareness.

Monitoring the process should ensure that the service delivery system is performing as it should, but it will not check the level of customer satisfaction with the service received. Therefore a checking system needs to be in place to measure the outputs from the system and the outcomes from the customers' point of view. A commonly used method is to use a mystery shopper or quality audit. Mystery shoppers visit the unit as normal customers but prepare a report on their experiences against established criteria. This technique is widely used in fast food operations, but also in commercial restaurants (Newton and van de Merwe, 1992) and international hotels. Another approach is to use some form of customer satisfaction survey (see Chapter 17). The SERVQUAL instrument (Zeithaml *et al.*, 1990) is currently being developed for lodging operations and a series of food and beverage applications (Knutson *et al.*, 1991).

Acting

The final stage of the cycle is to act on the information collected. Consistency involves acting on any non-conformance to established standards, i.e. making sure you are doing what you set out to do. Quality improvement to move toward zero defects is a continuing process. The introduction of quality improvement teams, quality control circles or corrective action teams may help this move. The focus here is on improving the process.

In looking at congruence, the focus is on ensuring that the food and beverage concept still matches the customers' requirements. Over time, customer expectations change and there must be some way of highlighting these gaps between expectations and delivery. Once identified, these new or changed requirements are passed on to the design team who then start the next round of the cycle.

Conclusions

Managing quality in food and beverage operations is difficult, complicated by the complex blend of production and service elements that need to be managed over the very short cycle of operations. There is an obvious need for a systematic and all-encompassing approach to the problem, but as yet only a few food and beverage operations have risen to the challenge. The potential rewards for the organization that does get it right, first time, every time, are enormous.

References

BS 4778 (1987). *Glossary of quality terms*. London : British Standards Institution.

Buzzell, R. D. and Gale, B. T. (1987). *The PIMS Principles – Linking Strategy to Performance*. New York: The Free Press.

Cassee, E. and Reuland, R. J. (1983) Hospitality in hospitals. In R. J. Reuland and E. Cassee (eds), *The Management of Hospitality*, Oxford: Pergamon Press, pp.143–163.

Crosby, P. B. (1984). *Quality Without Tears*. New York: McGraw-Hill.

Deming, W. E. (1986). *Quality, Productivity and Competitive Position*. Cambridge, Massachusetts: Massachusetts Institute of Technology, Centre for Advanced Engineering Study.

Fitzgerald, L., Johnston, R., Brignall, S., Silvestro, R. and Voss, C. (1991) *Performance Measurement in Service Businesses*. London: The Chartered Institute of Management Accountants.

Flood, R. L. (1993). *Beyond TQM*. Chichester UK: John Wiley.

Gummesson, E. (1992). *Quality Management in Service Organisations*. New York: SQA.

Heskett, J. L., Sasser, W. E., and Hart, C. W. L. (1990). *Service Breakthroughs – Changing the Rules of the Game*. New York: The Free Press.

Huelin, A. and Jones, P. (1990). Thinking about catering systems. *International Journal of Operations and Production Management*, **10**(8), 42–52.

Knutson, B., Stevens, P., Wullaert, C., Patton, M. and Yokoyama, F. (1991). Lodgserv – a service quality index for the lodging industry. *Hospitality Research Journal*, **14**(3), 277–284.

Lewis, B. R. (1989). Quality in the service sector: a review. *International Journal of Bank Marketing*, **7**(5), 4–12.

Lockwood, A. J. and Brunner, S. (1991). BS 5750 – Quality System Guidelines, *HCIMA Technical Brief*, No. 20, July.

Lockwood, A. J., Gummesson, E., Hubrecht, J. and Senior, M. (1992). Developing and maintaining a strategy for service quality. In R. Teare and M. Olsen (eds), *International Hospitality Management—Corporate Strategy in Practice*. London/New York: Pitman/Wiley.

Newton, S. and van de Merwe, C. (1992). Quality assurance and the mystery guest programme in Harvester Restaurants. In C. P. Cooper and A. J. Lockwood (eds), *Progress in Tourism, Recreation and Hospitality Management*, **4**, 169–174.

Nightingale, M. (1985). The hospitality industry: defining quality for a quality assurance programme – a study of perceptions. *Service Industries Journal*, **5**(1), 9–22.

Oakland, J. S. and Followell, R. F. (1990). *Statistical Process Control*. Oxford: Heinemann.

Parasuraman, A., Zeithaml, V. A., Berry, L. L. (1985). A conceptual model of service quality and its implications for future research. *Journal of Marketing*, **49**, Fall, 41–50.

Pearce, E. (1992). Taking quality on board! British Standard 5750. In C. P. Cooper and A. J. Lockwood (eds), *Progress in Tourism, Recreation and Hospitality Management*, **4**, 195–198.

Senior, M. and Randall, L. (1991). Hotel services in the NHS. *Managing Service Quality*, IFS Publications, July.

Shostack, G. L. (1981). How to design a service. In J. H. Donnelly and W. R. George (eds), *The Marketing of Services*. Chicago: American Marketing Association.

Shostack, G. L. (1987). Service positioning through structural change. *Journal of Marketing*, **51**(1), 27–43.

Tenner, A. R. and DeToro, I. J. (1992). *Total Quality Management: Three Steps to Continuous Improvement*. Massachusetts: Addison Wesley.

Walker, J. R. and Salameh, T. T. (1990). The QA payoff. *Cornell Hotel and Restaurant Quarterly*, **30**(4), 57–59.

Zeithaml, V. A., Parasuraman, A. and Berry, L. L. (1990). *Delivering Service Quality. New York: The Free Press*.

14 The role of operations research in the management of food and beverage operations with special emphasis on forecasting

Cliff Goodwin

Scope of the chapter

This chapter outlines the scope of operations research, concentrating on its potential usefulness to food and beverage in the areas of sales forecasting and labour scheduling. Having described some techniques and outlined their uses, it then looks at some applications in the industry, by looking at research on the use of such techniques in food and beverage operations in the USA.

Introduction

Management science, often referred to as operations research, consists of a series of tools which are available to management and which, when used appropriately, can assist in increasing decision effectiveness. It uses a range of sophisticated mathematical models and statistical methods in an attempt to make more meaningful use of the data collected by management about their operations. There is no doubt that data collection has become far more sophisticated in recent years, particularly within the areas of control of a food and beverage manager. This has largely been brought about by the range of readily available software for the microcomputers which are now commonplace within hospitality operations.

Other electronic point-of-sale equipment can now provide detailed sales analysis data; for example, a detailed sales mix by number of individual menu items sold, by their sales value, even an analysis of sales volume over a number of time periods. Yardsticks of productivity and asset utilization such as restaurant occupancy, sales revenue per employee, average spend, liquor and food sales mix, stock turnover, material cost percentages, and so on, are now generated with ease by commercial software. This has saved hours of work pouring over a calculator, and the quality of data is indeed high. However, much of the data that can be generated is not used to best advantage. Many managers, having obtained the data, then miss an opportunity of using it effectively to improve the performance of their operation.The increasing power of microcomputers, and their falling costs, has greatly expanded the possibilities of using the mathematical and statistical tools of management science. Computers make it possible to do quickly the extensive calculations that are often required. Mathematical models therefore can potentially be used to improve production planning and labour cost control. Some models and techniques also could be used to improve the quality of the data used for complementary approaches such as yield management and menu engineering. These techniques have received much attention over recent years, and sound quantitative forecasting, for example, could add to the accuracy of these approaches.

Scope of operations research

Operations research (OR) procedures have been used successfully in manufacturing industry for many years, but the service industries seem reluctant to take the techniques on board. This has probably been brought about by the fear of complex mathematical models, and also the decentralized nature of restaurant operations, with relatively small 'production outlets' spread over a large geographical area. The possible exception to this would be central production units for hospitals, social service meals on wheels and airline catering production. The scope of OR is extensive, but the following brief list will illustrate the potential:

- Help with the forecasting of production levels (and hence staffing and stock requirements) consistent with demand and cost.
- Determination of policy for maintenance of equipment, and its possible replacement.
- Optimization of stock levels with fluctuating demand.

- Solving problems where queuing occurs, as in self-service restaurants.
- Problems in sequencing, for example during the opening of a new facility or the running of a marketing campaign.

Application of operations research

In attempting to tackle a problem with the help of OR, the approach will vary with the particular circumstances and problem, but a simple five-step approach is usually applied (Figure 14.1).

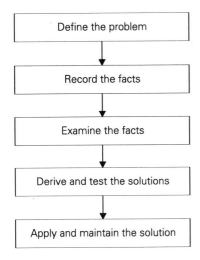

Figure 14.1 Operations research: the five-step approach

The first stage is to define the problem, and to be clear exactly what is to be improved. The necessary data then have to be collected and assembled in a suitable form. All variables (including quantities and costs) and all restrictions which may limit certain factors must be determined (e.g. legal restrictions on opening times, or on numbers of people allowed into a particular area, or storage limitations). When this is done models, mathematical equations and inequalities may be constructed. If any restrictions are overlooked, this could seriously affect the accuracy of projected results. In most cases the problems are modelled on past experience and results, and here data from electronic point of sale (EPOS) equipment could be particularly useful when dealing with problems of demand forecasting. If past records are non-existent, e.g. at the time of the set-up of a new concept restaurant, data may have to be created. For example, OR in its application to queuing problems : it is known that in self-service and fast food restaurants queues form and fluctuate with random arrivals and departures. This situation could be analysed by looking at existing facilities, or alternatively it could be simulated. This method of simulation, using queuing theory is described below.

Once the facts have been ascertained, then a hypothesis can be developed. This hypothesis, which may subsequently be found to be true or false, fills the gap between the observations and the known effects. This may be an inaccurate bridge, but experimentation and trial will indicate the way to the right path. The facts from the models and data equations are then analysed to present the facts in a mathematical form. The next stage is to process the data and derive the solutions. Increasingly this can be achieved on a microcomputer. The solution(s) can then be tested under operating conditions, and necessary modifications made. Finally, the solution is translated into practical and concrete terms and put into operation. It is important, however, that continual modification and adjustment take place in the light of new data or facts.

Some uses of operations research

A summary chart on the use of various techniques is given in Table 14.1. We will now look at them in outline, beginning with those concerned with forecasting.

Forecasting of demand for services and products

Forecasting is the process aimed at predicting changing conditions and future events that may significantly affect the business of an organization. As a process it is important to planning and decision-making, as both these

Table 14.1   Summary of uses of techniques

Simple moving average	Used in the prediction of future events, based on past data, but has the disadvantage of equally weighting all data. However, sensitivity can be adjusted by altering the value of N
Exponential smoothing	A refined prediction model which can have its sensitivity to the most recent events adjusted as required
Linear regression	Useful in predicting the future when there is a trend which is expected to continue
Linear programming	Used for the allocation of resources (human or physical)
Queuing theory	This simulation process is useful in predicting customer arrivals at service establishments, and therefore help decisions about staffing levels and service points

processes attempt to look into the future. Forecasting is used in a wide range of areas in food and beverage operations, including planning of food production, labour requirement estimation, budgeting, stock control, marketing planning, purchasing and new product development. Forecasting falls into three major groups: quantitative, qualitative, and judgmental. We will concentrate here on quantitative, i.e. that which relies on numerical data and mathematical models to predict future events. Three main methods are in use : time series, explanatory, and monitoring. In this chapter we will concentrate on time series methods.

These methods use historical data ('over a period of time' – hence the name) to develop forecasts of the future. The assumption here of course is that patterns or combinations of patterns (e.g. of consumer behaviour) will be repeated over time. Time series would therefore use data such as weekly sales figures to identify patterns and hence predict future demand.

Forecasting in food and beverage

Food and beverage management, like others in the service industries, is constantly make predictions about the future, particularly in the area of estimating future demand. Simple procedures may be used, such as looking at the most recent results, or perhaps, if it is a seasonal business, last year's figures may be consulted plus a figure for business growth. This relatively intuitive approach can be refined quite easily.

Simple moving average

One simple way of doing this is to use a simple (unweighted) moving average. This method will result in predictions based on the actual levels over a particular number of past periods. The result will be different dependent on the number of periods chosen, as the example below will illustrate. Let us assume that the number of meals sold over five sales periods were as follows:

Period	Sales
1	6,000
2	7,000
3	7,600
4	8,800
5	9,400
6	?

A three-period moving average for period 6 would be:

$$(9,400 + 8,800 + 7,600)/3 = 8,600$$

A four-period moving average would be:

$(9,400 + 8,800 + 7,600 + 7,000)/4 = 8,200$

It can be seen that these figures are substantially different, dependent on the sensitivity of the calculations. This sensitivity can be adjusted by varying the value of time periods used (N). As N is decreased, the model becomes more responsive to change in demand, as the data used are more recent. However, as N is increased, as in our second example, the model becomes less responsive to current changes. It can be seen here that 8,200 is much nearer to the earlier sales figures and this prediction does not take as much account of the growth trend. It could be argued that if the general trend was to continue, a simple chart (Figure 14.2) could be used to predict sales for the

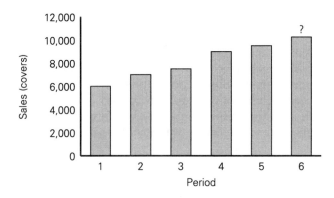

Figure 14.2 Sales bar chart

next period. A figure probably in excess of 10,000, assuming that the premises had the capacity, could be expected. There is a mathematical procedure for dealing with this approach, known as linear regression, which is briefly described later.

Exponential smoothing

To overcome the problems of time series, a major one of which is the equal weighting given to all information, it is possible to resort to exponential smoothing. This method allows us to vary the weighting on data, for example to give more weighting to the most recent data and less to the more historical. The new forecast is called the smoothed exponential mean or SEM. The SEM for a given period (SEM new) is calculated as:

SEM new = Forecast for the previous period (SEM old) plus an adjustment
                  for the error in the old forecast

SEM new = SEM old + α (Actual old − SEM old)

Because of the way that the SEM is determined, (SEM old) actually contains information about all the past level of the variable. As you will see from the formula, the error in the old forecast (Actual old − SEM old) is weighted by a constant α, called the smoothing constant. The higher the constant is set, the more weight is given to the error in the forecast for the last period, and thus to recent data. Suppose for the data presented that the smoothing constant α was set at 0.3. Below we can see the prediction for period 6 using this method. As we need an initial value for SEM old, we will assume this to be the actual level for period 1, that is 6,000. Using the formula

SEM2 = SEM1 + 0.3 (actual 1 − SEM1)
          = 6,000 + 0.3 (6,000 − 6,000)
          = 6,000

then

SEM3 = 6,000 + 0.3 (7,000 − 6,000)
          = 6,300

and

SEM4 = 6,300 + 0.3 (7,600 − 6,300)
          = 6,690

and

SEM5 = 6,690 + 0.3 (8,800 − 6,690)
          = 7,323

and

SEM6 = 7,323 + 0.3 (9,400 − 7,323)
          = 7,946

As exponential smoothing is based entirely on weighting of past data, it will lag any trend. With a low value of α, such as 0.3, the results can be seen in the example. Had the α constant been set higher, for example at 0.8, the result for period 6 SEM would have been 9,226. It can be seen that this latter figure, with a 0.8 constant, is a better prediction even than the three-period simple weighted average example above which gave an estimated figure of 8,600. The question may be asked 'How do we determine the level of α?' The answer is that as real data are collected, they are compared with the forecast, and α adjusted until it gives as accurate figures as possible. This value is then used for future forecasts. To further enhance our accuracy, where definite trends are apparent, we could draw the graph for the sales levels and then mathematically determine the formula for this sales line, and then use either this formula, or the graph itself to predict future sales level. This method is known as linear regression.

Linear regression

This method refers back to our idea of 'extending the current sales graph ' with a 'best fit' line, in order to take full account of the trends taking place.

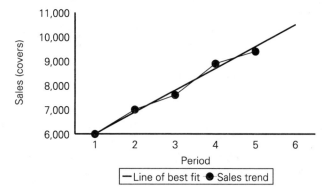

Figure 14.3 Sales trend graph

Figure 14.3 indicates this concept graphically. Using the basic formula for a straight-line graph of

$$Y = a + bX$$

where Y is the number we require for our forecasts, X is the independent variable, in this case period of the year, a is the intercept on the y axis, and b is the slope of the line.

Using a complicated calculation to arrive at the formula for the best line, we would get the formula

$$Y = 5,180 + 860X$$

Thus for period six the calculation would be

$$Y = 5,180 + (860 \times 6)$$
$$= 5,180 + 5,160$$
$$= 10,340$$

and for period seven

$$Y = 5,180 + (860 \times 7)$$
$$= 5,180 + 6,020$$
$$= 11,200$$

In order to make future predictions, one could continue to make calculations, and the alternative, of course, is to plot the graph and read off appropriate values. In calculating the formula for the line, an understanding of mathematics is required, but it is important to remember that many statistical packages are readily available for personal computers, thus simplifying the process considerably.

Thus it can be seen that linear regression is particularly useful in taking account of trends and using those to make predictions about the future.

Linear programming

Making predictions about expected sales levels is not our only concern in food and beverage management; sometimes we wish to make decisions about allocations. The mathematical technique used for this is called linear programming. The method determines the optimum combination of restricted resources in the attainment of some objective, which is usually of an economic nature (e.g. maximization of profit, minimization of cost, or maximization of benefit). The term linear implies proportionality, which means that the elements in the situation are so related that they appear as straight lines when graphed. It can therefore use both graphical and mathematical formulae to reach proposed solutions to problems. A typical use for this technique could be for the manager who wants to determine how best to allocate a fixed advertising budget among alternative media, such as radio, newspapers and magazines. The manager in this case would like to maximize the advertising effectiveness. An alternative could be the hospital dietician and catering manager, who have the problem of providing particular nutritional requirements at minimum cost. The variables would be the different nutritional content and costs of individual food items. A food and beverage manager armed with the appropriate nutritional data and material costs could construct simple data charts which could then be processed by computer.

Example

Part of the dietary requirement of the meal in the hospital is to provide 16 mg of vitamin A and 12 mg of vitamin B. By collecting data on various foods, we can establish how much of each foodstuff is required to provide the necessary vitamins. This is illustrated in Table 14.2. We then need to establish the decision variables. These are:

The number of eggs to be served   ($\times$1)
The number of bacon strips to be served ($\times$2)
Number of cereal portions to be served   ($\times$3)

Table 14.2   Dietary analysis of breakfast items

Vitamin	Mg/egg	Mg/rasher of bacon	Mg/cereal portion	Minimum daily need (mg)
A	2	4	1	16
B	3	2	1	12

The cost of an egg is 8p, bacon rasher 20p and a portion of cereal 4p.

The aim of the problem is to minimize the total cost of each breakfast. If this cost is said to be 'C' then we must minimize C = 8 ($\times$1) + 20 ($\times$2) + 4 ($\times$3), where

8 $\times$ 1 is the cost of eggs per serving
20 $\times$ 2 is the cost of bacon per serving
4 $\times$ 3 is the cost of cereal per portion

There is a vitamin requirement to be met for each vitamin, and it is not permitted to fall short of the required levels. Hence two more formulae could be constructed for

Vitamin A: 8 ($\times$1) + 20 ($\times$2) + 4 ($\times$3) = 16
Vitamin B: 8 ($\times$1) + 20 ($\times$2) + 4 ($\times$3) = 12

By minimizing the formula C = 8 ($\times$1) + 20 ($\times$2) + 4 ($\times$3) subject to these two 'vitamin formulae', the dietician will obtain the minimum total cost possible, while at the same time meeting the minimum requirements of vitamins A and B.

Queuing theory

We have all experienced waiting in queues, be it at a hotel reception, in a cafeteria, supermarket, or waiting to board a holiday ferry. The problem that the managers face in all these situations is one of balancing the cost of providing extra service points (e.g. till points, or staff in a cafeteria) against the problem of customers becoming dissatisfied by poor service speeds. Quantitative models have been developed to help with these decisions, and are often referred to as 'waiting line models'. Such models can be used to identify a given system's (e.g. new cafeteria design) characteristics, such as:

- The average number of people in a queue.
- The average time each person will spend in the queue.
- The percentage of time that the service facilities (service points and staff) will be idle.
- The average time a person would spend in the system (waiting time plus service time).
- The probability that a person arriving at the facility will have to wait.

Given such data together with service cost estimates, and customer waiting line limitations, the manager will be better equipped to make decisions that balance desirable service levels with service costs.

Method

Stage one is to observe a similar operation to that under investigation (e.g. a cafeteria in operation) and carefully time arrivals to and departures from the queues. A large sample over the period of normal operation would be required. From the data collected, cumulative histograms of arrival times and service times would be developed. Using random numbers to simulate customer arrivals, a situation at a service point can be simulated. An output of this simulation could be a chart as shown in Figure 14.4.

The data simulation tells us the following:

Customer 1 is served in 0.8 min.
Customer 2 arrives 0.2 min. after customer 1 and so must wait.
Customer 3 arrives 0.8 min. after the second, so joins the queue.
Customer 2 needs 0.6 min. of service time, and so on for all the customers simulated.

By looking at the diagram we can tell how many people are in the queue at a particular time. The mean waiting time can be calculated by adding all the waiting times and dividing by the number of customers. This technique then

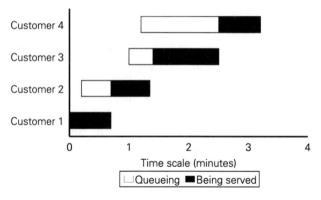

Figure 14.4 The queuing model

will construct a model of the pattern of waiting and service times from which decisions about staffing levels and service points can be made. This technique forms part of the labour planning system used by United Airlines, described later.

Research into food and beverage forecasting

Until recently, there had been little research carried out on the application of the above techniques to food and beverage operations. However, Miller *et al.* (1991a, 1991b) of Kansas State University have done some work in this area. We have seen several techniques, mentioned above, some of which are quite complex, but following the work of Cullen *et al.* (1978), Lawrence *et al.* (1983) and Armstrong (1986), we can conclude that:

1 Simple models have been found to be as accurate as complex ones in forecasting (Lawrence *et al.*,1983; Armstrong, 1986).
2 A comprehensive look at twenty-four techniques revealed that no particular method performed better than others for all classes of data (Lawrence *et al.*, 1983).
3 Forecasts produced by objective methods should not be adjusted on the basis of management intuition (Armstrong, 1986).

Miller *et al.* (1991b) tested and evaluated the use of time series forecasting using data from a university food service production area and concentrated on the prediction of uptake of particular menu items as the menu changed on a cyclical basis. The menu contained 60–80 regular entrées, and at most mealtimes customers could select multiple servings of all food items. Data in the form of selection of entrées was taken over a three-year period. Moving average and exponential smoothing models were employed and compared. This was done deliberately to keep the work 'user friendly', so that staff could use equipment that would normally be available to them, and therefore to other typical food and beverage operators.

Three measures were used:

- Simple moving average with $N = 3$ (used as it was more sensitive to recent changes):
- A naive method, where $N = 1$, i.e. follows the last period.
- Simple exponential smoothing with $\alpha = 0.3$.

Each daily menu offered two entrées from which the customers could choose. Both the total number of customers and entrée combinations were modelled, and a preference statistic was calculated for each entrée pair combination. You will see that in all cases the combination adds up to '1'. Thus in the first example, 28.4 per cent would choose the beef patty, but 71.6 per cent the pizza:

e.g.	Beef patty	0.284	with	French bread pizza	0.716
	Roast beef	0.541	with	Italian roast chicken	0.459
	Bacon burger	0.544	with	Shrimp creole	0.456

To ascertain the take up of particular entrées this statistic was applied to the modelled customer forecast. Eighteen different entrée combinations were tested and the results showed that the time series model outperformed the naive model sixty-four per cent of the time, with the simple moving average (with $N = 3$) outperforming simple exponential smoothing. The SMA model gave smaller but more numerous forecast errors, whereas SES did the reverse.This work then confirmed that carried out by Miller *et al.* (1991b), showing that mathematical models outperformed manual ones. In further studies, Athiyaman and Robertson (1992) carried out work on the use of time series forecasting for short-term planning in tourism and their findings indicated that the model of simple exponential smoothing provided the best one-month-ahead forecasts of visitors from Thailand to Hong Kong.

Application to manpower requirements forecasting

Manpower scheduling

A survey published in the *National Institute Economic Review* (NIER, 1986) reported that the growth in productivity in the service sector of the economy had been much slower than that within manufacturing. However, manpower scheduling in the service industries differs from that in manufacturing in that the idea of building 'stocks' of services does not apply, and hence 'reserves' are not available, and services have to be supplied in response to a request within a very short time-frame. Thus labour scheduling is focused on matching the number of employees to an uncertain and highly variable customer demand.

The process of manpower scheduling thus involves three stages:

- Demand forecasting
- Service level and hence labour requirement
- Workforce scheduling

The mathematical models for workforce scheduling can be very complex and several of these are described by Jacobs and Bechold (1993). To illustrate the level of analysis which could be required, such a system might, for example, require the following flexibility types:

1 Employees who work less than a full day (shift length flexibility).
2 Employees who work less than five days a week (working week flexibility).
3 Employees who may begin work at any time during the working day (shift start flexibility).
4 Employees who receive a meal break at one or more defined periods within their shift (meal break flexibility).
5 Individuals who can start work at different times of the day on different days of the week (start time float flexibility).
6 Employees who may receive days off on non-consecutive days of the week (non-consecutive days off).

Hence such models can become very complex, and therefore organizations often resort to the use of outside specialists for the production of such complex models. This usually involves the development of a purpose-designed computer program. Such systems have been developed using a variety of forecasting techniques, some of which are described in this chapter. One example of this approach is described below by reference to a forecasting system developed for United Airlines in the USA.

The United Airlines case

Much of the work on manpower forecasting emanated from the USA, and in particular in the airline industry. As airline traffic grew in the USA during the 1980s, major airlines, such as United Airlines, began to feel the strain of their then current workforce scheduling and planning systems. Holloran and Byrn (1986) report that as passenger volumes increased, so did their workforce, but as in many service industries, labour costs constitute a major part of operating costs.

To help with their scheduling, United Airlines turned to management science and its sophisticated mathematical and statistical methods. In the past, shift rotas within airports and reservation centres had been prepared manually. The system was based on the demands throughout the day, based on 30-min. time periods. A similar approach is used today within the McDonald's fast food organization to match staffing levels to customer demands with a heavy utilization of part-time staff working in short shifts in order to cover peak periods, particularly in the 12.00 to 1.45 time slot. However, in United Airlines the number of employees required was based either on the shift's peak requirements throughout the week or on its average requirements over the course of a week. The schedules based on peak requirements resulted in higher costs, and those based on average requirements did not provide adequate coverage during the peak periods, resulting in customer dissatisfaction with the service. In a competitive market, this dissatisfaction could not be tolerated, and so the 'peak based' strategy tended to be adopted. However, this was costly and it still had the problem that the whole process ran on the concept of a 'representative day'.

Due to the complexity of the problem, the new computer based system, the 'Station Manpower Planning System' (SMPS), involved several integrated parts. By linking with the air ticket historical sales data records, it was possible to forecast the expected telephone call volumes. As part of the forecasting process, a quantitative queuing model considering probable waiting times for customers' calls to be answered was developed. Then by referring to the company's 'quality' guidelines on waiting times, the number of employees that would be needed could be ascertained. In a similar way, staffing levels at airports were determined by using data on aircraft loads and arrival trends. Further sections of the SMPS system used the technique of linear programming. This helped determine possible shift start times and potential monthly shift schedules that minimized labour costs, while meeting employee working preferences and customer service needs.

Further sections of the program produce monthly shift schedules for the various locations and allow individual work schedules for each employee to be produced. This ensures, for example, that employees do not work for more than six days consecutively and contains an option to maximize the spreading of weekend days off among employees. This module has replaced manual functions that were extremely time consuming, and has produced more acceptable work schedules for the employees.

The SMPS has been a substantial success, and has resulted in a 6 per cent reduction in labour cost (representing some $6 million annually), while at the same time resulting in improved customer service and greater satisfaction among employees with their work schedules.

Summary and conclusions

Operations research offers an opportunity for management to improve the quality of data on which they make strategic and tactical decisions. Food and beverage management decision-making is becoming more sophisticated through the use of techniques such as menu engineering to help with pricing and promotion decisions. However, as is so often quoted 'if you put rubbish in, you get rubbish out!' Even methods such as menu engineering are rendered less useful if initial data are inaccurate. This chapter has introduced some alternative approaches, and the research quoted has stated that some of the less sophisticated models are perfectly suitable for most decisions. Targett (1989) states that time series methods 'are useful in a situation where the "product" is perishable and demand hard to predict. . . . They are used for short term forecasting where the variable has a momentum of its own i.e. before any management action has time to take effect'. He goes on to state that 'longer term forecasting methods such as regression analysis would be needed in situations where management was intervening to influence demand or there were external changes affecting demand'. The message for us all is to select the appropriate tool for the job, and not to be put of by the mathematics involved – the specialist and the computers can deal with that.

References

Armstrong, J. S. (1986). Research on forecasting : a quarter-century review, 1960–84. *Interfaces*, **16**, 77–89.

Athiyaman, A. and Robertson, R. W. (1992). Time series forecasting techniques: short-term planning in tourism. *International Journal of Contemporary Hospitality Management*, **4**(4), 8–11.

Cullen, K. O., Hoover, L. W. and Moore, A. N. (1978). Menu item forecasting in hospital food service. *Journal of the American Dietetic Association*, **73**(12), 640–646.

Holloran, T. J. and Byrn, E. B. (1986).United Airlines station manpower planning system. *Interfaces*, **16**(1), 39–50.

Jacobs, L. W. and Bechold, S. E. (1993) Microcompter-based workforce scheduling. *International Journal of Service Industry Management*, **4**(1), 36–48.

Lawrence, M. J., Edmunsen, R. H. and O'Connor, M. J. (1983). An exploration of some practical issues in the use of quantitative forecasting models. *Journal of Forecasting*, **2**, 169–179.

Miller, J. J., McCahon, C. S. and Miller, J. L. (1991a). Foodservice forecasting using simple mathematical models. *Hospitality Research Journal*, **15**(1), 43–58.

Miller, J. L., McCahon, C. S. and Bloss, B. K. (1991b). Food production forecasting with simple time series models. *Hospitality Research Journal*, **14**(3), 9–21.

NIER (1986). Productivity in services. National Institute Economic Review, No.115, February.

Targett, D. (1989). Management science in service industries. In P. Jones (ed.), *Management in Service Industries*.Oxford: Pitman, pp. 289–301.

15 Marketing and merchandising

Francis Buttle

Introduction

The fundamental purpose of marketing is to *create and keep customers*. There is growing recognition that improving customer retention levels should be a major marketing objective, equal in importance to expanding the customer base. The reasoning for this is quite straightforward. First, it is between five and twelve times as costly to win a new customer as it is to keep an existing customer (Buttle, 1992). Secondly, the longer the business maintains a service provider relationship with a customer, the more profitable that customer becomes. As customer defection rates fall, the average lifespan of an organization's relationship with its customers increases. The more enduring the relationship, the more profitable. One multi-industry investigation reports that a 5 per cent reduction in customer defections increased profits by between 30 per cent and 85 per cent! (Reichheld and Sasser,1990). It is therefore no surprise that 'although the shape of defection curves varies across industries, in general, profits rise as defection rates fall' (Reichheld and Sasser, 1990). The marketing challenge for food and beverage companies is to quantify the costs and benefits of customer retention.

Customer retention studies have provided new insights for marketing management. The old view of marketing is *transactional*. It didn't matter where demand came from as long as it produced the targeted profit. Market share was the means to this end. The new view of marketing is more *relational*.

Relationship marketing commits marketers to taking a longer term perspective of their association with customers. Market share is no longer enough. It does matter who the customers are. Customer retention has become an important external measure of customer satisfaction.

The old view dominates the marketing of fast moving consumer goods (FMCG). However, food and beverage marketing is not FMCG marketing.

Food and beverage organizations provide a service. Their outputs are acts, performances, deeds, *not* things. Like other services, food and beverage outputs are intangible-dominant products, highly perishable, and difficult to standardize because of the variability of human performance. Furthermore, they are generally consumed at the time and place they are produced, in an environment where there is a good deal of interaction between customer and service employees. These differences raise questions about the suitability of transactional marketing.

Relationship marketing is particularly well suited to business contexts where there is interaction between service providers and customers, and where quality is judged not simply by the technical performance of tangible goods, but by the interactive performance of customer contact staff. In these contexts, a high level of congruence between marketing, human resource and operations departments is essential to providing customers with a satisfactory experience. In relationship marketing, customers are individuals with identifiable and serviceable needs, not just market segments. These conditions accurately describe most food and beverage businesses, whether contract caterer, institutional feeder, high street retailer or lodging operation. With these issues in mind, the following definition of the *new marketing* is offered:

> Marketing's function is to create and maintain mutually satisfying long-term relationships with customers.

Compare this new definition with the long-established definition of the Chartered Institute of Marketing. 'Marketing is the management process responsible for identifying, anticipating and satisfying customer requirements profitably.'

To sum up, marketing's job in food and beverage operations is to identify the expectations and requirements of prospective customers, to provide the desired services through operations departments, and, by satisfying these customers, to retain them for the longer term. A growing weight of expert opinion claims that customer satisfaction is no longer enough. Customer delight should be the objective. This means providing exceptional service which goes beyond what was expected. The outcome? Higher levels of customer retention, higher levels of job satisfaction for contact employees, and stimulation of positive word-of-mouth.

The new marketing mix

The marketing mix is the box of tools that marketers deploy in their efforts to produce customer satisfaction. In FMCG-style transactional marketing, the tool-kit has become known as the 4Ps. For food and beverage-style relationship marketing, the tool-kit has been expanded. The original 4Ps of *product, price, promotion* and *place* have been retained and three more added. These new 3Ps are *process, physical evidence* and *participants*. For a review of the history of the evolution of the service marketing mix, see Bitner, M-J. (1991). This services marketing mix is an acknowledgement of the problems posed by the intangibility, heterogeneity, perishability and simultaneity (of production and consumption) of services. The three additional elements are defined as follows (Bitner, 1991):

1 *Process.* The actual procedures, mechanisms, and flow of activities by which the service is delivered.
2 *Physical evidence.* The environment in which the service is assembled and where the firm and customer interact; and any tangible commodities that facilitate performance or communication of the service.
3 *Participants.* All human actors who play a part in service delivery and thus influence the buyer's perceptions; namely the firm's personnel and other customers in the service environment.

These additional 3Ps enable the marketer to respond to the interactive nature of food and beverage service provision. Participants are the 'who' of the interaction, physical evidence is the 'where', and process is the 'how'. *Participants* are those persons with whom the customer interacts – customer contact staff – and other customers. *Physical evidence* includes both the physical environment in which the food and beverage service is performed and the tangible clues within the service delivery system. *Process* describes the content of the interaction.

It is becoming more common for food and beverage managers to stipulate the content of the interactions. Operations manuals spell out the procedures: how to handle a telephone request for a reservation, how guests shall be greeted and shown to their seats, how orders will be taken, how to handle disruptive or alcohol-impaired customers, how to handle complaints. This trend reflects a shift towards the industrialization of service (Levitt, 1976). Standardized specifications reduce the heterogeneity of the meal experience, and enable the customer to develop very clear expectations of future service performance. Because of the heterogeneity and intangibility of services, consumers are thought to perceive more risk. For many customers, risk is uncomfortable. The manuals help reduce perceived risk.

A few food and beverage companies are blueprinting interactions with customers. Blueprints are 'tools used to depict and analyze all the processes involved in providing a service' (George and Gibson, 1991). Essentially a blueprint is a flow-chart which details the sequential actions which need to be performed in order to produce service which satisfies the customer. Some portions of the blueprint involve interactions with the customer. The 'line of visibility' separates those parts which are visible to the customer from those

Table 15.1   The 7Ps in a restaurant context

Product
Core service: Provision of food and beverage away from home
Tangibles: Limited table d'hôte menu; full à la carte menu; extensive wine list
Intangibles: Plate service; very attentive

Price
Published menu price: adults, children
Prix fixe function menu
Party discounts
Frequent diner discounts

Promotion
Newspaper and radio advertising
Function selling by restaurant manager
Monday night specials
Early-bird specials
External illuminated menu
Merchandising
Public relations
Personal selling by waiting staff
Direct mail to local businesses and associations

Place
Restaurant location
Indirect distribution via travel agent reservations
Direct distribution to walk-ins

Process
Greeting process: hostess
Reservations process: phone
'Chef's specials' information provision by waiting staff
Ordering taking process by waiting staff
Complaints handling processes

Physical evidence
Table appointments
Decor
Lighting
Cleanliness
Comment cards
Waiting staff uniforms
China/silverware
Floor plan and table/seating orientation
Exterior appearance/architecture
Menu design

Participants
Hostess
Waiting staff
Maître d'
Restaurant manager

parts which are not. How a waitperson takes an order at table-side is visible. How that is communicated to the kitchen crew is not. Blueprints are particularly useful in identifying service system failpoints. Failpoints are processes or parts of processes where breakdowns occur, and the quality of the service provision is adversely affected. G. Lynn Shostack's work on service blueprinting has been at the leading edge; for example, Shostack (1984a, 1984b, 1987). A common failpoint in conference catering within hotels is the communication between hotel sales people who make food and beverage promises to the client, but fail to let the banqueting management know the full extent of those promises. Similarly, catering staff often fail to adequately brief salespeople on the capacity constraints and other operational limitations of food and beverage departments.

It is through the 7Ps that food and beverage marketers aim to create and keep customers for the long term. Table 15.1 illustrates the 7Ps in the food and beverage marketing context.

Food and beverage marketers, given the interactive nature of the experience they offer customers, are faced with a more complex set of marketing mix decisions. A useful way of approaching these decisions is to think in terms of assembling three different time-dependent marketing mixes out of the seven Ps. Implemented before, during and after the customer's food and beverage experience, these can be labelled the pre-contact marketing mix, the service performance marketing mix and the post-performance marketing mix. The objectives of these marketing mixes are as follows. The pre-contact marketing mix: to manage customer expectations of service performance, and to generate trial. The service performance marketing mix: to produce service which exceeds or matches customer expectations. The post-contact marketing mix: to develop and maintain long-term mutually satisfying relationships with customers, or, in other words, to promote customer retention. Table 15.2 describes typical contents of these three marketing mixes.

The relationship between the customers' perceptions of the performance of the service and their expectations of the service has been shown to be a primary determinant of their assessment of service quality. Where the performance is below that expected, dissatisfaction and negative evaluations of service quality are found. Where perceptions exceed expectations, food and beverage marketers can expect to find positive evaluations of quality, customer delight, high levels of customer retention and the generation of favourable word-of-mouth. Clearly, it makes sense for food and beverage marketers to measure and manage both expectations and perceptions. See especially the work of A. 'Parsu' Parasuraman, Len Berry and Valarie Zeithaml who developed the service quality model dubbed SERVQUAL (Parasuraman *et al.*, 1991). They also provide guidance for managing the gaps between expectations and perception (Berry and Parasuraman, 1991).

Table 15.2 Three services marketing mixes

PRE-PERFORMANCE MARKETING MIX

Objectives   to manage customer expectations of service performance; to generate trial

Elements   Product development
- tangibles
- intangibles

Service blueprinting
Pricing
Market communication
- internal
- external

Location
Distribution channel design and management

SERVICE PERFORMANCE MARKETING MIX

Objectives   to produce service which exceeds or matches customer expectations
Elements   Physical evidence
- consumables
- non-consumables

Participants–customer contact employees
- interactive performance; customer communication
- technical performance; service production

Process

POST-PERFORMANCE MARKETING MIX

Objective   to develop and maintain mutually satisfying long-term relationships with customers
to promote customer retention

Elements   Relationship marketing
Market communication
Performance and quality audits
Complaints management

In summary, food and beverage marketers should be managing customer expectations and the performance of the delivery system so that customers make a positive evaluation of service quality, i.e. their perceptions exceed their expectations. At worst, perceptions should match expectations, that is the food and beverage operation delivers what is promised, nothing more, but certainly nothing less. Once again, this emphasizes how important it is for marketers to influence restaurant design, menu structure and content, food and beverage production and delivery systems, and customer-contact staff recruitment and training. Customers' expectations of a food and beverage operation's performance are predominantly based on their previous experience of similar food and beverage outlets, and their exposure to both word-of-mouth and marketer-controlled communications, such as advertising and direct mail shots. It is important not to make promises which the service system cannot deliver. That is a certain route to dissatisfaction, negative word-of-mouth and customer defection.

Merchandising

Food and beverage marketers mediate the operation's relationships with its customers for two purposes – not only to ensure that *customer* expectations and requirements are met, but also to ensure that sufficient demand is generated to meet the *firm's objectives*. Marketing is a means to an end. It is not philanthropy.

The pre-contact marketing mix is designed to generate trial, to get customers onto the premises. Together with personal selling, merchandising is the principal means of converting this traffic into revenue. Food and beverage customers are captive for periods between two minutes (drive-throughs) and two hours (fine dining establishments). During this time, the operation has to raise the average check to a level which will achieve the firm's marketing and financial objectives.

Merchandising is any form of behaviour-triggering stimulus or pattern of stimuli, other than personal selling, which takes place at the point of sale (Buttle, 1984). Merchandising's goal is to influence customers to buy specified food and beverage products during their two-minute-to-two-hour captivity. In terms of the 7Ps, merchandising can be found disguised as 'physical evidence', and as a component of 'promotion'.

Merchandising works when customers have not made purchasing decisions before entering the outlet. Most diners do not decide on their food and beverage selections before entering restaurants. More often than not they will scan the menu and seek other clues before deciding. Obviously there are exceptions to this rule. Dunkin' Donut franchisees will tell of customers who have ordered coffee and a blueberry muffin for breakfast every workday morning for five years. However, it is this high incidence of impulse purchasing which enables merchandising to be effective.

Impulse purchasing takes two forms. Pure impulse purchasing occurs when a customer decides on both product class *and* item at the point of sale ('Yes, I think I *will* have a dessert. Nothing fattening. Fresh fruit salad, please.'). Item impulse purchasing occurs when, having decided prior to entering the food and beverage outlet to buy from a product class, say pasta entrés, the item decision is made on impulse ('I'll have the vegetarian lasagna, please.').

Merchandising has a reputation for being both inexpensive and effective (Buttle, 1987). Many of the techniques require nothing other than a better use of existing resources, e.g. a better designed menu. Table 15.3 lists many merchandising techniques that are used in food and beverage outlets. These techniques can be classified broadly into print and display options. On-table merchandising is predominantly print (an exception would be the suggestive display of wine glasses in the normal table set-up). Off-table merchandising is normally display. Merchandising works by making items more noticeable, accessible and attractive. For example, a coffee shop might vent the fumes of roasting coffee beans into the street (noticeable); a dessert cart may be wheeled to the diner's table (accessible); and a menu might contain photo-illustrations of selected entrés (attractive).

Table 15.3 Merchandising techniques in food and beverage outlets

External signage	Table tents
Display (or open) kitchen	Blackboard specials
Stemware on tabletops	Racked wines on display
Menu	Chiller cabinet displays
Menu inserts and clip-ons	Guéridon food preparation
Wine list	Dessert cart
Placemats	Salad bars
Napkins	Cheese board
Ashtrays	Table-top (printed laminate surface)
Buffet displays	Dining-room cooking stations
Smorgasbord	

Not all food and beverage products are worth merchandising. Selective merchandising of chosen items is in the best interests of both customer and outlet. The question is: which items to merchandise? Food and beverage products can be classified in three ways which are useful for making this decision.

- *Demand*: high annual; high seasonal; low annual; low seasonal
- *Margin*: high margin; low margin
- *Impulse*: high incidence of impulse purchasing; low incidence of impulse purchasing

The prime targets for merchandising attention are those items which are high margin, impulse items bought throughout the year. In many restaurants this means desserts, salads, coffee and wine. Because the main merchandising objective is to convert patronage into a high level of profitable sales revenue, the unit contribution, or margin, of each item is of paramount importance. Marketing management must know the unit contribution and direct costs of each menu item. Unit contribution is selling price less direct costs. Given the data in Table 15.4, other things being equal it would make sense for the marketer to merchandise pizza, despite it having a lower price than escargots Provençale. The reason is that it makes a greater unit contribution. In fact this restaurant would need to sell three of the higher priced items to equal the contribution from the lower priced item.

Other items to be merchandised are those with a short storage life, where spoilage and waste pose a threat to costs, and seasonal items which have a short-term appeal to customers.

Table 15.4   A comparison of menu item contribution

	Pizza £		Escargots Provençale £
Menu price		6.50		12.25
less:			
Food cost	1.20		8.70
Direct labour	0.30		1.20
Direct energy	0.50		0.85
Total direct costs		2.00		10.75
Item contribution		4.50		1.50

The principal print vehicle for merchandising food and beverage is the menu. Menu designers use sequencing, copywriting and graphic design as their main tools. Menus tend to be structured in such a way that they follow the sequence of a meal, typically, appetizers and soups, entrés, desserts. On folded menus, items on the external covers tend to be heavily merchandised because the material is visible to the diner for a longer period. Menu copy and illustrations for the selected items are designed to make them stand out from other, lower margin, menu items. The use of a larger typeface, mouthwatering description, illustration and white space is recommended. Menu inserts, extensions and clip-ons are also productive in drawing the diner's attention and raising interest.

Physical evidence

These print and display merchandising techniques are very specific in their application. They are not, however, the only physical environmental variables which impact upon customer behaviour and perceptions. Food service outlets are physical environments composed of walls, floors, ceilings, tables, chairs, sales fixtures, lighting and so on. These environments should be, and often are, designed to produce specific outcomes in selected customer markets. The outcomes may be behavioural (e.g. self service at a salad bar), affective (e.g. a feeling of pleasure) or cognitive (e.g. finding out about other restaurant locations in a chain).

The science of environmental psychology offers useful insights into the interrelationship between behaviour and the physical environment. Researchers have investigated the behavioural effects of many variables – noise, temperature, odour, colour, vibration, air characteristics (quality, movement, pressure, humidity), other people, architectural design, spatial arrangements, building size, space, environmental complexity, signage and information load. See, for example, Lynch (1960), Berlyne (1971), Sandahl (1972), Fisher (1974), Hershberger and Cass (1974), Mehrabian and Russell (1974), Murtha (1976), Canter (1977) and Hooper (1978). In the broader service industry context, environmental design variables have been found to influence the customers' image of the service organization, their expectations of the service experience, their perceptions of delivered service quality, and their behaviours within the service facility. It seems that the physical environment also impacts upon reported levels of overall customer satisfaction (Kemp, 1993). The work of Murtha and of Mehrabian and Russell may prove particularly useful for food and beverage marketers (Mehrabian and Russell, 1974; Murtha, 1976).

Murtha's research question was: what benefits do users seek from their presence or activity in a physical environment? Since the users of the food and beverage physical environment are employees and customers, the same question can be asked of both groups. Murtha identified four classes of user benefits common to most environments.

1 *Behavioural facilitation.* Does the environment enable successful completion of given tasks or activities? Does the spatial organization benefit users? The food and beverage environment must facilitate the task performance of both the service employee and the customer. Employees are not the only workers in the foodservice environment. Food and beverage managers often want customers to act as employees, for example, when they serve themselves or bus their dishes.
2 *Psychological maintenance.* Is the environment comfortable and safe? – not just for customers but for employees too.
3 *Perceptual maintenance.* Is the range of environmental stimulation appropriate to the tasks which have to be performed?
4 *Social facilitation.* Does the environment provide the desired opportunities for social interaction? Does the environment allow for privacy? The food and beverage environment must allow for appropriate levels of social interaction and privacy within both user groups.

Mehrabian and Russell argued that all emotional responses to environmental stimuli can be reduced to three basic dimensions – pleasure, arousal and dominance – which, when moderated by the actor's personality, are expressed in approach–avoidance behaviour towards the environment. They developed eighteen nine-point scales to access these three dimensions, as detailed in Figure 15.1.

Pleasure		
happy		unhappy
pleased		annoyed
satisfied		unsatisfied
contended		melancholic
hopeful		despairing
relaxed		bored
Arousal		
stimulated		relaxed
excited		calm
frenzied		sluggish
jittery		dull
wide awake		sleepy
aroused		unaroused
Dominance		
controlling		controlled
influential		influenced
in control		cared for
important		awed
dominant		submissive
autonomous		guided

Figure 15.1 The Mehrabian and Russell framework (*Source*: Mehrabian and Russell, 1974)

There is some evidence that the Mehrabian and Russell model can help management to create restaurant and other foodservice environments which produce 'approach' behaviour (Bitner and Booms, 1982; see also Bitner, 1990 and Bitner, 1992). Customers are more likely to want to try, and to continue to patronize, an outlet if it promises and delivers the desired levels of pleasure, arousal and dominance. Customers want to feel that they are in control (e.g. they do not want the uncertainty of not knowing whether to help themselves from the salad bar or to take a seat and wait to be served). They want a moderate level of arousal; too little is insufficiently interesting, too much produces stress and discomfort. Finally, they want a high level of pleasure. Of these three variables, pleasure is generally the strongest correlate of 'approach' behaviour.

Conclusions

Marketing food and beverage presents three challenges. One: how to persuade customers to try the outlet. Two: how to get them to spend so that average expenditure objectives are achieved. Three: how to keep them coming back. The key to meeting all these challenges is an intimate understanding of customers' expectations and behaviour, and an organizational commitment to providing a food and beverage experience which exceeds these expectations. Marketers must identify what customers want, manage customer expectations, lead and integrate the foodservice organization to ensure that these expectations are surpassed, monitor performance, and commit resources to the development of mutually satisfying long-term relationships with customers.

References

Berlyne, D. (1971). *Aesthetics and Psychobiology.* New York: Appleton-Century Crofts.

Berry, L. L. and Parasuraman, A. (1991). *Marketing Services: Competing Through Quality.* New York: Free Press.

Bitner, M-J. (1990). Evaluating service encounters: the effects of physical surroundings and employee responses. *Journal of Marketing,* **54**(2), April, 69–82.

Bitner, M-J. (1991). The evolution of the services marketing mix and its relationship to service quality. In S. W. Brown, E. Gummesson, B. Edvardsson and B. Gustavsson (eds), *Service Quality: Multidisciplinary and Multinational Perspectives.* Lexington, MA: Lexington Books, pp. 23–37.

Bitner, M-J. (1992). Servicescapes: the impact of physical surroundings on customers and employees. *Journal of Marketing,* **56**(2), April, 57–71.

Bitner, M-J. and Booms, B. H. (1982). Marketing services by managing the environment. *Cornell Hotel and Restaurant Administration Quarterly,* **23**, May, 35–39.

Buttle, F. A. (1984). How merchandising works? *International Journal of Advertising,* **3**, 139–148.

Buttle, F. A. (1987). Can you afford to ignore merchandising? *Management Decision,* **25**(6), 14–17.

Buttle, F. A. (1992). The George, Kelly and Marshall model of services selling: an empirical test. In *Proceedings of the Marketing Educators' Group Annual Conference.* North-West Centre for European Marketing: University of Salford, UK, pp. 505–520.

Canter, D. (1977). *The Psychology of Place.* London: Architectural Press.

Fisher, J. D. (1974). Situation-specific variables as determinants of perceived environmental aesthetic quality and perceived crowdedness. *Journal of Research in Personality,* **8**, 177–188.

George, W. R. and Gibson, B. E. (1991). Blueprinting: a tool for managing service quality. In S.W. Brown, E. Gummesson, B. Edvardsson and B. Gustavsson (eds), *Service Quality: Multidisciplinary and Multinational Perspectives.* Lexington, MA: Lexington Books, pp. 73–91.

Hershberger, R. G. and Cass, R. C. (1974). Predicting user responses to buildings. In D. Carson (ed.). *Man-Environment Interactions: Evaluations and Applications*, Part II. Stroudsberg, PA: Dowden, Hutchinson and Ross.

Hooper, K. (1978). Perceptual aspects of architecture. In E.C. Carterette and M. P. Friedman (eds). *Handbook of Perception*, Vol. 10. New York: Academic Press.

Kemp, A. J. (1993). Hotel design effectiveness: the relationship between design and behaviour – stage one research. In H.Hughes (ed.), *Proceedings of the Second CHME Research Conference*, Manchester Metropolitan University.

Levitt, T. (1976). The industrialization of service. *Harvard Business Review*, **54**, pp. 63–74.

Lynch, K. (1960). *The Image of the City.* Cambridge, MA: MIT Press.

Mehrabian, A. and Russell, J. A. (1974). *An Approach to Environmental Psychology.* Cambridge, MA: MIT Press.

Murtha, D. M. (1976). *Dimensions of User Benefits.* Washington, DC: American Institute of Architects.

Parasuraman, A., Berry, L. L. and Zeithaml, V. A. (1991). Understanding, measuring and improving service quality: findings from a multi-phase research program. In S.W. Brown, E. Gummesson, B. Edvardsson and B. Gustavsson (eds), *Service Quality: Multidisciplinary and Multinational Perspectives*. Lexington, MA: Lexington Books, pp. 253–268.

Reichheld, F. R. and Sasser, W. E. Jr (1990). Zero defections: quality comes to services. *Harvard Business Review*, Sept.–Oct., 105–111.

Sandahl, D. A. (1972). Conceptions of self as individual orientations to the spatial environment. In W. A. Mitchell (ed), *EDRA 3, 1, 2.3.1–2.3.10*. Los Angeles: University of California Press.

Shostack, G. L. (1984a). Designing services that deliver. *Harvard Business Review*, Jan.–Feb., 133–139.

Shostack, G. L. (1984b). Service design in the operating environment. In W. R. George and C. E. Marshall (eds), *Developing New Services*. Chicago: AMA, pp. 27–43.

Shostack, G. L. (1987). Service positioning through structural change. *Journal of Marketing*, **51**, Jan., 34–43.

16 Food and beverage purchasing

Colin Masters

Introduction

Few corporate activities have such a direct effect upon the profitability of a business enterprise as the purchasing function. It is true that marketing generates additional sales, so that a business can grow and develop; operational management ensures that those sales are satisfied efficiently; the personnel function provides the organization with the right people, properly trained. But all these activities normally have to use the company's financial resources to generate further income to achieve additional profit. To win more sales, a company may have to employ more people, produce more promotional literature, increase its purchases of raw materials and, perhaps, invest in plant and equipment.

The purchasing function also spends money – indeed, it is clearly a major spending department. But the purchasing manager approaches the function from the opposite direction. A rigorously controlled purchasing policy seeks to reduce an organization's expenditure on raw materials, goods and services. As a result, the organization does not need to invest funds to earn more profit, although systems may have to be improved and additional staff may have to be employed to further control the purchasing, the cost of which will be more than compensated by the savings effected.

By reducing purchasing costs to the lowest possible level, the organization is able to control its total expenditure very carefully, thus directly improving its profit margins. The benefit of this to the organization is clear: funds can be released for expansion and development and an organization can choose to become more price competitive than rival companies.

So the manner in which a catering organization purchases its food and beverage items has a crucial bearing on its competitiveness and ultimate profitability. We have only to look at the volume and value of the catering industry's food and beverage purchases, which are estimated at £6.6bn (Marketpower) to appreciate the enormous sums of money involved.

Moreover, in the hotel and catering industry, the value of these goods and services is a significant proportion of the total operating cost; in the non-commercial catering industry, that proportion is higher than in most other sectors of the industry. In 1993, the value of food and beverage purchases in contract catering, at £645m, amounted to 41 per cent of the industry's total turnover; combined with other purchases (e.g. cleaning materials) the value of goods purchases amounted to £794m, or 51 per cent (British Hospitality Association, 1993).

In commercial catering generally, the percentage value of food and beverage goods purchased to turnover will be only slightly less than that of the contract catering industry. And even in the hotel industry, where payroll expenses constitute the largest single item of expenditure at about 27 per cent, and where the provision of food and drink is normally a secondary activity to that of room sales, food and beverage costs amount to 11.9 per cent of total expenditure – third only to a hotel's fixed costs (14.5 per cent) (Horwath Consulting 1993).

Even a 1 per cent reduction in the industry's total purchases – £6.4m in the case of the contract catering industry – would make a massive impact on the industry's profits because the saving would go directly to net profit and to improve competitiveness, thereby contributing to increased sales. Bigger savings – by no means unrealistic – would make an even more significant impact.

Using the BHA figures, if we assume that a company earns £100,000 revenue, its gross operating profit (revenue – cost of sales) will be £59,000; to double its GOP, the organization would have to earn £200,000 revenue. But to achieve such a sales increase, the organization will need to buy in an additional £41,000-worth of raw materials and employ more staff to prepare and serve the meals produced. Moreover, to achieve such an increase in sales would take time, so that the additional revenue would not be gained immediately. In short, generating additional sales demands additional inputs of time, money and goods. But improvements in gross operating profit can also be achieved by reducing the cost of sales (i.e. purchases). These involve no additional labour inputs whatsoever, can be of immediate benefit to the organization, and go straight to the bottom line.

Clearly, then, when food and beverage purchases run into significant sums (Compass Group's own purchasing bill is £250m) per annum and represent such a large percentage of an organization's total costs, the purchasing function has a key role to play in maximizing profits. But this role demands clear policy guidelines which include setting out the specifications for key food items, ensuring quality is maintained, agreeing the number of deliveries which are needed per day or per week, regulating the way goods are checked, and controlling the manner in which they are stored and used.

Difficulty of fluctuating prices

As we have already emphasized, the greater the value of the goods purchased, and the greater their percentage of total cost, the greater the scope for more effective purchasing, for greater savings and for higher profits. On the other hand, the more an organization depends on the purchase of raw materials to make things to sell – to add value – the more vulnerable it is to outside influences which it cannot reasonably control. Food prices fluctuate according to season and availability; floods in one region and droughts in another affect supplies and prices. Few if any catering food buyers have the resources or the need to buy forward in order to spread the financial risk and they have to manage such price variations as best they can. They do this in a number of ways – by challenging price increase requests and ensuring that they are fully justified before any increase is agreed, or by changing the menu to offer more seasonal food items, or by changing the specifications of the goods required (always ensuring that the quality remains acceptable). In this way, the effect on the business of higher raw material prices, restricted availability of produce or poor-quality produce at certain times of the year is reduced to the minimum. In the final analysis, movements in raw commodity prices must always be matched by management action to contain costs and maintain profit. Additionally, we must always be sure that the full benefit is obtained when a seasonal glut reduces commodity prices.

In these circumstances, it is clear that the food buyer's relationship with other management functions is crucial. In commercial restaurants, increasing prices, changing the menu or offering more seasonal menu items will have an impact upon an organization's profile in the market place. But even in contract catering, the food buyer cannot act alone in choosing what to buy, because others are responsible for the preparation of the food items, the compilation of the menu and their marketing and promotion. And in contract catering, the client and his staff – the consumers – will have an input into these decisions. Thus, the role which the purchasing department plays in the organization has an impact on every other function and, in the catering industry, extends far beyond food and beverage items to include the purchase of services and equipment. But the complexity of the food and beverage purchase is such that it demands special attention, for the following reasons:

1 Fresh foods are expensive and can be subject to considerable daily/ weekly price fluctuations; their purchase thus requires tight management.

2 Fresh foods are perishable, easily and quickly spoiled; there is the potential for great wastage in preparation and cooking.
3 There can be a huge variation in the quality of food items, particularly fresh foods.
4 Even dry goods can vary significantly in quality and value for money from brand to brand.
5 The requirements of the Food Safety Act necessitate great care in choosing suppliers to ensure that the buyer is demonstrating due care in selecting both suppliers and products.

The chain of responsibility of the purchasing function, therefore, ultimately extends into the kitchen and other areas of the organization including the consideration of proper storage and security so that wastage is minimized and usage maximized. But the demarcation line between the chef's responsibilities on site and those of the purchasing manager at head office is necessarily long and tenuous, and it is normally the case that the purchasing manager assumes that when the goods reach a kitchen's delivery area, it is the chef who must check and accept them. But this can only be achieved if there is a commonly understood system of quality control, which is based on the establishment of written specifications.

Standard specifications are important

In many individually owned catering businesses, specification standards and food quality control procedures do not exist. Often it is the chef or the manager who will order the goods, check them in and put them into store. In doing so, he will satisfy himself that the goods reach his accepted standard. In small organizations, it is arguable that this is as much control as is needed; a more sophisticated approach would take time to introduce and implement and would probably be beyond the financial resources of the organization. In other words, the chef orders to the establishment's own needs and preferences. Provided that the prices charged are in line with expectations, and the quality of purchases appears to be of sufficient standard, there is little point in changing the supplier or method of purchase.

This is too haphazard an approach for a large-scale caterer. Any catering organization which has a number of outlets will need to take a more disciplined approach to the subject. We can consider deep-frying oil, a product used universally throughout the industry, to illustrate the complexities involved and the questions which need to be asked during the planning stage of the product nomination process.

The cost of the raw material is a major part of the equation, but it is certainly not the controlling influence. The cheapest oil is not the most economic and does not produce the best end-product; in fact, it is often the waste oil collector who will be the only party to profit.

Extensive technical evaluation is necessary, not only at source but in individual kitchens. Are the product management procedures in place and adequate at the point of usage? Do the temperature controls work properly? Are the load levels adhered to? What are the cleaning schedules and how do we know when the oil is past its life? At what temperature does the oil begin to smoke; what is the flashpoint or ignition temperature? Safety is certainly a major consideration and there is no point in choosing an oil that smokes below the recommended frying temperatures. But what products are we deep-frying on a regular basis? Recommended frying temperatures vary considerably – from pieces of chicken cooked from raw at 150°C to doughnuts at 200°C. Does the cooked food leave a greasy film on the plate? Is there a pronounced odour or flavour or is the product as it should be – clean, crisp and odourless?

The final decision is one of technical quality. The longer the life of the oil selected, the more cost-effective the decision becomes. It will be made when all these questions have been answered, and not before. The decision will be confirmed by creating an accurate product specification to be used as a yardstick by unit managers. Only in this way, can we ensure consistency throughout the life of the product.

Similar considerations apply to beverage purchases. The choice of coffee, for example, has to be based not only on the variety of coffee used, the cost, the quality, the blend, but on the method of brewing, because this will have a crucial impact on costs. Is the production method bulk brew or pour and serve? In some cases, coffee machines are supplied on the 'free on loan' principle, in which the cost of the equipment is incorporated into the cost of the coffee and milk supplies. The lower the turnover, the higher the cost of these supplies, so the throughput becomes a key consideration.

In this context, the brand of coffee is equally important. Will a well-known brand, even though it is more expensive than an own-label brand, encourage more sales? Is the additional cost worth the potential additional revenue? This brings us to a deeper consideration of brands.

Branded or non-branded – which to use?

There are many other considerations according to the type of item being purchased. One of the most important is the place of branded products in the catering industry. By their nature, branded products are normally more expensive than similar products which are unbranded; they may also be of a higher quality. The purchasing manager has to ask whether the high-quality product is worth the additional cost. Here, one key consideration is whether the product is to be used back-of-house or front-of-house – whether it is to be used as an ingredient in a made-up dish or whether the branded product will be sold to the customer directly.

In the former category, the customer will rarely be able to know whether a branded product ingredient is being used, so there would appear to be no strong argument for using the product, no matter how high its quality, when its high-value characteristic simply disappears in the preparation of the dish.

On the other hand, in certain cases, a branded product may deliver precisely the quality of ingredient which is so essential to the preparation of a dish. Tuna fish is an example here, where the considerations include whether the fish is packed in oil brine, its country of origin, the percentage of chunk against flake (value engineering), colour, smell, texture, yield and last but not least, flavour. In this case, the purchase of a branded, higher cost item could be justified, provided that the price sensibly reflects the quality.

Of course, where the high profile of a brand is a crucial factor in the purchase of certain goods at point of sale, then their purchase is clearly necessary. Examples here are brands of crisps, chocolate and other confectionery. Lesser known or own-label brands may not generate equivalent sales and will yield lower sales volume and profit.

These examples illustrate the range of factors which the purchasing department has to consider in the purchase of almost any item. Merely leaving decisions of choosing the brand to the supplier or distributor places the control of the purchasing function into the supplier's hands. The larger the catering organization, the more essential is the need to introduce and maintain standard specifications.

In the creation of standard specifications, the purchasing department will wish to research the products it wishes to use. This can be done in a variety of ways – using the manufacturers' test kitchen, the purchasing company's own test facility, or undertaking consumer trials in individual units and gauging customer reaction. Additionally, it may be possible to use an outside testing organization.

The extent of this research will depend on the information which needs to be obtained. Testing for the meat or fat content of dishes, for example, is a technical investigation and more straightforward than assessing customer views and attitudes on certain products. Major foodservice companies, not just contract caterers, recognize the need for product research and are spending increasing sums of money in this area as, clearly, it is a continuous process. Products need to be tested frequently to ensure that quality is maintained and specifications adhered to.

Importance of relationships with suppliers

We said earlier that the objective of the purchasing department is to reduce food and beverage costs to the minimum, while ensuring that quality standards and delivery requirements are met. The quality is achieved by setting standards and specifications, product testing and ongoing quality control; minimum pricing is achieved through a constant dialogue with suppliers and distributors to ensure that the delivery system is appropriate to the needs of the business.

It is important that the food buyer recognizes the importance of the relationship which exists between caterer, supplier and manufacturer. His aim is not to reduce the supplier's margins to such an extent that supply becomes unprofitable. Rather, the objective is to act in partnership so that new ways of working can be examined and introduced to the benefit of all parties. For a large catering organization, it may be possible to reduce the number of suppliers and giving more business to the best suppliers, to redesign product packaging or to vary a formulation of ingredients to make a product less expensive without reducing quality; alternatively, longer production runs may be introduced. The distribution system may also be reorganized so that it becomes more economic with fewer, larger drops. For the catering contractor, this is where the client's requirements and the availability of storage space in individual units become an important consideration. The client may require a daily delivery of certain goods, while few catering facilities have sufficient storage space.

None of these examples will lead to the supplier experiencing lower profit margins, but all of them will lead to the elimination of some cost which can lead to savings. Such a partnership with suppliers can usually only be achieved by catering companies which have significantly large annual purchases, but the partnership principle should be common throughout the industry.

In seeking the minimum cost, the purchasing manager is looking for value for money rather than mere cheapness. It is always possible to reduce food and beverage costs to such an extent that the caterer buys the least expensive goods and materials, but few will go down this route unless this is the market segment in which they are operating.

Value for money – always the objective

It is impossible to write about the purchasing function without defining what we mean by value for money because it is this, rather than low cost, which is what the purchasing department is constantly seeking. Certainly, quality is vital but what is even more important is the search for the appropriate quality. It is the relationship between quality and price which represents the food buyer's perception of value. This is the key relationship. A low-priced item may not represent value for a number of reasons: it may waste too much; it may be impossible to add sufficient value for the caterer to make a profitable sale; it may spoil or deteriorate too much or too quickly; its appearance and organoleptic properties may be wrong. So, while the item will be the cheapest, it does not represent value for money.

Conversely, a high-quality, high-priced item may represent outstanding value for almost exactly the opposite reasons. The waste is minimal, so more portions can be prepared; much greater value can be added to the item, so a higher price can be charged; the product may keep longer, so that more items can be prepared at the same time and stored in the right conditions – thus, maybe, enjoying some economies of scale in the production process; and it will look and taste so good that customers will want to come back for more – the ultimate objective of any caterer.

This relationship between cost and quality is the key to successful food and beverage purchasing and, indeed, to the purchase of any goods or services. The perception of value for money will vary from manager to manager, from company to company, from purpose to purpose. There is no universally accepted definition and individual caterers and catering companies have to make up their own mind on the subject. Naturally, between the two extremes of high quality and low price, most will want to steer a middle course for their own needs and circumstances. Although they will try to obtain the best of both these worlds – an item which is both low-priced and of high quality – they will realize that this is possible only within strict parameters: hence the need for quality control, standards and specifications. The wise middle course is to seek the high-quality item – or, at least, the appropriate-quality item – at the least cost. In doing so, the caterer is maximizing his purchasing efficiency and meeting client and consumer needs.

Of course, this implies that the caterer has only one market. This is certainly not the case with large contract catering companies who have to satisfy widely different markets – education, health care, staff restaurants, even commercial restaurants – all with different needs and requirements.

Challenges and constraints for the food buyer

Caterers, and particularly those who operate a multi-unit business which is geographically widespread, face challenges and constraints which are peculiar to the business in which they operate. We have already touched on some of the key difficulties facing the food and beverage buyer. One of the major constraints for most caterers – especially those operating many units – is that so much of what is purchased is highly perishable. This crucially affects buying procedures.

The caterer has to compromise between buying in quantity (which, almost alone, justifies low prices in the eyes of the supplier) with a limited throughput per unit and a very limited amount of storage space. In many catering facilities, space is one requirement which is most often lacking. Nor is it possible to store potatoes or bread or meat or fish in the same way that the car manufacturer can store rubber tyres or headlamp bulbs. Yet the car manufacturer, who has become an expert in materials management, bringing in components when required and storing the absolute minimum on site, has little to teach the large-scale caterer in the purchase and storage of materials. The manufacturer can keep his tyres and bulbs for a few days without any damage, the caterer cannot keep his components in the same way.

The caterer faces the problem of continuously supplying many different sites, each of a different size (in Compass' case, 3,000 individual units) with a constant supply of fresh or perishable foods, with the minimum of wastage and duplication. This is a formidable logistical exercise and one which shows (when it is properly executed) how inherently efficient some large-scale caterers are in the purchasing process. But, while the large-scale caterer can negotiate prices down because of higher purchasing volumes, no catering group has the purchasing power of the large supermarket groups. For the caterer, the element of cost represented by distribution is high in relation to the total cost of the product – much higher than it will be for the supermarket chain. Even so, suppliers will distribute to the major catering groups, but it is often uneconomic for them to make many small drops to the individual caterer. As a result, the independent caterer may shop locally at his cash and carry; this may not be so convenient, but it is the most economic method of buying in his goods. The same situation applies to the small retailer.

There is no doubt, however, that large catering organizations will be able to rationalize their sources of supply, so that the least number of suppliers are used to the greatest effect – to the extent that they have only three suppliers; one for frozen temperatures, one for chilled temperatures, and one for ambient temperatures. In this way, significant savings can be achieved. By making one distributor the source of purchases, rather than using a larger number of suppliers to deliver fewer items, the purchasing department may be able to achieve valuable economies of scale. This is the approach which large-scale, multi-unit catering companies are now taking and will do so, increasingly, in the future.

Nominated suppliers – two-tier purchasing

Multi-unit catering companies have traditionally controlled their purchasing function by designating a number of preferred national suppliers for long-life products such as flour and dry goods, while approving a much larger number of local suppliers for perishable goods such as milk, bread, meat and fish. In this way, the aggregated purchases of dry goods from the national supplier enables the caterer to demand bulk purchase terms on these items, even though local distribution is provided; at the same time, the approved list of items enables the caterer to control the standard and quality of these purchases. Control of perishable goods is more difficult because supply is localized and depends more on the catering manager, as purchaser, flagging up poor quality against specifications than on any national system of control. For a major catering chain, the number of nominated local bread suppliers may be as high as 100.

To paraphrase the famous dictum, purchasing in a large organization is too important to be left to individual catering managers. The potential savings that can be made through a carefully controlled central purchasing programme are too great for purchasing to be left to chance or to the personal preference of an individual manager. All catering managers must have an input into the purchasing function because only they know their customers, what they prefer, what they are willing to buy and how much they are willing to spend. In this sense, the unit manager must define what items to sell and what raw materials are needed. But if a company has 30 units – or 300 – or, indeed, 3,000 – with the same number of individual managers – it is leaving an enormous number of buying decisions to individual needs and preference when the *raison d'être* of a large company lies in its corporate purchasing power.

Of course, it is often argued, rightly, that the strength of any multi-unit catering operation lies in its individual managers. But even a company with 30 units has greater buying power than a single unit operation, and a company with 3,000 units unarguably has greater buying power than one with 300 units. So any catering company of any size, in its search for greater profitability, will be seeking to maximize its purchasing potential. In doing so, it will inevitably have to take away some element of choice from its operational management but, at the same time, provide a range of products from which the catering manager can make a reasonable selection.

A local manager may be keen to offer certain items, but if every manager took the same view the company's product list would be never-ending. As it is, a large catering company may have listed a choice of at least 10 different brands of mayonnaise or tomato sauce, all in different pack sizes and all at a different price. In these circumstances, it is little wonder that some rationalization becomes inevitable.

If the caterer can reduce the number of brands on offer and negotiate special terms with both the manufacturer and distributor, then it is possible to reduce purchasing costs. In a large company with hundreds, or even thousands, of units, the ability to achieve these kinds of savings on a large range of goods will lead to significantly reduced costs which, in turn, will lead directly to higher profits and improved competitiveness.

Nominating suppliers is, in effect, a two-tier purchasing system. The company will make the initial selection of products which it wants to be used based on all the factors mentioned earlier, but it also gives the local manager scope to choose whatever he believes will satisfy his clients' and his customers' requirements.

We have only to look at the major supermarket chains, with their highly efficient lines of distribution, distribution centres and rigorously enforced times of delivery plus product selection and range control, to realize that the catering industry has the potential to save significant sums of money if only it would take a more professional approach to the purchasing function. In this respect, the largest multi-unit caterers (both in the commercial hotel and restaurant industry and in contract catering) and the contractors' clients will be able to benefit from the experience of our major grocery retailers.

Purchasing policy and measurement of purchasing efficiency

We come to two final issues facing the purchasing department – introducing the company's purchasing policy and measuring its success.

Naturally, the purchasing policy will reflect the company's precise objectives. Not every company will have its policy determined in the same way, so the following outlines the main policy objectives which are common to most companies:

- To provide the most appropriate range of products, offering sufficient consumer choice in all the different markets in which the company operates.
- To provide optimum value for money.
- To regularly monitor the quality and price of purchases and to ensure that standards and value for money are maintained.
- To seek to deal directly with manufacturers, whenever possible (only possible for large-scale caterers).
- To rationalize the number of suppliers in order to focus the company's purchasing power.
- To seek partnership opportunities with manufacturers, suppliers and distributors, to improve customer awareness of the catering proposition and to drive up sales (again, only possible for large-scale caterers).

In the final analysis, it will be the improvement in sales which will be the ultimate – and most important – measurement of the purchasing department's policies. The consumer himself will make this measurement by choosing to accept (and continuing to accept) the company's catering offer.

Of course, there are other measures, too, which must be made during the purchasing cycle. For fresh produce fruit and vegetables, perhaps the most difficult area, prices can be checked against independent market reports from Covent Garden, daily auction prices in Holland, prices published in *Fresh Produce Journal*, and comparison with supermarket prices. For meat, prices can be compared to those published by the independent Meat and Livestock Commission.

Throughout this process of price checking, however, a company must depend on the experience and expertise of its buyers who will each have a common objective – to reduce the size of the company's purchasing bill while maintaining the appropriate quality of goods purchased. In this objective, the purchasing department will, itself, have some financial targets, primarily in terms of cost savings brought about by fewer distributors, fewer delivery drops and a more limited choice of products. Once these savings have been achieved, attention has to be paid to maintaining them. Purchasing cannot be regarded as a one-off activity, but a continuous and ongoing process which makes its own unique contribution to a company's financial success.

Conclusions

To summarize: the first priority of any purchasing department (or, indeed, any caterer who has responsibility for purchasing) is to focus on the number of nominated suppliers and then on the number of items which they carry. The product lines on offer to units must not be so large that the volume constitutes a needless cost to the organization and prevents prices being reduced.

Quality must be ensured through a quality control programme which, in the largest companies, will demand a test kitchen and sample testing. The buyer will work with distributors and manufacturers so that the relationship becomes one of partnership not confrontation; in doing so, the overwhelming aim will be to reduce costs while maintaining and often enhancing quality and service.

References

British Hospitality Association (1993). *Annual Contract Catering Survey*. London: British Hospitality Association.
Horwath Consulting (1993). *UK Hotel Industry: 1993*. London: Horwath Consulting.

Part Four

Controlling Operations

17 Monitoring customer satisfaction

Abraham Pizam

What is customer satisfaction?

In recent years the concept of customer satisfaction/dissatisfaction has been extensively studied by marketing researchers and students of consumer behaviour. Several conferences were devoted to the subject and extensive literature reviews were published (Day, 1977; Hunt 1977; LaTour and Peat, 1979; Smart, 1982; Ross, *et al.*, 1987).

Customer satisfaction is a psychological concept that involves the feeling of well-being and pleasure that results from obtaining what one hopes for and expects from an appealing product and/or service (WTO, 1985). While there are a variety of approaches to the explanation of customer satisfaction/dissatisfaction, the most widely used is the one proposed by Richard Oliver who has developed the expectancy disconfirmation theory (Oliver, 1980). According to this theory which has been tested and confirmed in several studies (Oliver and DeSarbo, 1988; Tse and Wilton, 1988), customers purchase goods and services with pre-purchase expectations about anticipated performance. Once the product or service has been purchased and used, outcomes are compared against expectations. When outcome matches expectations, confirmation occurs. Disconfirmations occur when there are differences between expectations and outcomes. Negative disconfirmation occurs when outcome is less than expectations or in other words when product/service performance is less than expected. Positive disconfirmation occurs when outcome is greater than expectations, or in other words when product/service performance is better than expected. Satisfaction is caused by confirmation or positive disconfirmation and dissatisfaction is caused by negative disconfirmation.

A minority of researchers perceive the satisfaction process to be subjective in expectations but objective in the perceptions of the product attributes, or outcome. Thus, Klaus (1985, p. 21) defines satisfaction as 'the customer's subjective evaluation of a consumption experience, based on some relationship between the customer's perceptions and objective attributes of the product'. Others point out that both what is perceived (outcome) and what is expected are subjective and therefore psychological phenomena – not reality (Maister, 1985). The importance of the subjective nature of the process cannot be overstated. Since both expectations and perceptions are psychological phenomena, they are both susceptible to external influences and manipulation. As an illustration of how expectations can be explicitly manipulated Sasser *et al.* (1979, p. 89) note that: 'Some restaurants follow the practice of promising guests a waiting time in excess of the "expected time". If people are willing to agree to wait this length of time, they are quite pleased to be seated earlier, thus starting the meal with a more positive feeling' (Maister, 1985, p. 114). Another example of creating low customer expectations is a restaurant in Orlando, Florida which calls itself Warm Beer & Lousy Food. Once a customer has experienced a reasonable meal at the above restaurant he/she is pleasantly surprised and comes out very satisfied. Manipulating perceptions of outcome is also a common practice in some restaurants where waiting staff mention nonchalantly that a particular dish that was just consumed by the customer is a favourite of a noted restaurant critic or a famous personality. The intention here is to influence the perception of the customer that the dish must be good since an 'expert' said so.

Satisfaction is not a universal phenomenon and not everyone gets the same satisfaction out of the same meal experience. The reason is that customers have different needs, objectives and past experiences that influence their expectations. To a student on a limited budget, a lunch composed of fast food items at the crowded and noisy school cafeteria may be a highly satisfying experience, while the same experience may be perceived as totally dissatisfying to an affluent executive discussing a business transaction. The same customer may also have different needs and expectations on different meal occasions, or at different times of the day (Davis and Stone, 1985, p. 31). The student in our previous example will not be highly satisfied when his college friends take him out for a birthday meal celebration at the school cafeteria.Therefore it is important to gain a clear idea of the customer needs and objectives that correspond to different kind of satisfactions. This necessitates the segmentation of the market, because no service or product can offer everyone the same degree of satisfaction (WTO, 1985).

To recapitulate, what we have established by now is that an individual's satisfaction with outcomes received from a meal experience results from a comparison of these outcomes with expectations. Expectations can be described as a mutable internal standard which is based on a multitude of factors including needs, objectives, past personal or vicarious experiences with the same restaurant, with similar restaurants, and the availability of alternatives (i.e. are there any other restaurants in town?). This view is supported by Mazursky who suggests that

> experiences beyond those with the focal brands may lead to different normative standards employed by consumers in evaluating performance. Possible norms, according to this view, include perceived best brand, the most recently used brand, a brand used by a reference person, products competing for the same needs, and the like. (Mazursky, 1989)

Changes in satisfaction with the meal experience may result from changes in the perception of the actual quality of outcomes received, or from changes in the expectations against which these outcomes are compared. Alterations in the expectations can result from change in needs (i.e. hungry versus full) change of objectives (i.e. business luncheon versus anniversary dinner), new personal or vicarious experiences (i.e recently had a superb meal experience at another restaurant) and any other influences that make salient a particular quality of outcomes (i.e. it's a very hot day and the restaurant is not air-conditioned) (McCallum& Harrison, 1985).

The importance of customer satisfaction

The concept of customer satisfaction which is classified by marketing specialists as post-purchase behaviour is recognized as of great importance to all commercial firms because of its influence on repeat purchases and word-of-mouth recommendations (Berkman and Gilson, 1986).

> Satisfaction, reinforces positive attitudes toward the brand, leading to a greater likelihood that the same brand will be purchased again . . . dissatisfaction leads to negative brand attitudes and lessens the likelihood of buying the same brand again. (Assael, 1987, p. 47)

Or as others put it:

> . . . if consumers are satisfied with a product or brand, they will be more likely to continue to purchase and use it and to tell others of their favourable experience with it . . . if they are dissatisfied, they will be more likely to switch brands and complain to manufacturers, retailers, and other consumers about the product (Peter and Olson, 1987, p. 512)

Satisfaction of customers also happens to be the cheapest means of promotion. As Knutson (1988, p. 17) states:

> . . . it costs more to get a customer than to keep one. The ratio is about ten to one. For every $10 you spend on advertising, public relations, price incentives, and other promotions to get a new customer, it costs about $1 to get a current customer to come back. Moreover, word-of-mouth advertising is free.

The components of satisfaction

Unlike material products or pure services, the meal experience is an amalgam of products and services. Therefore it is *possible* to say that satisfaction with a meal experience is a sum total of satisfactions with the individual elements or attributes of all the products and services that make up the meal experience.

There is no uniformity of opinion among marketing experts as to the classification of the elements in service encounters. Reuland *et al.* (1985, p. 142) suggest that hospitality services, including meal experiences, consist of a harmonious mixture of *three* elements: the material *product* in a narrow sense which in the case of a restaurant is the food and beverages; the *behaviour* and attitude of the employees who are responsible for hosting the guest, serving the meal and beverages and who come in direct contact with the guests, and the *environment*, such as the building, the layout, the furnishing, the lighting in the restaurant, etc.

Czepiel *et al.* (1985) on the other hand, suggest that satisfaction with a service is a function of satisfaction with *two* independent elements. The *functional* element, i.e. the food and beverage in a restaurant, and the *performance-delivery* element, i.e. the service. To prove the independence of the two elements from each other, the authors claim that 'restaurant clients are quite capable of having responses to each element that differ one from the other. "The service was great, the food poor" or conversely. . . .' (p. 13)

Davis and Stone (1985, p. 29) divide the service encounter into *two* elements: *direct* and *indirect* services: *direct* services being the actual service of the food and beverages to the customer, while the *indirect* services include the provision of cloakroom facilities, parking, telephone for customer use, etc.

Lovelock (1985) divides the service attributes into two groups: *core* and *secondary*.

> Airline service provides a good example, with customers first making inquiries and reservations, then checking in their baggage, getting seat assignments, being checked at the gate, receiving on-board service in flight, and retrieving their baggage at the destination airport. Each of these activities is an operations task that is secondary to the core product of physically transporting passengers and their bags between two airports. But these secondary tasks have a greater potential to generate customer dissatisfaction if performed poorly. (Lovelock, 1985, p. 272).

In a restaurant situation Lovelock's *core* will be composed of the food and beverage, while his *secondary* will be composed of everything else, including service, environment, etc.

Lewis (1987), too, classifies the service encounter attributes in two groups: *essential* and *subsidiary*. The *essential* attributes are identical to Czepiel's *functional*, Davis and Stone's *direct*, Reuland and colleagues' *product*, and Lovelock's *core*, i.e. the food and beverage in the meal experience. On the other hand Lewis's *subsidiary* attributes are more comprehensive than either Davis and Stone's *indirect*, Czepiel's *performance-delivery*, or Lovelock's *secondary*, and include such factors as: accessibility, convenience of location, availability and timing and flexibility, as well as interactions with those providing the service and with other customers. It is equivalent to a combination of the *behaviour* and *environment* elements in the Reuland and colleagues model.

Yet other researchers support the idea that the service encounter attributes are situation-specific and as such cannot be classified into universal elements. For example, Fiebelkorn (1985) doing a study at Citybank found that overall satisfaction with Citybank as one of the customer's banks (or his bank only) is based on satisfaction with the last encounter with the bank in five main areas: teller encounter, platform encounter, ATM (automatic teller machines) encounter, phone encounter, problem encounter. He then concludes that 'the common thread running through all five service-encounter types is that customers want: prompt service by people who know what to do and how to do it, and who care about them as valued customers. . . .' (Fiebelkorn, 1985, p. 185).

Overall satisfaction vs. satisfaction with individual attributes

In the previous section we indicated that it is *possible* to say that satisfaction with a meal experience is a sum total of satisfactions with the individual elements or attributes of all the products and services that make up the meal experience. Though superficially the above statement makes sense, in reality the matter is more compounded. The question that we have to ask ourselves is whether when customers experience the attributes of the meal experience they form a set of independent impressions on each and compare those with the expectations of the same attributes. And, is the resultant *overall level of satisfaction* determined by the arithmetic sum total of these impressions? The answer to the above question is dependent on one's belief about the process of consumer choice. More specifically, it is related to whether one believes that consumer choice behaviour could be explained by *compensatory* or *non-compensatory* models.

Non-weighted compensatory models presume that customers make trade-offs of one attribute for another in order to make a decision, i.e. a weakness in one attribute is compensated by a strength in another. In a restaurant example, if the food was poor, the atmosphere was pleasant but the service was good, the resultant overall satisfaction with the meal experience might still be high; poor food was traded-off with good service, because both of them were of equal importance to the customer. *Weighted compensatory* models (sometimes referred to as *expectancy-value* models) also assume that people have a measurement of belief about the existence of an attribute, but that each attribute has an importance weight relative to other attributes. Using this model in our previous example, we might conclude that because food was rated higher in its relative importance than service was, and the relative importance of atmosphere was rated lower than the other two, the resultant overall satisfaction with the meal experience will be dissatisfaction.

Non-compensatory models (no trade-offs of attributes) can take one of two forms: *conjunctive or disjunctive*. In *conjunctive* models consumers establish a minimum acceptable level for each important product attribute and make a choice (or become satisfied) only if each attribute equals or exceeds the minimum level. In our previous example each of the three attributes – food, service and atmosphere – will have to pass a threshold before overall satisfaction will occur. If atmosphere did not pass this threshold, no matter how good the food and the service was, the result is overall dissatisfaction.

Disjunctive models, are similar to conjunctive models, with one exception. Rather than establishing a minimum level on all important attributes, in conjunctive models consumers establish such levels only on one or a few attributes, e.g. food (Lewis and Chambers, 1989, p. 157).

Research evidence conducted in tourism and hospitality enterprises (Mazursky, 1989; Cadotte and Turgeon, 1988) support the disjunctive models. In a study conducted in 1978 among 432 foodservice firms representing 22,000 foodservice units, Cadotte and Turgeon asked company executives to list the type and frequency of their guests' complaints and compliments. As indicated in Table 17.1, the data from the surveys suggest that:

> ... some restaurant attributes are more likely to earn guest complaints than compliments. Availability of parking, hours of operation, traffic congestion, noise level, and spaciousness of the establishment all appear in the top-ten complaint list. ... In contrast, guests express appreciation for high performance in some areas, but rarely complain when performance is so-so. The survey results suggest that guest react favourably to a clean neat restaurant, neat employees, ample portions, and responsiveness to complaints. The quality and quantity of service, food quality, helpfulness of the employees, and the prices of drinks, meals and other services appear in both the list of most frequent complaints and the list of the most frequent compliments. (Cadotte and Turgeon, 1988, p. 47)

Following these findings, Cadotte and Turgeon divided the attributes into the following four categories: *satisfiers, dissatisfiers, critical* and *neutral*.

Satisfiers, in the researcher's opinion, were those attributes where unusual performance apparently elicited compliments and satisfaction, but average performance or even the absence of the feature did not cause dissatisfaction

Table 17.1   Comparative rankings of food-service attribute compliments and complaints

Attribute	Complaint rank	Compliment rank	Satisfier/ dissatisfier
Availability of parking	1	19	Dissatisfier
Traffic congestion in establishment	2	26	
Noise level	5	24	
Spaciousness of establishment	8	18	
Hours of operation	9	20	
Cleanliness of establishment	14	4	Satisfier
Neatness of establishment	11	5	
Size of portions	12	5	
Employee appearance	17	7	
Responsiveness to complaints	20	9	
Quality of service	3	1	Critical
Food quality	7	2	
Helpful attitude of employees	6	3	
Quantity of service	10	8	
Prices of drinks, meals and service	4	10	
Management knowledge of service	23	11	Neutral
Availability of food on menu	16	12	
Beverage quality	24	13	
Variety of service	21	14	
Uniformity of establishment appearance	26	15	
Quality of advertising	25	16	
Convenience of location	15	17	
Quietness of surroundings	18	21	
Accuracy of bill	19	22	
Litter outside restaurant	22	23	
Reservation system	13	25	

Source: Cadotte and Turgeon, 1988 p.46.

or complaints. Large-size food portions, smartly dressed employees, clean and neat restaurants are all examples of a restaurant satisfier. Normal food portions, regularly dressed employees and not so neat restaurants do not cause dissatisfaction. In contrast, large food portions and well-groomed and smartly dressed employees please the restaurant guest. 'Satisfiers, represent an opportunity to shine, to move ahead of the pack, and to stand out from the crowd . . .' (Cadotte and Turgeon, 1988, p. 51).

Dissatisfiers were more likely to earn a complaint for low performance or absence of a desired feature than anything else. But an operation that exceeds the threshold performance standard apparently will not receive compliments on the attribute. Parking and excessive noise are good examples of dissatisfiers; they have to be provided and maintained at a minimum or sufficient level. But efforts to achieve a higher performance level will not be appreciated by customers nor will it cause them satisfaction. 'Dissatisfiers particularly require management control to prevent poor performance. Minimum standards should be established, and the focus should be on maintaining these standards. . . . Be as good as your competition, but do not waste resources trying to be better . . .' (Cadotte and Turgeon, p. 51).

Critical attributes were capable of eliciting both complaints (dissatisfactions) and compliments (satisfactions), depending on the situation. Quality of service, food quality and helpful attitude of employees ranked high in eliciting both complaints and compliments. Critical factors deserve special attention, because of their potential for both hurting and helping a business. 'Like dissatisfiers, minimum standards must be set to avoid negative responses to your service. . . . For the critical attributes, the objective is to raise performance beyond the norm' (Cadotte and Turgeon, p. 51).

Neutral attributes neither received a great number of compliments nor many complaints, therefore probably indicating that they were either not salient to guests or easily brought up to guests' standards.

Cadotte and Turgeon draw our attention to the fact that the classification of these factors is not permanent but constantly changes. Some dissatisfier-type attributes were probably critical at one time. Higher industry standards, though, may have improved performance to the extent that most restaurants are able to meet guest requirements on these factors. For example, in warm climates, the availability of reliable air conditioning in restaurants was a critical factor; today, with the advent of modern refrigeration technology, all restaurants in such climates will have it. Having more of it will not satisfy anyone, but when it breaks down, suddenly everyone becomes dissatisfied.

If Cadotte and Turgeon's findings will be confirmed by other studies, we might indeed revise our theory about the nature of customer satisfaction/dissatisfaction and reject the notion that satisfaction and dissatisfaction are two extremes on one continuum. Instead, we might accept a modification of a theory that was advanced some years ago on the subject of job satisfaction. In this theory, Herzberg *et al.* (1959) proposed that job satisfaction and dissatisfaction are two extremes on two continua. On one continuum – the motivation continuum – we have satisfaction versus no-satisfaction, while on the other – the hygiene continuum – we have dissatisfaction versus no-dissatisfaction. In Herzberg's opinion, the variables the presence or absence of which cause satisfaction or no-satisfaction, are not the same that cause dissatisfaction or no-dissatisfaction. While Herzberg confirmed his theory by using a particular research method – the critical incident – few other researchers managed to duplicate his results by using alternative methods. In the majority of cases, it was found that though some variables operate solely on one continuum (i.e. working conditions were found to be a hygiene factor, or dissatisfier), others (i.e. salary) appeared in both the hygiene (dissatisfier) continuum as well as the motivator (satisfier) continuum. Applying the same rationale to Cadotte and Turgeon's findings, one might conclude that if supported by other studies, customer satisfaction/dissatisfaction could also be explained as a process operating in three continua: the first for satisfaction, the second for dissatisfaction and the third (critical) for common factors that can cause both satisfaction as well as dissatisfaction.

But until such time we must still operate under the assumption that satisfaction and dissatisfaction are two extremes that operate on one continuum. Therefore we propose that customers' overall satisfaction with a service encounter is a sum total of the difference between their perceived outcome and expectations relating to a group of weighted attributes, some of which carry minimum thresholds, plus an additional mysterious factor which Gronroos (1984) calls *image* and Lewis calls *overall feeling* (Lewis, 1987, pp. 84–85). The following equation (modified from Lewis and Chambers, 1989, p. 157) gives a mathematical depiction of overall customer satisfaction:

$$A_{jk} = \Sigma^n \, W_{ik} \, B_{ijk} \qquad \text{with } B_{ijk} > I$$

where A_{jk} = consumer k's overall satisfaction score for restaurant j, W_{ik} = the importance weight assigned by consumer k to attribute k to attribute i, B_{ijk} = consumer k's rating of the amount of attribute i offered by rest j, n = the number of product/service attributes, and I = a minimum level (threshold).

As to the question of identifying the individual attributes in the meal experience, and determining their relative importance weights as well as their minimum threshold levels, the answer to that has to be determined by each restaurant for each customer segment. However, based on previous research findings we can suggest what some of these attributes *might* be and how important they generally have been found to be among consumers.

The product/service attributes of the meal experience

Following Reuland *et al.* (1985) we suggest that the meal experience consists of the following elements which can be classified in three groups: the *material product* – the food and beverage – the *environment*, and the *behaviour and attitude* of the employees (Table 17.2).

Table 17.2   Product/service attributes in the meal experience

Material product: food and beverage	Environment	Behaviour and attitude
1 Quality of F&B	1 Cleanliness of rest	1 Friendliness
2 Portion size	2 Location and accessibility	2 Competence
3 Variety of menu choices	3 Size and shape of room	3 Courtesy
4 Food and Beverage consistency	4 Furniture and fittings	4 Efficiency and speed
5 Range of tastes, textures, aromas and colours	5 Colour scheme	5 Helpfulness
6 Correct F&B temperature	6 Lighting	6 Professionalism
7 Appearance of F&B	7 Temperature and ventilation	7 Responsiveness to special requests
8 Price of meal/ drinks/ service	8 Acoustics (noise level)	8 Responsiveness to complaints
9 Availability of menu items	9 Spaciousness of restaurant	
	10 Neatness of restaurant	
	11 Employees' appearance	
	12 Availability of parking	
	13 Hours of operation	

Several research reports (Davis and Stone, 1985; WTO, 1985; Cadotte and Turgeon, 1988; Mintel, 1989), indicated that the following factors were rated by many restaurant customers as relatively high in their importance:

- *Material product.* Quality of food and beverage, portion sizes, and price of meals/drinks.
- *Environment of the restaurant.* Cleanliness, spaciousness, neatness, employees' appearance, availability of parking.
- *Behaviour.* Helpfulness of employees, responsiveness to special requests, responsiveness to complaints.

Measuring satisfaction

The measuring instrument

To measure satisfaction with a meal experience we recommend that each establishment measure both the global or overall satisfaction with the meal experience as well as measure the satisfaction along the various product/service attributes contributing to overall satisfaction. Global measures involve questions such as:

(a) On balance, how satisfied are you with the meal that you had?

    5. Very satisfied
    4. Satisfied
    3. Neither satisfied nor dissatisfied
    2. Dissatisfied
    1. Very dissatisfied

(b) In comparison with your expectation how good was your meal experience?

    5. Much better than I expected
    4. Better than I expected
    3. About what I expected
    2. Less than I expected
    1. Much less than I expected

(c) How likely are you to return to this restaurant within the next year?

    5. Will definitely return
    4. Likely to return
    3. Maybe
    2. Not likely to return
    1. Absolutely will not return

(d) Would you recommend this restaurant to friends or relatives?

    5. Will definitely recommend
    4. Will probably recommend
    3. Maybe I will recommend
    2. Will probably not recommend
    1. Will definitely not recommend

To measure satisfaction with particular product/service attributes, the use of questions similar to the following is recommended (WTO, 1985):

(a) Please evaluate the quality of the main course and kindly list what it was (main course: ....)

    5. Excellent
    4. Good
    3. Average
    2. Below average
    1. Poor

(b) Please evaluate the speed and efficiency of the service:

   5. Very efficient but not too quick
   4. Efficient
   3. Neither efficient nor inefficient
   2. Slow and inefficient
   1. Very slow

(c) How helpful would you say was our waiting staff?

   5. Very helpful
   4. Helpful
   3. Neither helpful nor unhelpful
   2. Unhelpful
   1. Most unhelpful

Measurement scales and profile variables

Satisfaction scales

In addition to the satisfaction scales presented above, researchers and practitioners use a variety of other scales for global or attributes' measurement. Among some of the most popular are: critical incidents, graphic scales, delighted/terrible, and faces. Following are some examples of questions relating to these scales:

I. Critical Incident

(a) Could you kindly tell us what did you find *good* about your meal experience in this restaurant?

   ....
   ....
   ....

(b) Could you tell us what you find *bad* about this restaurant?

   ....
   ....
   ....

II. Graphic

(a) Place an 'X' on the line to show how satisfied you were with your meal today:

   0   10   20   30   40   50   60   70   80   90   100
   | | | | | | | | | | |

   Not at all   Totally
   Satisfied   Satisfied

III. Delighted/Terrible (DT)

(a) How did you feel about your meal experience today?

Delighted	Pleased	Mostly satisfied	Mixed (about equally satisfied and dissatisfied)	Mostly dissatisfied	Unhappy	Terrible
7	6	5	4	3	2	1

IV. Faces

(a) Please mark the face that shows how you feel about your meal experience at this restaurant (Maddox, 1985).

(A set of five drawings of faces ranging from a fully smiling face to a very sad face)

Importance scales

To determine the relative *importance* of each of the product/service attributes, it is possible to add another scale next to each of the previous questions that asked individuals to rate their *satisfaction* with a particular attribute.

For example, in one of the previous sections consumers were asked to rate their *satisfaction* with the speed and efficiency of the waiting staff with the following question:

(a) Please evaluate the speed and efficiency of the service:

5	4	3	2	1
Very efficient but not too quick	Efficient	Neither efficient nor inefficient	Slow and inneficient	Very slow

If finding out the relative *importance* of service speed and efficiency is of interest, the following questions could be asked:

(b) Could you also tell us how important is the speed and the efficiency of service to you:

5	4	3	2	1
Very important	Important	Neither important nor unimportant	Not really important	Not important at all

Profile variables

Some basic demographics, such as sex, education, income, profession, geographical origin, etc., should be determined for the purpose of identifying the profile of the customer. Other relevant variables should include: number of individuals in the party, frequency of eating out, frequency of eating at this establishment, etc.

Frequency and method of measurement

It is recommended that questionnaires containing some of the above measurements be distributed either on a continuous or periodic basis to all customers at the end of their meal. Under no circumstances should the questionnaires be left on the table before the meal was completed. Leaving the questionnaire on the table in advance will result in it being completed by only those who have either had an exceptional experience or a very poor one. The waiting staff should distribute the questionnaire at the end of the meal with a request to complete it. To increase the rate of completion we recommend giving customers some form of incentive such as a 20 per cent discount on the next meal, etc.

If the establishment cannot afford to distribute questionnaires to every customer, then a method should be devised so that random sampling be achieved. For example, every third customer at dinner and every fifth customer at lunch should be approached and asked to complete a questionnaire. The customers to be approached should be seated throughout the restaurant so that all waiters will be represented in the sample. Questionnaires should be distributed throughout the seven days of the week so that both weekdays and weekends are included. All questionnaires should be coded in advance for date, meal (lunch or dinner), and table number, to enable analysis by day, menu items, and waiting personnel.

Data analysis

The analysis of the data should be conducted on a weekly basis and the results compared with previous weeks. The mean and standard deviation should be computed for the global/overall satisfaction variable(s) as well as for each of the product/service attributes. To understand better the satisfaction/dissatisfactions of each market segment, we recommend that separate analyses be conducted for each identifiable market segment (i.e. lunch, dinner, banquets, themed meals, frequent versus occasional diners, etc.).

To determine the relative importance (weights) of each product/service attribute, an establishment can either conduct a periodic study to determine how customers themselves rate these, or alternatively determine the weights by running a multiple regression with the global satisfaction variable as the dependent variable and each of the product/service attributes as the independent variables. The beta weights for each independent variable in the regression will be equivalent to the importance rates of the attributes. Since the relative importance of product/service attributes changes from time to time, we recommend that these weights be computed at least once a year and if possible twice per year.

To conclude, if properly designed, administered and analysed, the process of monitoring customer satisfaction can be beneficial to any restaurant and make the difference between offering a mediocre quality product and an excellent quality product. For a further discussion on the subject of quality and its relation to customer satisfaction see Chapter 13.

References

Assael, H. (1987). *Consumer Behaviour and Marketing Action*, 3rd edn. Boston: PWS-Kent.

Berkman, H. W. and Gilson, C. (1986). *Consumer Behaviour: Concepts and Strategies*, 3rd edn. Boston: Kent.

Blackman, B. A. (1985) Making a service more tangible can make it more manageable. In *The Service Encounter: Managing Employee Customer Interaction in Service Business* Lexington, MA: Lexington Books, pp. 291–302.

Cadotte, E. R. and Turgeon, N. (1988). Key factors in guest satisfaction. *Cornell Hotel and Restaurant Quarterly*, **28**(4), 45–51.

Czepiel, J. A., Solomon, M. R. Suprenant, C. F. and Gutman, E. G. (eds.) (1985). Service encounters: an overview. In *The Service Encounter: Managing Employee Customer Interaction in Service Business* Lexington, MA: Lexington Books, pp. 3–15.

Davis, B. and Stone, S. (1985). *Food and Beverage Management*, 2nd edn. Oxford: Butterworth-Heinemann.

Day, R. (1977). Consumer satisfaction, dissatisfaction, and complaining behaviour. In *Symposium Proceedings*, 20–22 April, R. Day (ed.). School of Business, University of Indiana, Bloomington, Indiana.

Fiebelkorn, S. L. (1985). Retail service encounter satisfaction: model and measurement. In J. A.Czepiel, M. R. Solomon, C. F. Suprenant and E. G. Gutman (eds), *The Service Encounter: Managing Employee Customer Interaction in Service Business*. Lexington, MA: Lexington Books, pp. 181–194.

Gronroos, C. (1984). A service quality model and its marketing implications. *European Journal of Marketing*, **18**(4), 36–44.

Herzberg, F., Mausner, B. and Snyderman, B. (1959). *The Motivation to Work*, New York: Wiley.

Hunt, K. H. (ed.) (1977). *Conceptualization and Measurement of Consumer Satisfaction and Dissatisfaction*. Cambridge, MA: Marketing Science Institute.

Klaus, P. (1985). Quality epiphenomenon: the conceptual understanding of quality in face-to face service encounters. In J. A. Czepiel, M. R. Solomon, C. F. Suprenant and E. G. Gutman (eds), *The Service Encounter: Managing Employee Customer Interaction in Service Business*. Lexington, MA: Lexington Books, pp. 17–33.

Knutson B. J. (1988). Ten laws of customer satisfaction. *Cornell Hotel and Restaurant Quarterly*, **29**(3), 14–17.

LaTour, S. A. and Peat, N. C. (1979). Conceptual and methodological issues in consumer satisfaction research. In W. L. Wilke (ed.), *Advances in Consumer Research*. Ann Arbor, Michigan: Association for Consumer Research, pp. 431–437.

Levitt, T. (1981) Marketing intangible products and product intangibles. *Harvard Business Review*, May/June, 94–102.

Lewis, R. C. (1987). The measurement of gaps in the quality of hotel services. *International Journal of Hospitality Management*, **6**(2), 83–88.

Lewis, R. C. and Chambers, R. E. (1989). *Marketing Leadership in Hospitality*. New York: Van Nostrand Reinhold.

Lewis, R. C. and Nightingale, M. (1991) Targeting service to your customer. *Cornell Hotel, Restaurant Administration Quarterly*, **32**(2), 18–27.

Lovelock, C. H. (1985). Developing and managing the customer–service function in the service sector. In J. A. Czepiel, M. R. Solomon, C. F. Suprenant and E. G. Gutman (eds), *The Service Encounter: Managing Employee Customer Interaction in Service Business*. Lexington, MA: Lexington Books, pp. 265–280.

Maddox, R. N. (1985). Measuring satisfaction with tourism. *Journal of Travel Research*, **23**(3), 2–5.

Maister, D. H. (1985). The psychology of waiting lines. In J. A. Czepiel, M. R. Solomon, C. F. Suprenant and E.G. Gutman (eds), *The Service Encounter: Managing Employee Customer Interaction in Service Business*. Lexington, MA: Lexington Books, pp. 113–123.

Mazursky, D. (1989). Past experience and future tourism decisions. *Annals of Tourism Research*, **16**(3), 333–344.

McCallum, J. R. and W. Harrison (1985). Interdependence in the service encounter. In J. A. Czepiel, M. R. Solomon, C. F. Suprenant and E. G. Gutman (eds), *The Service Encounter: Managing Employee Customer Interaction in Service Business* Lexington, MA: Lexington Books, pp. 35–48.

Mintel (1989). *Eating Out: Special Report*, London: Mintel.

Oliver, R. L. (1980) A cognitive model of the antecedents and consequences of satisfaction decisions. *Journal of Marketing Research*, **17**, 460–469.

Oliver, R. L. and DeSarbo, W. S. (1988). Response determinants in satisfaction judgments. *Journal of Consumers Research*. **14**, 495–507.

Peter, P. J. and Olson, J. C. (1987). *Consumer Behaviour: Marketing Strategy Perspectives*. Homewood Illinois: Irwin.

Reuland, R., Coudrey, J. and Fagel, A. (1985). Research in the field of hospitality. *International Journal of Hospitality Management*, **4**(4), 141–146.

Ross, C. K., Frommelt, G., Hazelwood, L. and Chang, R. W. (1987). The role of expectations in patient satisfaction with medical care. *Journal of Health Care Marketing*, **7**(4) 16–26.

Sasser, W. E., Olsen, J and Wyckoff, D. D. (1979). *Management of Service Operations*, New York: Allyn and Bacon.

Smart, D. T. (1982). Consumer satisfaction research: a review. In J. U. McNeal and S. W. McDaniel (eds), *Consumer Behaviour: Classical and Contemporary Dimensions*. Boston: Little Brown, pp. 286–306.

Tse, D. K. and Wilton, P. C. (1988). Model of consumer satisfaction formation: an extension. *Journal of Marketing Research*, **25**, 204–212.

WTO (1985). *Identification and Evaluation of those Components of Tourism Services which have a Bearing on Tourist Satisfaction and which can be Regulated, and State Measures to Ensure Adequate Quality of Tourism Services*. Madrid: World Tourism Organization.

18 Management information systems for food and beverage operations

Peter A. Jones and L. Ferroni

Introduction

Information is the key resource for business decisions and increasingly is a major factor in developing competitive advantage. Computer based information systems (IS) represent the knowledge revolution. They impact on the business, economic and domestic lives of the developed world. Banking financial markets, retail operations and travel agencies are all entirely dependent on computer systems for the collection, collation and processing of data affecting all elements of their businesses. Porter and Millar (1985) referred to the impact of information technology as the provider of the key business resource – information – and as a result the use of that information will affect the structure, increase the competitive advantage and provide new business opportunities when recognized and used effectively.

However, in the hotel and catering industries, one of the major industries in the UK, the utilization of computers in one of the most important areas of that business – food and beverage – has had little impact on the nature of food and beverage operations or on the conduct of the function. If comparators are made with the banking and retail industries, food and beverage operations and their manual control systems would be unsustainable in direct competition. The 'system' for the collection, storage and processing of this information is increasingly based on the computer. This technology has had a most significant impact on the handling of information, an impact that in measure has been slow to penetrate the hospitality industry. Yet the benefits were identified by Gamble (1984, 1992).

The wider use of computers and IS in the hospitality industry has focused on the accounting and reservation activities more as a recording and control device than as a key resource in deriving either operational or competitive advantage.

The role of systems in food and beverage has been limited in both development and utilization. The concept of computers as IS capable of supporting management decision-making has been commented upon by many authors. Within this wealth of writings, others have proposed developments that move from the management information systems (MIS) to decision support systems (DSS) and executive support systems (ESS). While the actual level or target for such systems may change, the basic premise remains – timely, pertinent information on which to base management judgement and decisions.

This work will focus on the use of MIS to better inform the food and beverage decision-maker, whether he or she is a manager or a chef (Jones, 1983). Various authors, including Jones (1983), Kinton and Ceserani (1989) and Ryan (1989), have classified the catering industry into groups in an effort to categorize and understand the variety of management styles and approaches. They acknowledge that hospitality is a multi-faceted industry, but have divided it into two broad sectors: the so-called 'commercial/profit orientated' sector and the 'non-commercial/cost orientated' group. The intention here is to draw together the common strands which have brought MIS to their present form.

Most managers, including some senior members of the hospitality industry such as Lord Forte, believe that this industry very much depends on quick and decisive actions involving strategic management decisions often being made on 'intuition' rather than systematically collected data. El-Sawy (1987), in his study of chief executives in 1984, found that most relied on external information drawn from personal sources in the decision process rather than systematic or internally provided information.

Intuitive decision-making

One of the observations that can be made of the 'intuitive' decision-maker is that the 'thinker' is an experienced professional in a particular field who calls on past experience when making decisions. The more experienced the individual, the more credible the decision may be considered to be. The most important aspect of this, is that the person doing the thinking is in fact recalling data and subjective opinion as the basis for that decision. So, for example, a simple decision such as pricing a menu item may only involve the recollection of the latest price of the main components of that dish. A more complex decision on the pricing of a formal banqueting menu will require the recall of significant elements of data relating to the costs of many items, including staff costs. Or for a more long-term decision, such as the employment of extra staff, such judgements will be based often on perceptions of need rather than a systematic analysis of recorded internal data. The ability to store and recollect information is one of the major influences on the intuitive decision-maker. While it may appear a reasonable way of conducting everyday business, it is by no means as successful when it comes to long-term strategic planning (Mockker, 1987).

The common pattern emerging is that the underlying intuitive decision process relies mainly on professional experience. The database of information that could better inform judgements is not widely available or easily accessible and even in cases where the data are meticulously collated, the analytical process is a slow one, often rendering the information obsolete at the time of use.

Information systems

These and other similar limitations have prompted the introduction and use of computer based systems as a tool to collate, store, retrieve and assist in the analysis of data. While the computer is the hardware on which the tool is based, the overall approach is for one of using the computer technology as the platform for the provision of information for managers; thus the term 'management information systems'. Before the case is made for the use of computerized MIS, it is necessary to highlight some of the difficulties associated with this approach. As in every new area of development, the computer software packages developed for the hotel and catering industry have come in various shapes and sizes. In some cases the 'software programs' have proved to be unreliable, to the extent that the overall system has been discarded. However, not all the failures can be attributed to unreliability. The most common problem has been one of lack of planning and incompatibility of perception between the software designer and the end-user.

The general conclusion to be drawn from some of these difficulties is that the management of new technologically based information systems is not an easy task: 'Management of information technology (IT) is no easy task, as any data processing executive will admit' (Emberton, 1987).

Management information systems

Computerized MIS, compared with the manual model, are fast, can provide statistical information on almost any key areas of management and, most importantly, can be used as a forecasting tool. However, there are a number of factors which influence the efficiency of this process, each requiring careful consideration. For the purpose of this chapter, these factors will be broadly divided into two. First, the computer based IS, and secondly the 'human' aspect of the interface between the system and the user.

In their research paper 'Issues in information systems planning', Lederer and Mendelow (1986) state: 'Numerous difficulties face information systems managers as they develop IS plans'. Not surprisingly, they narrow the difficulties down to human perception and prioritization:

> Top IS managers were concerned most with learning the objectives of top general management. Middle IS managers were concerned most with adopting a methodology for planning. Operating IS managers were concerned most with understanding the perceived needs of the user.

Any system has therefore to meet the requirements of users at differing levels within the organization structure. Technologies have been described by Burns and Flam (1987) as 'artefacts which extend the capabilities of human action and are therefore sources of power', and

> those artefacts of technology are to a great extent used instrumentally, that is to achieve certain objectives or to solve certain problems, where improvements in performance (speed, reliability, quality etc) can be ascertained.

In this sense the food and beverage 'system' is a technological artefact. It has the characteristics described above. It extends the capabilities of differing levels of user in its instrumental use in assisting in solving problems and increasing the speed, reliability and quality of the output; in this case, relevant information concerning food and beverage business activity. This, of course, presupposes that the input data are accurately collected.

Planning for information systems

Information systems practitioners consider 'IS planning' to be the most important issue for the field in the 1980s (Raghunthan, 1988): '. . . firms now have so many diverse opportunities to develop and use information technology that they must rationally plan for those activities.'

The main reason for this approach is to avoid huge sums being spent, only to find that the systems do not suit the business. The rational planning must include key issues arising from the nature of the business, the functionality of the system and the fit of that functionality against the business activity and organization. However, what is clear is the 'planning' required must also include the systems implementation. The most sophisticated systems will be redundant if they are not carefully and successfully implemented.

They must enjoy the support of management, be immediately usable at all levels and be recognized as extensions of human capability that will improve on and benefit human performance. In a review of implementation strategies, Rhodes (1991) identified a number of common themes. These related to:

- Failure to design systems in line with business and operational policies.
- Failure to rationalize and simplify operational procedures in advance of systems implementation.
- Over-eagerness to adopt over-sophisticated systems rather than build systems on basic user needs.
- Failure to involve all of the users and stakeholders in the systems development and installation.
- Failure of management to recognize stakeholders' needs for operational systems rather than centralized bureaucratic systems.

The user and use of information systems

The term 'user' or often 'end-user' refers to anyone who uses the information a system provides in whatever capacity. Much of what goes on in the food and beverage department has a direct bearing on the totality of the business operation, in the sense that it contributes to the service provided to the customer. In a hotel, for example, a guest staying for one night will involve the services of the accommodation department, the services of the food and beverage department and finally the accounting department. This integration of services means that the 'information' derived from the operational activity of each department is crucial to the overall financial management and control needs of the hotel.

Food and beverages are the most complex of the operational activities. They require the purchase and storage of a wide range of raw materials, complex processing to demand, and the delivery to customers in a variety of service interactions. The control of this system relies on considerable volumes of data drawn from a wide variety of sources.

In analysing a manual food and beverage system through recording the flow of material through that system, the resultant model shown in Figure 18.1 illustrates the complexities of the sources of data and the inherent difficulties in presenting any processed data as information in a pertinent timely manner.

The nature of the manual operation requires the processing and storage of data in a number of discrete areas of the operation. The files within which this is stored will be in a variety of formats, locations and styles and may or

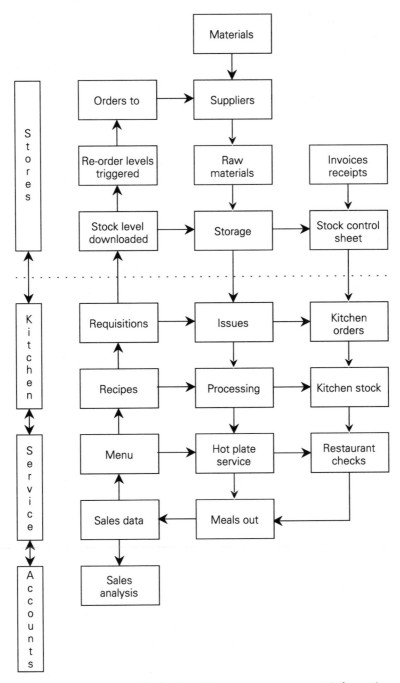

Figure 18.1 Major elements of a food and beverage management information system

may not be readily usable for other than the primary purpose. Some examples of the variability of data stores can be seen in the following:

1 *Stores*. Orders, receipts, invoices, stock control sheets, issue vouchers, supplier price lists.
2 *Kitchen*. Recipes, stores orders, kitchen orders, menus.
3 *Restaurant*. Menus, order pads, customer bills, credit card vouchers, cash summaries.

The interaction between the data, the storage systems and ownership of the data inhibits the flow of information and the effective system to provide meaningful information on which to base management decisions. An MIS must overcome these inherent difficulties and provide, for the stakeholders, the confidence that the manual system provides. It will extend the current capability by allowing the concurrent accessing and processing of the data drawn from this wide variety of sources. Thus a computer based system that can provide that degree of facility through common storage and access to data relevant to all of the facets of the food and beverage operation will significantly enhance the operational capability and managerial effectiveness.

The major components of a food and beverage system of any kind are the 'ingredients' and 'recipes'. The ingredients are items of stock used in quantities suitable for processing into products through the control mechanism of a recipe. This principle applies equally to beverages as it does food. From this simple premise the entire production, monitoring and control system and cycle can be seen in terms of the interrelationships between the ingredients and recipes. Provided that data relating to all aspects of the ingredients and recipes can be captured and stored in a coherent systemized and accessible way, all of the relevant management information required can be provided. In developing a computer based MIS, therefore, the ingredients and recipes are key. The classification of the data and the structure of the files in which the data are stored provide the mechanism by which the food and beverage system accesses, retrieves and processes the data into meaningful information. Examples of the data structure of the computer files are shown in Table 18.1, which indicates the data stored against each file.

The ingredients relate to stock items, the recipe to the combination of ingredients required for the production of recipes into meals elements and thence those elements combined into meals. The ingredients costs are identified through the stock control system, that in turn derives those costs from suppliers.

The recipe costs are calculated from the sum of the ingredients costs and the meal costs from the sum of the recipe costs. Thus cost as a control activity can be monitored throughout the process. Sales revenue derived

Table 18.1   Data structures of computer files

Ingredients	
Item type	Vegetables, fresh
Name	Potatoes
Unit of purchase	20 kg sack
Unit of use	lb/kg
Supplier 1	Covent Garden
Supplier 2	Market Supplies plc
Cost per unit of purchase	£5.98
Stock reorder level	3 sacks
Stock level	1 sack
Locations	
Location type	Supplier/store/kitchen/sales
Address	
Stockholding	Yes/no
Recipes	
Recipe type	Fish
Name	Salmon en croute
Ingredient 1	Salmon
Quantity	1 whole
Ingredient 2	Puff pastry
Quantity	2 lb
Ingredient 3	
Portions	10

from selling meals is then able to be directly related to the individual units of production – the recipe, dish or complete meal.

The following shows the major features of the food and beverage MIS system:

Ingredient/stock sub system
- Control and document all food-stock items (ingredients) by classification and individual item.
- Record and cost all food-store transactions throughout the unit.
- Calculate values of stores issued, held and demanded, within automatic updating on price changes.
- Maintain food stores levels in all stock locations.
- Record automatically, at the point of entry or exit from stores, all stock movements by destination, ingredient, types and costs.
- Generate purchase orders based on reorder levels.
- Record purchase orders status, i.e. deliveries awaited, and those partially fulfilled.

- Update stock levels on receipt of purchase orders.
- Calculate stock-usage data and generate stock-usage report.
- Prompt for unit stock checks and generate period-end reports.

Recipes/menu planning subsystem
- The compilation of menus from an index of recipes.
- The storage of cycle of menus.
- The calculation of the specific ingredient requirements based on compiled menu.
- The generation of a stores requisition to meet the ingredient requirements.
- The costing of individual recipes.
- The costing of total meal requirements.
- The ability to plan costed meals for routine and special functions.
- The analysis of historical data to indicate food usage by type, and to provide a database for developing a demand model.

Other features of the MIS could include: selling price tariffs that can be set at any given percentage. For example, if the aim is to make 25 per cent GP plus VAT (@17.5 per cent), a calculation formula of 42.5 per cent is set up, and the selling price could be recalculated at any time and would recognize all changes in ingredient costs.

The use of such a system does not mean that the intuitive 'decision-making' becomes redundant; on the contrary, the manager can still call upon his intuition but it means that he can reduce the margins by accessing all of the relevant information, thus making him more competitive. Equally, a production manager can plan a production run for any given number of customers without actually using any food items, this resulting in a more accurate costing and ordering of food item. The food once ordered and distributed to various locations can, if required, be tracked down and its usage assessed.

For example, food ordered to produce x number of portions must be verified when the production has been completed; thus any variances would be pinpointed to a specific location and usually narrowed down to specific individuals. The system can therefore monitor operational activity in terms of the cost of ingredients, recipes, production and sales all against established targets. Such variances against targets provide not only a measure of operational performance, but indicate the effectiveness of the discrete elements of the entire food and beverage area. These measures of performance against budgets or norms are critical to the decision process and the role of an MIS in improving managerial effectiveness. The presentation of relevant information within an appropriate timescale allows for management intervention to correct operational variances almost immediately, to avoid delayed and often dramatic control measures to

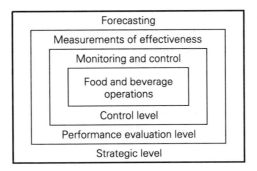

Figure 18.2 Model of MIS functions

reduce variances. Thus the system is a management tool that has direct and immediate control functions and is a storage device from which historical data can be drawn to assist in the long-range and strategic planning process. This range of functions is shown in Figure 18.2.

Such a system can provide information at each operational level, or micro level, for the better management and control, at each level, while also providing the overview of the whole. At the top, or macro level, the holistic view of the food and beverage operation also can provide consolidated information for longer term and strategic decisions.

The micro level

At this level, the nature of information required is precise and usually relates to a single element or activity. For example, it may be the price of a specific food item or the cost of an individual recipe. This affects the ownership of that information. That is to say, while the information may be available to those who have access to the system, it may only be relevant to the chef and the storekeeper. Equally the cost of beer may only be of importance to the barkeeper. The food and beverage manager, on the other hand, may use the information both for 'micro level' and 'macro level' use. That is to say, he or she may wish to point out to the storekeeper or chef that the fillet of beef is cheaper elsewhere, while at the same time make use of the same information when pricing menus for a function or using the stock figures derived from the stock control sheet to control expenditure. The significant factor here is the comparative speed by which the information is available.

Such information could be available soon after the processing of an invoice. Once the visual and manual check for accuracy has been carried out, the information on the invoice can be entered into the system. A flexible and integrated package allows this information to be used at micro and macro level. The data management facilities contained within the software allow the operator to set up the system, and change the parameters when necessary, in such a way that provides control at every level. For example, cost parameters can be set at various percentages, so that when an invoice is processed the system flags any prices which are either higher or lower than the preset parameter, thus providing the 'user' with the opportunity to accept or reject the item based on price comparisons. Compared with the traditional model, where the information may not have come to the surface for a considerable length of time, this instant flagging of price variances means that the operator can make a more learned judgement instead of relying on instinct.

Because the data inputted, when processing the invoice, automatically updates the cost of recipes it means that the food and beverage manager can rely on current recipe costs and not on cost based on historical information.

The macro level

Managing an MIS is not an easy task. Anecdotal evidence from a number of studies seems to support this view. It is often reported that rather than seeing computerized MIS as a helpful tool to achieve efficiency, it can be perceived as a threat to the power, status or authority often derived through the control of data. Once this data and the resultant information are more widely disseminated, the ownership changes and this could affect the current nature of the food and beverage operation. This was noted in the study conducted by Norton and Jones (1992), where the introduction of an MIS into a rigid hierarchical system resulted in significant changes in the power and authority within that organization, highlighting the role of information as the source of power.

There are no easy solutions to this; however, a phased process where key members of staff are involved from the development stage not only provides the opportunity to encourage its use, but also helps to smooth out some of the operational problems, thus making staff feel less threatened.

The use of the system as a forecasting tool, the integration between the operational controls and the recording through the accounts function, the measurements of variances against that planned, are all examples of the utilization of the system at a macro level. It is at this level that the data collected and stored are processed into information to aid the management decision process. The key to effective operation is, however, the skill of the manager to recognize and use the material presented. The sophistication of the system should be such to allow the manager to present the relevant information in a variety of ways to aid that decision process. Unwieldy cumbersome reports and lack of flexibility in interrogating the data will inhibit the use of the system and therefore its effectiveness at this level.

The future

Considerable advances in technology can now integrate food and beverage MIS with other administrative and accounting systems. Direct linkages with suppliers, sophisticated point-of-sale systems, intelligent credit cards, automatic stores recording of receipts and issues using bar code scanners, are all technologies well tried and tested in banking and retail industries. These indicate the potential sophistication for food and beverage systems and the implications for the management of this operational function. Advances in computing power and the opportunities that the development of 'intelligent' systems could bring have even greater potential. It would not be unrealistic to suggest that the entire stores stock order, monitoring and control process would be automated and initiated on the basis of actual sales. Similarly all of the accounting activities could be automatically initiated entirely by an operational transaction. The staff tasks and responsibilities would be significantly affected by these developments and it could be argued that this would displace administrative staff to the benefit of the customer service and operational staff.

The outputs from future systems would combine many of the facilities now found in different software packages: the presentation of menus and wine lists direct from the food and beverage system; dietary and nutritional labelling of menus taken from an integrated dietary and nutritional analysis package; menu and sales optimization based on ingredient availablity related to forecast sales mix and target profits; automated stock management systems that would check supplier availability and price comparators through on-line access to supplier databases and then order in economic order quantities based on forecast stock usage. All these are realistic and realizable developments. As with all such systems, the benefits and advances are entirely reliant on the sophistication of the user. The hotel and catering industry is not noted for its sophistication.

The major implications for the future of food and beverage systems will be the increasing sophistication of software, the speed and processing power of the hardware platforms and the opportunities for the wide-scale network and data integration for the acquisition and transference of information, both internal and external, to the food and beverage operation.

Conclusions

Food and beverage MIS are complex systems that broadly replicate the manual control systems and procedures. They add functionality, and provide timely, pertinent and relevant information to aid the decision process at operational and strategic levels. In addition to the obvious controls, the systems can aid management through: identification of variances against planned targets; improving stock and inventory systems; minimizing stock levels; improving supplier responses; and improving cash flows. The crucial factors of the success of such systems lie entirely with the implementation and the utilization of the system both by the management and the users or stakeholders who can benefit from the system. To optimize the use requires a level of user sophistication in terms of understanding the functionality, the benefits and future opportunities. Such a level of understanding derives largely from the use of the system and a sense of imagination. As Benjamin Disraeli once said: 'Success is a product of unremitting attention to purpose.'

References

Burns, T. R, and Flam, H. (1987). *The Shaping of Social Organization.* California: Sage, 297.

El-Sawy, O. A. (1987). Personal information systems for strategic scanning in turbulent environments. In R. Long (ed.), *New Office Information Technology.* London: Croom Helm.

Emberton, J. (1987). Effective information systems planning and implementation. *Information Age*, **3**, July.

Gamble, P. R. (1994). *Small Computers and Hospitality Management.* London: Hutchinson.

Gamble, P. R. (1992). Corporate strategy in practice. *International Journal of Contemporary Hospitality Management*, **3**(1), 10–15.

Jones, P. (1983). *Food Service Operations.* Eastbourne, UK: Holt, Reinhart and Winston.

Jones, P. A. (1983). The computer and the chef. *International Journal of Hospitality Management*, **3**, 179–180.

Kinton, R. and Ceserani, V. (1989) *The Theory of Catering*, 6th edn. London: Edward Arnold.

Lederer A. and Mendelow, A. L. (1986). *Issues in Information Systems Planning.* North Holland: Elsevier.

Mockker, R. J. (1987). Computer information systems and strategic corporate planning. *Business Horizons*, May–June, pp. 32–37.

Norton, J. and Jones, P. A. (1992). A catering information system in the Armed Forces. In R. Teare, *et al.*, (ed.), *Managing Projects in Hospitality Organisations.* London: Cassell.

Porter, M. E. and Millar, V. E., How information gives you competitive advantage. *Harvard Business Review*, **63**, 149–160.

Raghunthan, T. S. (1988). The impact of information systems planning on the organization, University of Toledo, USA. *Omega International Journal of Science*, **16**(2), 85–93.

Rhodes, D. J. (1991). The facilitator – an organisational necessity for the successful implementation of IT and operations strategies. *Computer-Integrated Manufacturing Systems*, **4**(2), 109–113.

Ryan, D. A. (1989). *Business Aspects of Catering.* Harlow, UK: Longman.

19 Managing profitability

Paul Merricks

Introduction

Planning and control need each other. Alone they are useless. Together they enable managers to improve profitability.

Setting long-term objectives, such as return on capital employed, is the starting point for profit planning and control. These objectives need to be translated into integrated operational, marketing and financial plans. Performance standards are essential for the day-to-day guidance of supervisors and operative employees. A management information system is needed to generate performance information. The control function is that part of management activity which keeps performance in line with plans by comparing actual performance with standards so that corrective action can be taken. This hierarchy of objectives, plans and performance standards is necessary to enable short-term progress to be directed towards the achievement of long-term objectives (Figure 19.1).

Restaurant control techniques have evolved in response to changing environmental pressures. When material costs were the dominant problem area, emphasis was placed on standardized recipes as a foundation for daily calculation of cost and gross profit percentages. Increasing use of convenience foods, with more stable prices, has simplified the material cost control problem for many restaurants.

As wage levels increased, attention turned to labour cost control. Short-term measures of labour utilization highlighted productivity problems for many firms. The resulting search for improvement led to the development of flexible employment structures and more emphasis on employee scheduling. More recently, increased competition has resulted in restaurant control becoming increasingly market orientated, with sales mix analysis techniques such menu engineering focusing attention on pricing and sales promotion issues. Furthermore, the widespread use of computer point-of-sales systems has allowed more accurate and more rapid production of control information, and in many cases has facilitated a shift from post-operational to pre-operational control.

However, outstandingly successful restaurant firms cannot attribute their success to control procedures alone. The key to profitability lies not only with keeping business performance in line with plans, but with the nature of the plan itself. Restaurant chains, with their closely defined concepts, high standardization, limited product ranges and use of convenience foods, have designed out many of the common control problems. For them, profitability is mainly an outcome of their business policies.

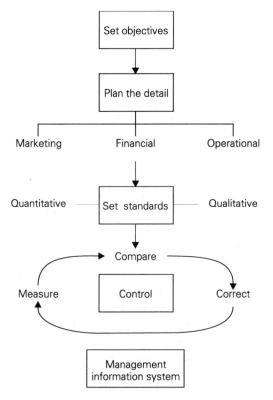

Figure 19.1 The management process

This chapter will, first, examine two case studies of profitable restaurant firms and then will attempt to analyse the policy factors which have contributed to their profitability. Both of the cases illustrate very profitable concepts. Both of the chains are now over twenty-five years old and the facility design, operating procedures and menu have changed little in that time. They have survived and prospered despite heightening competition and turbulent business environments.

Case studies

1   *Courte-Paille – a well tried recipe*

Courte-Paille is a chain of steak houses located at major road intersections in urban and commercial areas in France. Its formula is based on a limited menu of grilled meats, with quick table service.

The first restaurant started in 1966 and the chain developed rapidly. Now part of the Accor Group, the eighty-eight units served 3.5 million meals in 1986.

The Courte-Paille chain relies on a high degree of standardization (Figure 19.2). Each restaurant is a small, round thatched building, with similar layout and décor. In the restaurant, a large wood burning grill with a brick canopy forms the visual focus. A long table runs across the restaurant and smaller tables of four are grouped around the perimeter. The ground floor

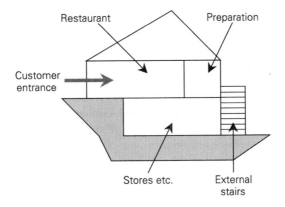

Figure 19.2 Courte-Paille – typical cross-section

contains the restaurant, customer toilets and a small kitchen. Below, reached by external stairs, are the stores, preparation areas and staff facilities. The site is often elevated and is pleasantly landscaped with adequate parking spaces. All units are of the same size, seating sixty-five people inside, with extra tables outside during the summer. All units are open from 10.00 a.m. until 10.00 p.m., seven days a week.

The same menu is served in every unit, and this has changed little since the 1960s. All main courses are meat and are cooked on an open wood fire in the restaurant: andouillette (a sausage made of pig's tripe), chicken thighs, lamb filets, pork chop, sirloin steak, rump steak and entrecôte steak. A salad and french fries are included in the price. Four starters and eight desserts and cheeses complete the standard menu. There is a separate children's menu of beefburger or chicken thighs with fries, followed by apple pie or ice cream. Variation is provided by the short-term promotion (for one, two or three months) of regional dishes and wines, and seasonal foods, e.g. duck or strawberries. There is no bar licence and alcohol can only be served with a meal.

There are four price zones – a minimum tariff, a motorway tariff, Paris tariff, and a tariff for large towns in general. In 1986, average spend was around FF80, and usually consisted of two courses and a drink. The clientele tend to be young; during the day they are mainly people working nearby, and in the evening local residents. In the summer months car travellers constitute a large part of the market for Courte-Paille. During a busy month a unit may serve 6000 meals, with a peak of 300 per day, while during a quieter month only around 4000 meals may be served. A typical day consists of 150–160 meals.

Each unit is staffed by a team of eight employees. The average age of the employees is 26. All training is done at the unit, and the training programme takes one month, except for the grill operator which takes two months. Most of the staff are 'polyvalent', or multi-skilled. They are trained in several aspects of the preparation and service tasks. Exact standard recipes, identical equipment and rigid purchasing specifications enable the production of training videos. Food preparation requires the ability to prepare and grill meat, prepare fries and salad and make apple pie. There are no computerized point-of-sale systems, and little advanced equipment.

Accor's central supplies company, Société Centrale d'Achâts de Produit Alimentaire (SCAPA), can provide all of the supplies necessary to operate a Courte-Paille unit. However, the local manager has no restrictions on using other suppliers if they can be shown to provide purchases of equal specification but lower price. SCAPA provides meat to all of the eighty-eight units and supplies all commodities to forty of the Courte-Paille chain. SCAPA delivers three times each week, from one of their three distribution centres.

All red meats and andouillettes are delivered 'sous-vide' or vacuum packed, and white meats and mince for the burgers are delivered frozen. All meat is delivered pre-portioned and is cooked in full view of the customers. The grill burns birch wood and is lit every morning at 10.00 a.m.

Each unit has a budget of FF1200 for local sales promotion. This may comprise a mix of local radio and cinema advertising. Promotions are often directed at children, with personality visits – such as Father Christmas or free Easter eggs.

The chain has a strong growth record. In recent years, sites for Courte-Paille have been shared with Accor's budget hotel, Formule 1. This eighty-bedroom hotel provides a simple breakfast but no other catering facilities. Courte-Paille is promoted in the hotel, and a Courte-Paille typically gets about fifteen customers per day from an adjacent Formule 1.

2   Benihana comes to London

The first Benihana restaurant opened in Manhattan in 1964. By 1986 there were eighty restaurants, located in most major American cities, and the founder, Rocky Aoki, was a billionaire. The first Benihana in Europe opened in London's Swiss Cottage in August 1986.

The Benihana menu, although based on authentic Japanese cuisine, is far removed from the raw fish associated with a Sushi Bar or traditional Japanese restaurants. In Benihana the dishes are based on steak, chicken, prawn, scallops and lobster, cooked in front of the customers on a teppanyaki or griddle. The stainless steel teppanyaki uses very little oil, making Benihana food both light and low on calories.

In 1986 the inclusive menus were priced at £11.25 to £24.95; this included a starter of light onion soup and a salad. Desserts were priced separately and did not feature strongly on the menu. Saki was £2.85 a bottle, house wine £6.00 and vintage wine up to £27. Average spend was reported to be about £27, or £22 after VAT and service charge is deducted.

What made Benihana quite distinctly different from other Japanese restaurants was the way in which its chefs combine the culinary and performance arts to create the concept of the 'theatre of the table'. Each of the dining tables – or hibachi – seats eight people and their design incorporates a chef's workstation which is used for preparing and cooking the raw ingredients (Figure 19.3).

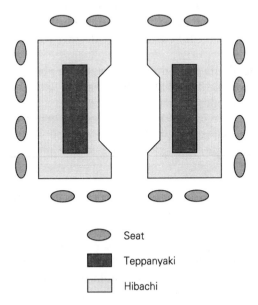

Figure 19.3 The Benihana seating arrangement

On average only 22 per cent of the Benihana's total floor space is devoted to back-of-house areas (kitchen, stores, staff rooms, etc.). The kitchen itself is very small. The main items of kitchen equipment are a rice boiler, stock pot, boiling table, preparation tables and refrigerated storage. The 560 m^2 (6000 ft^2) site at Swiss Cottage has a sixty-seat bar and a restaurant with fourteen teppanyaki, giving a maximum of 114 seats. The teppanyaki are arranged in seven pairs, which is the usual size and configuration for a Benihana restaurant. Rent is typically 7 per cent of sales.

Advertising and promotion costs are reported as about 8 per cent of sales. Word of mouth is the most common way of discovering Benihana and repeat usage is very high. Most customers make reservations and on arrival they are shown into the bar. They typically wait thirty minutes before being shown to their table. Tables of eight people are made up with customers from two or more groups. A sophisticated point-of-sale system – a Remanco RMS 1500 – is necessary to keep track of the complex billing. On average, customers spend ninety minutes at the table, and often on Friday or Saturday nights between 350 and 450 covers are served.

During Friday and Saturday evenings, seven chefs will be working. They pre-portion the food before service and then cook at the teppanyaki during the meal periods. Each chef works with a dining-room assistant. The assistant brings the guests from the bar, then takes their order. The drinks, salad and soup are served by the assistant, who then brings a trolley from the kitchen with the ingredients for the main courses.

The chefs prepare the main courses, employing spectacular knife-work and artistic food presentation, as well as occasional juggling tricks with the utensils. Once the main courses have been served, the assistant clears the teppanyaki and offers a limited choice of desserts. Coffee is served in the bar.

For a typical Benihana restaurant, beverages are about 30 per cent of total sales. Food costs are 30–35 per cent of food sales, and beverage costs are 20 per cent of beverage sales. Labour costs are reported between 10 and 12 per cent of total sales. The unit is run by a team of general manager, deputy manager and two assistants.

Discussion

Is there a common thread which can explain these two different examples of profitable businesses? It would be difficult to transfer ideas from one to the other with success; Courte-Paille could not employ Benihana's reservation and customer scheduling system, neither would Benihana benefit from Courte-Paille's multi-skilled staff. Profitability seems to result from the way in which specific techniques have been fitted together in response to the external environment of the businesses.

Heskett (1986) proposes a 'Strategic Service Vision' (as a framework for analysing a service business. Heskett identifies four basic elements which must fit well together: the target market segments, the service concept, the operating strategy, and the service delivery system.

Target market
- How can the total market for similar products be segmented to allow more specific understanding of customer needs, values and behaviour?
- Which are the most potentially profitable segments and how are their needs being met by competitors?

Service concept
- What benefits and outcomes does this business intend to produce?
- How is it intended that the market perceives the business and these outcomes?

Operating strategy
- How are resources deployed to deliver the service concept to the target market profitably?
- What part is played by operations, financing, marketing, organization, human resources and quality and cost control?
- How should the business perform in relation to the competition?
- What results are expected in terms of quality, cost profile, productivity, employee commitment?

Service delivery system
- What is the capacity of the system and how can it respond to fluctuations in demand?
- How does the system provide differentiation and barriers to entry in respect of competitors?
- What are the important features of the system?
- How do employees, technology, facilities, location, procedures, materials and customers contribute to success?

Ingenuity in one element alone will not guarantee success. Profitability should follow when all these elements are individually well conceived, and when they fit together to make a coherent business system.

Both Benihana and Courte-Paille have established themselves as leaders in closely defined target market segments. Courte-Paille is aimed at French motor travellers who like grilled meat. Benihana aims at people out for an unusual and entertaining meal, both for business purposes and family celebrations.

Benihana's service concept is to provide an intensive, exotic and entertaining experience with little perceived risk. The image is of luxury and personal service. The 'Japanese-style' food is prepared in front of customers from familiar prime ingredients. The work of the chef provides the entertainment element, in an oriental atmosphere. Courte-Paille creates a welcoming French farmhouse kitchen with familiar, plain food cooked to order and served promptly. Children are looked after and lone travellers given the opportunity to join others at the long table. The priority given to car parking and toilets recognizes the needs of motor travellers.

The business strategy of the two firms differs considerably. Courte-Paille is largely limited to the French hexagon and relies on support from corporate resources. In particular, it gains economies of scale through SCAPA's one-drop delivery system, enabling better margins on grilled meats than most competitors. The polyvalent workforce is supported by carefully designed operating procedures and centrally supported training packages. Local managers are encouraged to develop the business, including control of local advertising initiatives, but with support from central marketing which produces materials for building brand loyalty, such as route maps, and 'shells' for local press or radio advertising. Site search and development are important centralized functions, but each new unit is largely a repeat of the standard designs. Developing improved building methods is important, as improved designs allow earlier payback and more efficient operation. Quality audit is given emphasis and a management training centre builds a chain culture among a geographically dispersed team.

Benihana is a worldwide chain which aims to have only one or two very large units in each major city. The highly specialized technology and skills needed to set up and run a Benihana unit require the support of mobile senior management who can undertake trouble-shooting and training assignments. Resourcing for materials and human resources needs to be undertaken independently by each unit. Strong public relations and international advertising support is necessary, particularly aimed at the international traveller. The large sites are often difficult to find in prime city centre sites and each scheme requires separate and detailed treatment. The highly skilled Hibachi chefs are critical to the success of the chain; the organization structure, reward and training systems must recognize this.

Of course, the design of the service delivery systems is essential to the profitability of each chain. Benihana needs a high-technology investment per seat, not only for the teppanyaki but also for the efficient air conditioning necessary to allow cooking in front of customers. This high investment needs a high capacity. The bar acts as a store of customers queuing to enter the restaurant, and of customers who have completed their meal. The arrival in the bar is timed well before the restaurant table is scheduled to be vacant; this allows the opportunity to sell drinks and to assemble the table of eight guests. Sitting strangers together probably would not be successful for an intimate meal, but Benihana is in some respects more like a theatre than a restaurant and table-sharing creates no problems.

The menu offers a number of set meals comprising the same basic ingredients, at a wide range of prices allowing for selling up. The preparation and service time for each set meal is similar. The timing of the meal is largely controlled by the service staff and at the end of the meal customers are charmingly moved to the bar. Complex scheduling such as this is made easier by an appropriate point-of-sales system, but the payoff is high. This batch processing allows very high-capacity utilization.

The Benihana service delivery system also facilitates very high labour productivity. Part of this is due to capacity scheduling, but job design plays a major part. The job design of the chef and the waiting assistant, and the timing of the meal, allow the two staff to serve two tables in a synchronized delivery; while the chef is working at one table, the waiter is usually working at the other. Furthermore, the labour costs can easily be varied in relation to forecast variations in demand; when five pairs of Teppanyaki are in operation, only five pairs of chefs and waiters are needed. The kitchen brigade, which normally represents a fixed cost, is minimal.

The limited number of food commodities which are used in Benihana require minimum pre-preparation and there is little resulting waste. The limited range of foodstuffs make stock control relatively simple, and this is aided by the sales and stock analysis functions of the point-of-sale system. Preparation equipment is highly specialized, but a limited range of equipment is used.

In Courte-Paille, customers are shown directly to a table. Orders are taken, and food prepared to order. The Courte-Paille service delivery system also achieves high levels of labour productivity, but unlike the specialization of Benihana, this system relies on the functional flexibility of polyvalent employees who can perform any and all of the operative tasks. Unlike Benihana, Courte-Paille uses little modern technology, matching the wood-burning grill with its farmhouse image. The facilities' design allows rapid construction of a unit which finally appears to have been built on high ground beside the road; with its distinctive pointed roof it is easily seen from a long way off and this creates instant merchandising.

In summary, each of these restaurants is profitable, but the factors leading to success in each case are different. However, each of them has synergy between its target market, service concept, business strategy and service delivery system. It is not the individual policies alone which lead to profitability, but their integration into a coherent business idea.

Both Benihana and Courte-Paille demonstrate how robust concepts can continue to be profitable despite changes in competition and a turbulent business environment. From the customer perspective, their menus have hardly changed in twenty-five years. Interestingly, neither has tried to differentiate its product by the style of the food alone. In fact both of them prepare a limited number of high-quality ingredients with simple culinary techniques. Like the menu, the interior design concept has changed little.

Over time, both chains have replaced some traditional building materials with more functional and durable modern equivalents. Benihana's antique Japanese artefacts have been replaced with a modern symbolic Japanese interior design; Courte-Paille have found a fireproof and long-life roofing material to replace thatch – but the look and feel of the units are unmistakable.

Both chains have found a 'best operating level' – a seating capacity and configuration which allows optimum profitability. It is doubtful if any chain hits this ideal at first attempt – of course, informed management is important, but the benefits of chain development include the opportunity to get it righter next time.

Heskett (1986) also stresses the importance of 'Value/Cost Leveraging' as a component of a successful service. By this he means the deployment of resources in a way which adds maximum perceived value to the service concept with minimum cost. The application of a little cost to lever up the perceived value should be accompanied by healthy profit margins and high repeat sales, as demonstrated by both Benihana and Courte-Paille. Unique atmosphere and distinctive personal service are used to advantage, adding value and profit margins to ordinary food ingredients. Courte-Paille's wood-burning grill forms a focal point in the restaurant design and reinforces the farmhouse image, but at the same time adding interest. Benihana serves cocktails in white china tankards in the shape of various Japanese mythological figures. Not only does this help sell high-margin drinks, but the tankard can be taken home and displayed as tangible evidence of the experience and will provide a prompt to the all-important word-of-mouth promotion.

A further factor in the Heskett's 'Strategic Service Vision' concerns positioning, or the creation of an image and product offer that enables the market segment to understand the difference between the business and its competitors. Benihana has established itself in a luxury product position and stresses the entertainment value – 'The Theatre of the Stomach'. The communication channels selected reflect its position, with heavy use of 'aditorial' in glossy magazines. It has also positioned itself as a slightly exotic experience but with limited risk; a previous advertising campaign promised 'No icky, slithery, slimy stuff', explaining that this was a Japanese restaurant with steak and lobster but no raw fish!

In London, it proved impossible for Benihana to find the required large site in the West End. However, the Swiss Cottage location – adjacent to some of the best residential accommodation in London – provided an interesting opportunity. Many restaurants use special promotions to fill capacity in the early evening. However, with a luxury, high-margin product, price reduction could merely result in potential customers trading down and even worse could destroy some of the perceived value. Benihana adopted a different position for its early evening business. It aimed early evening promotions for children at a much reduced price. Not only did this fill the restaurant with up-market children's birthday parties, but the resulting word-of-mouth promotion reached the affluent parents who were the prime target market.

Courte-Paille established itself in a high-value position, with a limited menu of grilled meats of consistently high quality at a competitive price. The theme of the restaurant and the cooking method established gave it a traditional image, which differentiated it strongly from other roadside chains. The distinctive building was associated with the brand and provided its own promotion to the target market of motor travellers.

Conclusions

Benihana and Courte-Paille are profitable, but each has very different business policies which lead to success. Heskett's 'Strategic Service Vision' provides a useful framework for analysing the factors leading to success and the way in which they fit together.

Both businesses have evolved operating systems which deploy resources in an efficient and effective manner – without waste and without prejudicing quality. However, neither of them seems to derive great benefit from the traditional techniques of restaurant control. Meticulous attention to market segmentation, the communication of the service concept, the refinement of operating strategies and the design of the service delivery system hold the key to the management of profitability.

Reference

Heskett, J. L. (1986). *Managing in the Service Economy.* Boston: Harvard University School Press.

20 Productivity improvement

Jim Pickworth

Introduction

Foodservice, like many other service industries, has shown lacklustre productivity performance. In fact, from 1979 to 1985, hotels and catering were the only sector with a fall in the output per head (Medlik, 1989). Yet, managers, economists and academics all seem to agree on the importance of productivity improvement (Ball and Johnson, 1989; Jones, 1990; Lundberg, 1991). So why is there such a discrepancy between intent and performance?

Implicit in the above question is an assumption that we all agree on what productivity means. Although few people would disagree that productivity focuses on the ratio of inputs to outputs, it is when the need for further clarification arises that differing schools of thought emerge. For some, productivity improvement is principally a matter of training, monetary incentives and management style; while for others, it is primarily a question of time and motion studies and of acquiring labour-saving equipment.

Essentially, it would appear that how we set about improving productivity depends on what we conceive it to be in the first place. In fact, it seems our notions of productivity tend to reflect our disciplinary predispositions. Before we can really tackle the issue of productivity improvement, we need to reconcile these differing notions by briefly reviewing how economists, management scientists and behavioural scientists have each made contributions to this area, while also identifying those issues that seem to confuse us.

The economist's contribution

The concept of productivity originated with economists as a means to assess how well a company managed its factors of production, e.g. capital and labour. Over time, two basic types of productivity have emerged – total factor and partial factor. Total factor productivity relates to how well a company uses all of its combined resources, whereas partial factor productivity focuses on the performance of a specific factor of production such as labour.

For the most part, relatively little attention has been directed towards total factor productivity, primarily due to measurement difficulties. (For a fuller discussion of the issues involved here, the reader is referred to two studies by Brown and Hoover, 1990 and 1991.) Much more emphasis has been placed on partial factor measures such as labour productivity, and there are a number of reasons for this. First, the labour-intensive nature of the industry encourages this focus. Secondly, it is easier to measure employee productivity compared with capital productivity, since the latter may be defined in varying terms either as capital invested or capital employed, and also has to be measured over time. Thirdly, national economic statistics highlight labour output per hour, and this, it can be argued, leads us to equate productivity with employee productivity.

This tendency to consider productivity in terms of employees imposes constraints on management that can restrict our approach to productivity improvement. Unfortunately, many improvement programmes rely on exhorting employees to work harder, only to find it difficult to sustain such strategies. After a while, employees realize that management is having another 'push' on productivity and, if they just 'go through the motions' it will fade away.

Worse still are improvement strategies which, at first sight, seem to boost productivity when in fact they might do the reverse. For instance, one frequently hears foodservice managers say that 'we purchased some new labour-saving equipment and productivity shot up'. In the short term, labour productivity may well have increased, but capital productivity will have declined because more money is now being ploughed back into the operation without necessarily increasing sales. Whether *overall* productivity improves in the long term depends on the extent to which the savings generated exceed the original capital outlay, as well as on the operating and opportunity costs incurred. In short, by focusing unintentionally on labour productivity, foodservice managers may delude themselves into thinking they have improved total factor productivity.

Even measuring labour productivity can be problematical. It is generally agreed that productivity improvement cannot be at the expense of quality. However, due to the difficulty of measuring quality, the accepted practice has been to assume that the quality of inputs and outputs remains unchanged. In other words, quality is usually regarded as a constant with quantity being the variable.

The practice of ignoring quality considerations has now been widely questioned (Leonard and Sasser, 1982; Thor, 1983). Also, the intangible nature of the foodservice product, i.e. the meal experience, raises a number of questions. Should managers think of 'output' as 'meals produced' or 'customers satisfied'? For instance, has labour productivity improved if one food server handles twenty customers in an hour while another serves thirty customers? Can quality be assumed to be constant? Lundberg (1991) argues that 'the key to productivity in services becomes a matter of quality as much as quantity'. Indeed, the widely held notion that productivity can only be raised at the expense of quality, and vice versa, is also being challenged. Companies do not have to consider productivity and quality improvement as an 'either/or' proposition. The convergence of these two concepts and their potential for creating synergy has been discussed by Pickworth and Haywood (1988).

The implicit issue being raised here is whether productivity should continue to be viewed primarily as an economic concept when behavioural factors are so influential in determining quality levels.

The management scientist's contribution

For many years, industrial engineering techniques have been used to measure and improve productivity. Despite the negative connotations of time study, management scientists have developed increasingly sophisticated and effective techniques for improving operational efficiency.

Yet, the question arises as to whether the focus should be extended beyond efficiency to encompass effectiveness. The traditional emphasis has always been on how efficiently an operation converts its inputs, such as food, beverages and labour, into outputs. Another school of thought argues that management needs also to focus on how well objectives have been identified and resources deployed in the first place (Mali, 1978; Shetty and Buehler, 1985).

To be efficient is not necessarily to be effective. For instance, a restaurant could be managed very efficiently, yet be heading for bankruptcy due to poor financial structuring. Should such a company be rated highly on its productive use of resources? Also, we should bear in mind Ellsworth Statler's well-known adage regarding the secret of successful hotel management, 'location, location, location'. Doesn't this suggest that operational efficiency will not make up for ineffective strategic decisions?

The issue here, then, is whether our conception of productivity should be broadened to include an effectiveness dimension. If so, it follows that we should view productivity from a strategic as well as from a tactical operational perspective.

The behavioural scientist's contribution

Behavioural scientists have tended to place less emphasis on measurement issues and have focused instead on improving employee output. From its earliest days, behavioural researchers have been aware that improving working conditions, e.g. the Hawthorne experiments, or applying time and motion studies, will not necessarily enhance employee productivity. If employees are poorly selected, ill-trained and demotivated, then no matter how well-designed and well-equipped an operation may be, productivity can only be improved to a certain degree.

For these reasons, behavioural scientists have studied closely the relationship between job satisfaction and productivity. While many studies indicate that high employee satisfaction does contribute to long term productivity by reducing absenteeism, pilferage, staff turnover, etc., the relationship in the short run is confused (Sutermeister, 1976). For example, some employees may work very hard to get a promotion or transfer from one restaurant because of intense job dissatisfaction, whereas other employees may have high job satisfaction because they can sit and socialize all day! Thus, satisfied employees may not be productive employees, and vice versa.

What seems to be established beyond much doubt is the element of 'contingency' in many behavioural techniques. The impact of such techniques as quality circles, empowerment and pay for performance seems to depend (i.e. be contingent) on the situation. What may work well in some situations, may not work very satisfactorily in others. Although this 'contingency' element is a source of ongoing confusion, several studies have pointed to management ineffectiveness and middle management resistance as one of the most serious obstacles to productivity improvement (Judson, 1982; Schlesinger and Heskett, 1991).

Increasing management effectiveness has long since been the focus of organizational development programmes. However, it is now becoming clear that improvements in productivity (and for that matter, quality as well) are the result of 'a new way of thinking' that needs to be infused into the organizational culture. Further, changing an organization's culture implies more than changes in its structure and processes; it really does mean a realignment of management and employee expectations. Indeed, from a behavioural scientist's perspective, it could be argued that productivity improvement is a process of social change in which the inputs are expectations and the outputs are satisfactions.

In reality, a more pragmatic approach predominates, and productivity only comes into 'vogue' during recessions as a 'cover' for cost cutting. However, the severity of the recent recession has forced top management to view productivity from a more strategic and long-term perspective, as opposed to series of quick fixes. Sheer necessity has forced this long overdue reassessment of the importance of productivity. The process of redeploying resources, e.g. closing operations and de-layering, has been very painful with the benefits barely yet in evidence.

The contribution of behavioural scientists, then, has been to challenge some underlying assumptions about productivity improvement. Should it be viewed from a strategic, proactive perspective as well as from a tactical, operational perspective? If so, shouldn't productivity improvement extend beyond being primarily technique-oriented to stress the importance of changing corporate culture?

Reconceptualizing productivity

Until now, the organizing principle behind productivity has been largely drawn along disciplinary lines. This framework is now becoming less helpful. In an extensive review of the factors or variables influencing productivity (Pickworth, 1982), it was concluded that these could be summarized most logically according to their area of impact on the organization (Figure 20.1).

A basic premise in reconceptualizing productivity is to state that it should consider *all* inputs and *all* outputs. Consequently, the concept has to be broadened beyond solely economic concerns to include social dimensions. By thinking of productivity as a multidisciplinary concept that focuses on optimizing social as well as economic inputs and outputs, new insights begin to emerge. It is possible to reconcile a number of issues raised earlier, if we view productivity as an aggregate concept consisting of a hierarchy of components (Figure 20.2).

The most important component of productivity has been termed 'corporate productivity'. It is concerned with how *effectively* corporate objectives have been identified and how *effectively* resources have been deployed. Since these decisions are strategic and long term in nature, they are of prime concern to top management.

Assuming that corporate productivity is being optimized, the next priority is to focus on partial factor productivity to ensure that each resource, e.g. capital and human resources, is being administered competently. Accountants, human resource managers, etc., have an abundance of techniques available to them to audit the performance of their respective resources.

The next component in the hierarchy encompasses the traditional notion of productivity, namely, efficiency. The term 'operational productivity' has been used, since the focus here is basically tactical, and it is of concern primarily to middle and unit managers. Numerous industrial engineering and behavioural science techniques have been applied in this area to reduce costs consistent with quality standards, while marketing techniques have similarly been applied to boost sales – the output dimension.

The final component, 'employee productivity', is concerned with the actual performance of each employee compared with his/her potential. By selecting and training effectively, an organization can build up a core of capable employees. However, whether they will actually perform according

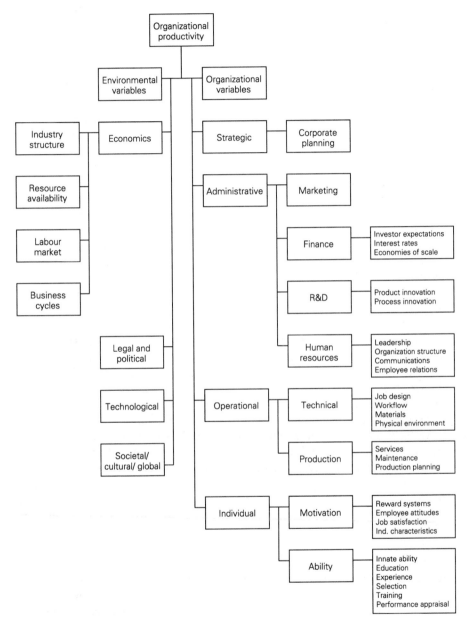

Figure 20.1 Framework of the main variables influencing organizational productivity

to their potential capacity, i.e. be empowered, would seem to be largely a matter of motivation.

By thinking of productivity as an aggregate concept consisting of a hierarchy, a more comprehensive approach to its productivity improvement can be pursued. The first step is to ensure that corporate productivity is on track; otherwise efforts aimed at improving other productivity components will be misdirected. Next, each productivity component in the hierarchy needs to be assessed and strategies for improvement identified. Some of the major approaches to productivity improvement have been summarized in Table 20.1.

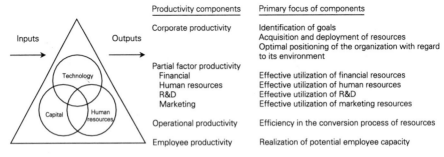

Productivity components	Primary focus of components
Corporate productivity	Identification of goals
	Acquisition and deployment of resources
	Optimal positioning of the organization with regard to its environment
Partial factor productivity	
Financial	Effective utilization of financial resources
Human resources	Effective utilization of human resources
R&D	Effective utilization of R&D
Marketing	Effective utilization of marketing resources
Operational productivity	Efficiency in the conversion process of resources
Employee productivity	Realization of potential employee capacity

Figure 20.2 Hierarchy of components in organizational productivity

Indeed, it would be possible to extend this summary much further by listing the many improvement techniques that are available. Many of these approaches have been discussed elsewhere (Witt and Witt, 1989; Jones, 1990). Although such techniques can make a significant contribution to raising productivity, they are essentially reactive inasmuch as the focus is usually directed at improving an *existing* operation. An alternative, and more proactive, strategy is to build productivity (and quality) *into* the basic design of an operation. The value of a more systematic approach to productivity improvement has been stressed by others (Schlesinger and Heskett, 1991; Jones 1993).

A systematic approach to productivity improvement

Hospitality operations, like most other service businesses, share a common characteristic, namely that the marketing and production activities are integrated at the service delivery level. In fact, the term 'service delivery system' is often used to describe an operation in which products/services are created and delivered to the customer almost simultaneously.

Table 20.1 Major strategies for productivity improvement

Corporate productivity	Partial factor productivity	Operational productivity	Employee productivity
Primary focus • Identification of goals, acquisition and deployment of resources, optimization of short- and long-term utilization of resources	*Primary focus* • Effective utilization of each resource, e.g. financial, human resources	*Primary focus* • Efficient conversion of resources into products/services	*Primary focus* • Realization of potential employee capacity
Possible approaches • Primary emphasis on raising outputs, i.e. growth through acquisitions, increased sales; capital expenditure to increase capacity; product R. & D., etc., with effective marketing being a critical activity • Primary emphasis on lowering inputs, e.g. cost effectiveness through downsizing; reducing costs; improving supplier productivity; capital expenditure to lower operating costs, e.g. automation process R. & D., etc., with effective control being a critical activity • Primary emphasis on instilling employees at every level with the need to improve productivity through establishing a conducive organization climate including appropriate reward systems, effective communication, etc., with the continual projection of corporate values being a critical activity	*Possible approaches* • Financial: reduce capital requirements, e.g. down-sizing, leasing, franchising • Human resources: reduce labour requirements through capital substitution, i.e. automation; improve performance of all employees in terms of quality and quantity; subcontracting work • R. & D.: reduce costs or improve quality through an appropriate balance of product and process innovation; develop R. & D. internally or externally; focus on larger projects or a series of smaller ones • Marketing: increase profitablity through manipulating the marketing mix to provide larger market shares (volume) or to provide greater margins (prices); reduce marketing costs, e.g. reduce product range, promotion, distribution costs	*Possible approaches* • Problem orientated to remove specific obstacles to improving operational productivity, e.g. industrial engineering • Systems orientated to optimize the overall conversation process, e.g. service delivery systems; sociotechnical analysis; just-in-time deliveries • Capacity orientated to align demand to supply, e.g. manipulating demand, raising process speeds and throughput	*Possible approaches* • Human resource management orientated to develop and maintain appropriate selection, training, performance, feedback, etc. • Structurally orientated to improve the work environment, e.g. job redesign • Gain-sharing orientated to share the benefits of increased productivity and to align employee goals closer to organizational goals, e.g. incentive schemes • Participation orientated to foster employee contributions and commitment, e.g. quality circles, MBO, empowerment, etc.

A vital key to developing any successful service delivery system is to build in desirable productivity and quality features from its inception. Such a process may take the form of 'blueprinting', whereby specific bottlenecks in service delivery systems can be identified during the design stages (Shostak, 1984). However, in order to apply such techniques it is helpful to have a conceptual framework to facilitate the critical examination of any proposed service delivery system.

The value of conceptualizing a service delivery system in this fashion lies in the ability to provide a structured way of analysing the relationships between various activities within an operation. The basic components of a typical service delivery system and some of the basic design issues are shown in Figure 20.3 (Pickworth, 1988).

The starting point in the design process is to develop the overall marketing strategy. It is essential to clearly define the product concept. Schlesinger and Heskett (1991) stress this point, 'at the heart of this new approach to service are the needs and expectations of customers as customers, not the operating system and its constraints, define them'. They continue by citing the example of Taco Bell.

> Taco Bell's new model is based on a very simple premise: customers value the food, the service, and that is all. Everything that helps the company deliver value to customers along these dimensions deserves reinforcement and management support. Everything else is a non-value overhead. The brilliance of this strategy lies in its execution: Taco Bell's management examined every aspect of the restaurant operation.

Although an operation's production strategy will reflect basic marketing strategies, a series of decisions have to be made concerning service levels. For example, service levels relating menu variety, waiting times and hours of operation need to be translated into operational performance standards. Indeed, service levels will often be used as a means of product differentiation, e.g. guaranteed service and/or delivery times, degree of customization, freshness, speed, convenience, etc.

The choice of technology for a service delivery system also has important implications. For instance, a lack of equipment flexibility can limit the ease with which new markets can be pursued; Kentucky Fried Chicken would be one example. Some companies have incurred considerable costs in retrofitting their delivery systems with equipment to serve additional menu offerings. As might be expected, much thought needs to be given to the layout component to ensure appropriate flows of materials, information, employees and customers. Various techniques may be used to this end, such as CAD, flow charts, etc.

The management of capacity is another critical issue because production and seating capacities have to be balanced with demand. Determining the

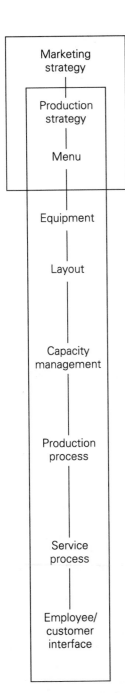

Marketing strategy	▸ customization as opposed to speed and standardization ▸ determination of service levels ▸ use of product differentiation
Production strategy	▸ finish-to-order rather than ready-to-serve ▸ degree of on-site v. off-site production ▸ attaining a fundamental system balance
Menu	▸ degree of menu flexibility ▸ identification of dayparts ▸ differentiating menu items
Equipment	▸ degree of built-in quality control ▸ labour-saving potential ▸ technological flexibility
Layout	▸ allocation of space between service and production areas ▸ appropriate seating configuration ▸ provision for ancillary service facilities ▸ number of service stations
Capacity management	▸ capacity analysis to ensure supply matches potential demand ▸ reliable forecasting methods ▸ ability for the system to operate with the fewest possible employees during off-peak periods ▸ built-in provisions to deal with excess demand
Production process	▸ extensive use of specifications ▸ centralized vs. diffused control of the production system ▸ accurate and reliable communications system ▸ establishment of standard service times ▸ use of self-service techniques to maximize throughput and minimize costs
Service process	▸ use of service blueprints to identify potential problem areas ▸ provision of features to shape customer expectations ▸ procedures to minimize the adverse impact of queuing
Employee/ customer interface	▸ effective employee scheduling ▸ use of suggestive selling ▸ appropriate management culture that engenders commitment to organizational goals ▸ socio-technical system that facilitates employee motivation

Figure 20.3 Model of a service delivery system (*Source*: Pickworth, 1988. Reproduced with the permission of the *International Journal of Hospitality Management*)

size or capacity of a service delivery system is an extremely important decision. From a productivity perspective, the issue is one of effectiveness rather than efficiency. If an operation is too large, even though it may be efficiently managed, it may nevertheless be unprofitable due to lack of customer throughput. Insufficient revenue is being generated to provide an adequate return on a capital investment that is larger than necessary. On the other hand, if the operation is too small, quality might be compromised as customers are expedited through the system in order to generate sufficient revenue.

However, once the operation is built, it becomes important to manage capacity by manipulating *demand* through the use of such techniques as off-peak pricing, coupons, etc. Likewise, thought needs to be given as to how *capacity* can be manipulated using techniques such as self-service, cross-training, preset menus, etc. The significance of thinking through capacity management issues is that it provides for future operational flexibility (Brotherton and Coyle, 1990). For instance, the provision of outside patio seating builds in additional capacity (weather permitting), while also providing customers with a choice as to their location of eating.

The remaining components of the service delivery system model relate to the service process and the consumer experience. The term 'consumer experience' is used to describe the combined physical and psychological impact of all the specific service experiences or encounters that occur during the entire service process. Whenever a customer and an employee interact, there is a 'moment of truth' (Carlzon, 1987). Will the employee behave in a way that will reflect the company's concern for customer satisfaction? The manner in which employees do, in fact, actually respond is subject to many variables such as the existing level of business, their own personality, supervisory styles, etc. However, it can be asserted that, if the service delivery system is poorly designed with built-in hassles, inefficiencies and friction points, the likelihood of a positive employee response is con-siderably diminished. Indeed, service productivity has been defined as 'a function of the efficient use of non-human resources on the one hand and customer perception of quality service on the other hand. ... It is the ratio of service-enhancing encounters which creates a perception of quality service' (Lundberg, 1991).

In a perfectly designed service delivery system, there should be equilibrium between supply and demand within each component of the system. For instance, customers would not have to wait for service, employees would not stand idle, etc. Inevitably, of course, there will be imbalances and the test of any service delivery system is how quickly it regains its balance. Many foodservice operations seem to be perpetually 'out-of-sync', and are characterized by haphazard service quality, an inconsistent product quality and a level of productivity that cannot be maintained unless there is constant supervision.

The essential argument being made here is the need to view productivity improvement from a strategic perspective. The current tendency is to conceive of productivity at an operational level, and also to think in terms of applying a host of techniques to improve productivity in an existing operation. Such an approach will frequently prove beneficial, but may be limited in its impact.

An alternative approach is to adopt a broader conception of productivity as consisting of a hierarchy of components that each have to be assessed systematically. By thinking of productivity improvement from a truly multidisciplinary perspective, it is then possible to use the concept of a service delivery system as a means of enhancing both productivity and service quality.

References

Ball, S. and Johnson, K. (1989). Productivity management within fast food chains – a case study of Wimpy International. *International Journal of Hospitality Management*, **8**,(4), 265–269.

Brotherton, B. and Coyle, M. (1990). Managing instability in the hospitality operations environment. *International Journal of Contemporary Hospitality Management*. **2**(3) 24–32.

Brown, D. and Hoover, L. (1990). Productivity measurement in foodservice: past accomplishments – a future alternative. *Journal of American Dietetic Association*, **90**, 973–981.

Brown, D. and Hoover, L. (1991). Total factor productivity modelling in hospital foodservice operations. *Journal of American Dietetic Association*, **91**, 1088–1092.

Carlzon, J. (1987). *Moments of Truth*. New York: Harper & Row.

Jones, P. (1990). Managing foodservice productivity in the long term: strategy, structure and performance. *International Journal of Hospitality Management*, **9**(2), 143–154.

Jones, P. (1993). Foodservice operations management. In *VNR's Encyclopedia of Hospitality and Tourism*. New York: Van Nostrand Reinhold, pp. 27–36.

Judson, A. (1982). The awkward truth about productivity. *Harvard Business Review*, **60**, 92.

Leonard, F and Sasser, W. (1982). The incline of quality. *Harvard Business Review*, **60**, 163–171.

Lundberg, C. (1991). Productivity enhancement through managing the service encounter. *Hospitality Research Journal*, **14**(3), 63–71.

Mali, P. (1978). *Improving Total Productivity: MBO Strategies for Business, Government and Not-For-Profit Organizations*. New York: Wiley.

Medlik, S. (1989). Profit from productivity in tourism. *Tourism*, no. 61, Jan./Feb., pp. 14–15.

Pickworth, J. (1982). *A Multi-Disciplinary Literature Survey of Micro-Level Productivity.* Canada: University of Guelph.

Pickworth, J. (1988). Service delivery systems in the foodservice industry. *International Journal of Hospitality Management,* 7(1), 43–62.

Pickworth, J. and Haywood, M. (1988). Connecting productivity with quality through the design of service delivery systems. *International Conference on Services Marketing,* 5, 261–273.

Schlesinger, L. and Heskett, J. (1991). The service-driven service company. *Harvard Business Review,* 60, 71–81.

Shetty, Y. K. and Buehler, V. M. (1985). *Productivity and Quality Through People.* Conn: Greenwood Press.

Shostak, G. L. (1984). Service positioning through structural change. *Journal of Marketing,* Jan./Feb., pp. 33–39.

Sutermeister, R. (1976). *People and Productivity.* New York: McGraw-Hill, p. 51.

Thor, C. (1983). Productivity measurement in white collar groups. In R. N. Lehrer (ed.), *White Collar Productivity.* New York: McGraw-Hill.

Witt, C. and Witt, S. (1989). Why productivity in the hotel sector is low. *International Journal of Contemporary Hospitality Management,* 1(2), 28–34.

21 Electronic data interchange introduction in the service environment: prerequisites, problems and possibilities

Nicholas Alexander

Introduction

Information technology has already had a major impact on the service environment. The new information technologies are today building on an infrastructure of existing technology-based information systems. Electronic data interchange (Edi) systems are of the new generation of technological development, which are providing organizations with the ability to control operations efficiently, and, more significantly, to more effectively manage interaction with trading partners.

While the introduction of information technology is clearly not limited to the service sector, and has had, through such as computer integrated manufacture (CIM), value added data services (VADS) and Edi (Fleck, 1990), a considerable impact in other sectors of the economy, the development of the service sector and the exploitation of information systems are essentially inseparable (Child and Loveridge, 1990). The fundamental importance of information exchange within service operations has been long recognized. Bell (1973) acknowledged that the exchange of information would be crucial to the creation of value within a service-based economy. However, the potential impact of information technology, while long recognized, has made and continues to make slow progress in some service contexts. Indeed, it is axiomatic that within the process of information technology introduction and exploitation, there exist considerable time lags, between the development of technologies capable of exploitation and their utilization, as there is a time lag between the realization of technological development and organizational response. Observers may well be forgiven for believing that, as far as technology is concerned, much heralded 'revolutionary' developments take a considerable amount of time to appear, and when they do, they are soon superseded by 'new generation' technology. Debit cards, for example, were technologically although not commercially superseded by smart cards by the time electronic funds transfer at point of sale (Eftpos) systems were introduced in the UK.

How the process of change which surrounds the introduction of technology is conceptualized is important in predicting future change and understanding current and past developments. Fleck (1990) has suggested that two broad interpretations appear in the literature. The first asserts that technology is itself a force for change; that is, new technology contributes to the creation of new organizational forms. This follows from the approach of Perez (1985) and Freeman (Freeman *et al.*, 1982), in which new technology is employed by organizations and that an efficient method of exploitation is arrived at through usage. The second approach views technology as the answer to problems which have been caused by social and economic changes. Fleck (1990) notes the work of Beniger (1986) and Hughes (1983) in this respect. Here technological development is a response to a lack of control. Social and economic developments have created situations which demand new technological innovations so that control may be more effective. Innovation following the approach of Hughes (1983) must address the 'reverse salient' which is created through uneven technological development (Fleck, 1990).

According to Fleck (1990, p.11) both interpretations may be considered to be 'partly right and both partly wrong!' Nevertheless, these two approaches provide useful reference points for attempting to understand the process of technological innovation. They are particularly useful in a context where the innovation itself may be utilized to a considerable degree in one commercial context, or role, but remains unemployed or underemployed in another. In such a context, it is easy to assume that technology has not been adopted because it is not suitable to the particular conditions of the industry which has not yet fully adopted the technology. However, if for example the interpretation of Perez (1985) and Freeman *et al.* (1982) is adopted – that industry experiments with technology in order to discover its most efficient uses – then to look at other industrial applications may well lead to a better understanding of its potential uses in another context. Similarly, to adopt the approach of Beniger (1986) and Hughes (1983), then the stresses which have been eradicated or relieved in one context may well still exist in another, but for organizational or environmental reasons the technology has not been employed.

Electronic data interchange: a definition

Edi is a facilitating technology which empowers management and enables management to more fully exploit and control existing technology-based systems, human resources and operational facilities, to respond quickly to customer needs and responses through the exploitation of a technology-based infrastructure and network. It is an inter-company rather than an intra-company technology which involves electronic communication systems.

Cunningham and Tynan (1990, p.3) observe that practitioners often use the expression Edi to describe 'any electronic link which exchanges information between trading firms'. Acknowledging the DTI/Vanguard initiative approach, Cunningham and Tynan (1990) favoured a definition of electronic trading which covered electronic non-verbal communication systems where communication is between person and person (Email), computer and computer (Edi, Eft, common systems), and person and computer (interactive and online systems). This definition draws a distinction between electronic trading and Edi. Edi is one form of electronic trading: in Cunningham and Tynan's definition, computer to computer communication.

Unlike electronic point of sale (Epos) systems, Edi is an inter-company communications system rather than an intra-company system. Edi therefore facilitates enhanced communication between businesses. Whereas Epos allows an individual business to gain information for internal company purposes, Edi systems facilitate the flow of information between organizations. Edi is also, as has been noted above with reference to Cunningham and Tynan's definition, one form of electronic trading and depends on compatible systems within the communicating organizations.

As Epos depends on an infrastructure of bar codes which are universally recognized, so Edi depends on a recognized system, and technology, which drives an Edi approach to trading relationships. Child and Loveridge (1990) point to the establishment of a universal product code (UPC) in the USA, and the European article numbering (EAN) system in Europe, as a prerequisite for the widespread use of Epos systems. They see the lack of a dependable infrastructure as one of the reasons why there is slow or limited roll-out of such systems. The other reasons they note are, the limited capital available for investing in technology systems, and the organizational learning process. These observations, which are based on the adoption of Epos systems, may be transferred to the situation pertaining to Edi system development. The key point, however, within the Edi context would appear to be the willingness of players to accept the new technology and clearly this willingness is based on awareness of and experience of the benefits of new technology systems. Thus, players familiar with the use of in-house systems such as Epos are aware of the information and operational benefits which are received from the system and are therefore willing to advance to the next stage of electronic communication. The next stage in this context is electronic trading, communication between companies, which makes use of the information derived from the in-house information systems already deployed by some players. Therefore, for those players who understand the value of information technology there is the added impetus to move on to the next level of technology. Indeed, there exists the imperative that further development should take place in order to derive the full benefit from previous phases of technological innovation, leaving the organization predeterminedly responsive to new technological developments.

Implementation

Electronic trading and Edi systems introduction is limited by controlling factors: the existing relationships among trading partners; the cost of implementation and the competing demands on financial resources, which are fundamental to any commercial context; but the most crucial issue is the willingness of companies to introduce a technology-based system and the infrastructure on which to base such a system. The development of Edi systems is, therefore, predetermined by the conditions within an industry.

The hotel and restaurant industry has not seen the rapid development of systems (Jesitus, 1991) to the same degree as other industries. Nevertheless, changes have occurred where business needs, systems and operational approaches are such that Edi introduction has proved to be a suitable response. The hotel industry depends on the maximum use of facilities, a crucial issue where there exists an over-supply of rooms (Durocher and Niman, 1991). Adopting the approach of Beniger (1986) and Hughes (1983) to technological introduction, noted above, the industry has reacted to this problem through the use of information systems. Electronic reservation systems are one way that business-to-business electronic trading will impact on the hotel trades' efforts to increase occupancy rates (Salomon, 1992a). The Sheraton Corporation has installed a reservation system which it will seek to utilize as a marketing tool, in recognition of the efficiencies of target marketing (Jaben, 1992). Holiday Inn has claimed it is five years ahead of its rivals with its central reservation system which the organisation claims will help to better manage room nights (Salomon, 1992b). The more efficient use of capacity within the hotel industry is one means by which electronic communication will be employed. However, other needs will demand other responses in different operational areas.

An electronic support system (ESS) provides automated support for Burger King's supply system (Yetter and Bowman, 1990). The development of the ordering systems has been combined with the introduction of improved technology at the point of sale, which will drive the system and lead to supply-based benefits through the creation of information which will support ordering, stocktaking and sales forecasting. For the manager of the Burger King outlet, the Edi system will seek to provide system which reduces the problems of human error.

Also, within the fast food industry, McDonald's, through the use of portable data capture devices (PDCDs) and a unit-based modem, has developed a data communications system, which sends information direct to the payroll coordinating and processing office (EIU, 1990). The system utilizes data entered once at the time of an employee's arrival or departure.

The introduction of Edi systems has been limited in the hotel and restaurant sector. However, it should not be assumed that introduction elsewhere has been evenly spread. In the retail sector, introduction has been uneven, and has been linked to a complex array of organizational, inter-organizational and inter-sectoral contexts.

Ordering systems

In the retail sector, electronic communication networks are closely asso-ciated with supply chain management. The large superstore groups have invested considerable resources in the introduction of Edi technology (Ody and Newman, 1991). Edi technology, Tesco claims, has provided the basis for the most efficient replenishment system in the UK, which, by 1992, had allowed the company to establish Edi links with more than 900 suppliers (Anon., 1992). This has been experienced both on a national and inter-national level. Marks and Spencer has increased its European stores operation in recent years and consequently experienced the need to integrate the operation across borders. In 1985, the company undertook a £250m investment in information technology and established an inter-national link between stores and suppliers (Ogilvie, 1991).

The major replenishment system benefit of Edi is the shorter cycles between ordering and delivery. This has led to better control of stock levels and, in consequence, reduced stockholding levels, with the result that the costs have been reduced, and efficiency improved by both supplier and retailer (Harris, 1991). However, retailers who have introduced Edi systems have also benefited from the reduction in administrative costs. As McKinnon (1990) has pointed out about '70% of computer output is re-entered into other computers'. Therefore, the human errors, the costs of printing out invoices, and personnel costs can be, and have been, reduced through the introduction of Edi.

Investment in Edi, which is driving innovation within the superstore sector, and better utilizing existing information, must be considered in context. Developments in the retail sector support the contribution of Child and Loveridge (1990) that a willingness to introduce new technology is dependent on an existing infrastructure, capital investment and the organizational learning process. The company-to-company links which such organizations as Sainsbury and Tesco have established are driven by in-store technology, which has been introduced prior to Edi, as serving particular needs within the organization. The intra-company communications network has therefore been used as a basis for inter-company communication. Retailers have, through the introduction of Epos technology and the cost benefits associated with the introduction of that level of technology (IGD, 1974; Dawson *et al.*, 1987), been encouraged to develop further information-based technological systems. The Epos systems themselves have, in part, provided a structure on which to build Edi systems. UK superstores have progressed through the learning process with the technologies that they began introducing in the early 1980s and which now form a basis for the introduction of Edi technology in the early 1990s.

Edi developments in the retail sector are an example of how technology is introduced where there exists limited control, and where operations have progressed beyond a point where technology is necessary to remove the 'reverse salient' (Hughes, 1983) of development, but these developments also exemplify how the technology itself has altered relationships within the distribution channel. Marks and Spencer, it is claimed (Ogilvie, 1991), was one of the first retail companies to introduce electronic trading in Europe. Marks and Spencer is renowned for its supplier relationships (Tse, 1985) and it is consequently not surprising to see the company able to introduce the system, to the benefit of the retailer and the supplier, into a context where close links already exist between supplier and buyer. For other retailers, this has involved a changing relationship. The impact of Epos on the role of the buyer, and the location of the buyer within the retail organization, shows how technology has effected this function (Swindley, 1992) which the development of Edi and the need for suppliers to have compatible systems to receive electronic messages have taken one stage further. It is a feature of the development of Edi that integrated operations such as Marks and Spencer, but more notably still in this context, Benetton, have developed networks because of the existing relationships already established within the distribution channel, or even within the same company, where that company operates at different levels within the classic distribution channel. Benetton uses Edi as a means to control the flow of goods within a complex structure of subcontractors and franchise operations. Edi is central to the decentralized structure (Zottola, 1990).

The major initiatives have come from the large retailers who have gained substantial market share and, through their growth, contributed to concentration within that sector. Retailers with considerable buying power are simply able to demand that suppliers conform to the retailer's standards of Edi communication, or be delisted. Nevertheless, Edi should not be considered the preserve of large operators. As Epos technology has been utilized by smaller operations, so Edi, as common systems are introduced and become widespread, will become available to the smaller operator. This is shown by the development of Eftpos systems, where again the large operators have shown their influence in the market, both in terms of their influence on suppliers, but also their effect on the level of technology introduced, with the implications that this has had for other users.

Payment systems

As Cunningham and Tynan (1990) indicate, Eft is like Edi, another form of electronic trading, where communication is computer to computer. This is electronic trading in its purer form. The similarities between the two systems are considerable and, given the acknowledged fluidity of terms, an inappropriate distinction should not be drawn. The use of Eftpos technology, however, involves the participation of a third party, namely the bank customer, at the point of retail sale, so that for the purposes of conceptualization, Eftpos should be perceived as essentially a triadic rather than a dyadic relationship (Alexander *et al.*, 1992). That is, whereas Edi communication between supplier and retailer in respect of the physical distribution of goods is dyadic in nature and is affected and affects the relationship described by Piercy (1983), where there exists a flow of information between two parties concerning the actions of a third, the consumer, the consumer is directly involved in the electronic communication process in the context of Eftpos, and is thus an active participant in what is a triadic relationship.

Eftpos introduction in the UK (and this experience is mirrored elsewhere) has shown how relationships within the socio-technical constituency (Molina, 1989) may be affected by the introduction of new technology. However, it should not be assumed that the technology system itself has repositioned members of the constituency; rather, that changes in the power relationship are emphasized by the new technology.

The introduction of Eftpos technology in the UK is an example of how the initiator of the technology, the banks, at first assumed an influence within the socio-technical constituency which was eroded by other players, the retailers. It also shows how a widely accepted infrastructure is essential to any scheme involving Edi, if that technology is to be widely used and the full benefits received. The UK banks' attitude toward the retail sector was such that the retailer was perceived as a facilitator rather than a partner in the process of Eftpos introduction. The banks assumed that they would be able to retain full control over the design considerations surrounding Eftpos introduction.

There were other schemes before the UK banking sector attempted to introduce a unified scheme under the auspices of Eftpos UK. Indeed, the incorporation of Eftpos UK Ltd, in 1985, as a clearing company and as part of the Association of Payment Clearing Services, was an indication that banks recognized the need for unified action. Given the nature and history of the banking sector within the UK (Hine and Howells, 1993), such a move toward concerted action appears not only logical, but given the ultimate requirements of a nationally acceptable and usable system there were good reasons grounded on technological considerations for adopting this approach. However, throughout the 1980s individual banks had been experimenting with their own systems (Sparks, 1984; Anon., 1985, 1986) which in itself built up an organizational knowledge independently of other banks and because of competitive pressures which helped to create tensions within an ultimately less than united banking community.

Ultimately, the banks' failure, inability or reluctance to gain the co-operation of the retailers in a partnership led to the collapse of the pilot schemes established by Eftpos UK Ltd and 'undermined the national system' (Howells *et al.*, 1993). The result was competing bank schemes which led to the acceptance of retailer demands.

Future

The banks failed to establish a unified system through Eftpos UK Ltd because of inter-bank rivalry and the failure to assess the power and interests of the retailers. In that, there are lessons to be learned as far as electronic communication and Edi systems are concerned. The experience of introducing Edi communication systems within the retail-supplier context also indicates that there are lessons that should be learnt from the introduction of Edi technology.

First, within the socio-technical constituency there will exist pressures which must be fully appreciated in the context of changing roles and power within the constituency. The banks made assumptions about the introduction of Eftpos which ignored the major organizational and market-based changes that had occurred in the retail sector during the 1970s and 1980s.

Secondly, the design features of the system sponsored, if not introduced, by a unified body capable of establishing universally acceptable standards and systems requirements, will lead to the introduction of company-specific systems, which will ultimately compete for pre-eminence. The result may well be less than perfect.

Thirdly, the organizational players' experience of technology, and specifically previous generations of information technology, will be crucial in the introduction of a system demanding intra-company communication. Retailers, both in the context of ordering and payment systems, based on electronically communicated messages, have been able to draw on their experience of introduction and usage but also have found themselves constrained by that technology. This has been the case, both in the sense that certain technological options become less attractive, but also in the sense that opportunities provided by existing technology will not be fully utilized unless a new generation of technology is introduced. Implementors' willingness to invest (Child and Loveridge, 1990) will depend on this experience or lack of it.

Fourthly, the fundamental motivation behind change is driven by the need of organizations to address pressures which technology is capable of alleviating (Fleck, 1990). This has been the case in the control of the movement of both goods and funds. However, it may be argued that in the case of the movement of funds, the benefits to the banks were disproportionately high, compared with the benefits to the retailers. In the case of the movement of goods, there have been sufficient shared benefits. This interpretation, however, would have to accommodate an awareness that it is in the interest of suppliers to accept retailer demands simply because it would not be in the suppliers' interests to disregard them. Certainly it may be said that the banks needed the retailers more than the retailers need the banks in the context of Eftpos introduction. Indeed, it was not until the establishment of a national system that the retailers needed access to the established payment system, because of competitive rivalry among retailers, although, even then large retailers such as Marks and Spencer have been prepared to forgo membership of electronic payment schemes, and favoured the use of in-house financial services.

Conclusions

Electronic communication between companies may take a number of forms: in its purest state it is defined by computer-to-computer communication (Cunningham and Tynan, 1990) and that context may be described as Edi. This may be subdivided to the point where distinctions based on technology or context may suggest a separate term such as Electronic funds transfer, whether at point of sale or not. Essentially, what is described is a system which removes the need for human-based processing in a context where regular exchanges are involved. Therefore, in a buying situation, repeat buys will be well served by the system and may be sales-based, so that a thorough utilization of existing facilities such as Epos may be achieved.

The immediate benefit of the system is speed of processing, which should ultimately provide cost savings in one form or another, whether clerical or directly related to such as stockholding costs. The information processed may also be used for marketing planning purposes, but the benefits thus derived will be constrained by organizational information systems and an organization's marketing orientation.

Within the retail sector, Edi has been used to deliver benefits through the more efficient flow of physical items in such contexts as the grocery sector, where repeat orders are frequent. In the banking context, the system has been used to speed up the flow of funds, although, given off-line processing systems, it has not always ensured the guaranteed flow of funds with low fraud levels. In the hotel and catering sector, while operations such as Burger King have been able to adopt an approach similar to that adopted in the retail sector, other operations have focused more on the marketing benefits derived from systems which provide customer information.

The introduction of Edi technology supports the notion that change demands technological answers (Hughes, 1983; Beniger, 1986; Fleck, 1990). Both in terms of the control of the flow of goods and funds, it may be argued that the systems within the commercial environment had passed a point where ideally new methods of control needed to be employed. However, it should also be noted that where there existed an uneven set of benefits for participants in electronic communication process – Eftpos – various applications were introduced into the commercial environment. This supports the notion that where the most appropriate application of the technology is not immediately appreciated, the experience of technology usage will in itself indicate suitable applications (Freeman *et al.*, 1982; Perez, 1985; Fleck, 1990).

The nature of the industry employing Edi will define those operational areas where swift information flow is most beneficial. In the context of hotels, this may prove to be primarily the flow of service information, whereas in catering operations, where the flow of physical goods demands and facilitates Edi communication, then benefits to management may accrue. Operations within a vertically controlled channel, where there are regular movements of a limited range of physical items, are a case in point. Therefore, breweries with tied chains, and fast food operations, are ideal for the controlled development of Edi communication.

Whatever the context of Edi introduction, there does, however, remain one common factor and that is the establishment of universally recognized standards. The development of UPC and EAN codes is a classic example of the considerable benefits which will result not only in the initial phase of technological introduction but also in subsequent phases. Edi must follow this example.

References

Alexander, N., Howells, J. and Hine, J. (1992). EFTPoS: impact on channel relationships. *International Journal of Bank Marketing*, **10**(6), 38–44.

Anon. (1985). Tradenet launched by ANA and ICL. *Retail and Distribution Management*, **13**(3), 42–43.

Anon. (1986). Retailers assess EFTPoS state of play. *Retail and Distribution Management*, **14**(3), 34–38.

Anon. (1992). At Tesco in the UK, sales based ordering by EDI raises efficiency, profits. *Supermarketing Business*, **47**(8), 26.

Bell, D. (1973). *The Coming of Post-Industrial Society.* New York: Basic Books.

Beniger, J. (1986). *The Control Revolution; Technological and Economic Origins of the Information Society.* Cambridge MA.: Harvard University Press.

Child, J. and Loveridge, R. (1990). *Information Technology in European Services.* London: Basil Blackwell.

Cunningham, C. and Tynan, C. (1990). Electronic trading and retail supply chain relationships: a network approach. *Henley Management College, Working Paper Series*, HWP1/90.

Dawson, J., Findlay, A. and Sparks, L. (1987). The impact of scanning on employment in the UK food stores: a preliminary analysis. *Journal of Marketing Management*, **2**(3), 285–300.

Durocher, J. and Niman, N. (1991). Automated guest relations that generate hotel reservations. *Information Strategy: The Executive's Journal*, **7**(3), 27–30.

EIU (1990). *Retail Business*, Economics Intelligence Unit, London, No. 388 June.

Fleck, J. (1990). The development of information integration: beyond CIM. Working Paper series 90/2. University of Edinburgh: Department of Business Studies.

Freeman, C., Clark, J. and Soete, J. (1982). *Unemployment and Technical Innovation: A Study of Long Waves and Economic Development.* London: Pinter.

Harris, D. (1991). Fast orders help traders net profits. *Accountancy*, **108**(1179), 104–105.

Hine, J. and Howells, J. (1993). The UK banking context for EFTPOS development. In J. Howells and J. Hine (eds), *Innovative Banking: Competition and the Management of New Networks Technology.* London: Routledge, pp.6–26.

Howells, J., Alexander, N. and Hine, J. (1993). The Design of EFTPoS and the bank-retailer industry relationship. In J. Howells and J. Hine (eds), *Innovative Banking: Competition and the Management of New Networks Technology.* London: Routledge, pp.62–89.

Hughes, T. (1983). *Networks of Power: Electrification in Western Society, 1880–1983.* Baltimore: Johns Hopkins University Press.

IGD (1974). *Evaluating Feasibility of SPNS in the UK Grocery Industry.* Watford, UK: Institute of Grocery Distribution.

Jaben, J. (1992). Tapping new tools. *Business Marketing*, **77**(6), 20–22.

Jesitus, J. (1991). Restaurant uses for Pos technology grow. *Hotel and Motel Management*, **206**(19), 59, 64, 68.

McKinnon, A. (1990). Electronic data interchange in the retail supply chain: the distribution contractor's role. *International Journal of Retail and Distribution Management*, **18**(2), 39–42.

Molina, A. (1989). *The Social Basis of the Microelectronics Revolution*. Edinburgh: Edinburgh University Press.

Ody, P. and Newman, S. (1991). Speeding up the supply chain. *International Journal of Retail and Distribution Management*, **19**(5), 4–6.

Ogilvie, H. (1991). Electronic ties that bind: Marks and Spencer's pan-European JIT inventory system. *Journal of European Business*, **3**(1), 48–50.

Perez, C. (1985). Microelectronics, long waves and world structural change: new perspectives for developing countries. *World Development*, **13**(3), 441–463.

Piercy, N. (1983). Retailer marketing – informational strategies. *European Journal of Marketing*, **17**(6), 5–14.

Salomon, A. (1992a). Hospitality industry battles quality questions, discounting. *National Real Estate Investor*, **34**(13), 26–49.

Salomon, A. (1992b). Holiday abuzz with Hiro/Encore. *Hotel and Motel Management*, **207**(7), 33–34,60.

Sparks, L. (1984). Electronic funds transfer at point of sale – an overview. Scotland: University of Stirling Working Papers, No. 8406.

Swindley, D. (1992). Retail buying in the United Kingdom. *Service Industries Journal*, **12**(4), 533–544.

Tse, K. (1985). *Marks and Spencer: Anatomy of Britain's Most Efficiently Managed Company*. Oxford: Pergamon Press.

Yetter, M. and Bowman, R. (1990). Computers: logistics' productivity tool. *Distribution*, **89**(4), 66–72.

Zottola, L. (1990). The United Systems of Benetton. *Computerworld*, **24**(14), 70.

22 Food hygiene and HACCP

Anita Eves and Michael Kipps

Introduction

The 1980s–90s has been an era in which food and the food industry (in its broadest sense) have come under close scrutiny. The media has been active in publicizing the shortcomings of the industry and also of food production systems, prompted by scares over contamination of everyday foods such as eggs and of 'new' pathogens affecting even the unborn child (e.g. *Listeria monocytogenes*). So successful has been this publicity that almost every consumer is now aware of at least two micro-organisms (*Salmonella* and *Listeria*). While the industry may be irritated by such attention, it has highlighted problems that must be addressed.

At a time when consumer confidence in the food industry is at an all time low, and confidence in the government to control it even lower, it is particularly important that the industry should do everything possible to ensure the safety of the food it produces, whether that be from a factory or from a catering outlet. This is the basis on which the new defence of 'due diligence' has been introduced in the UK Food Safety Act 1990 (HMSO, 1990). The Food Safety Act recommends that a systematic approach should be taken to ensure the production of safe food. Hazard analysis and critical control points (HACCP) is such an approach.

HACCP is a proactive management tool that aims to prevent foods becoming unsafe, rather than relying on final product testing to ensure the same. There has been some question as to how fully it can be implemented outside of a food manufacturing environment, but the principles should be applicable in any situation. The following will discuss the recent rise in food poisoning cases, and the responsibility of the catering and retail sectors for this, the legal requirement for hygienic practices and the use and feasibility of the HACCP approach as a means of ensuring safe food.

Food poisoning – the scale of the problem

Cases of food poisoning have increased rapidly over the past ten years, with numbers of reported cases increasing from 14,253 in 1982 (Social Services Committee, 1989) to 53,881 in 1991 (Public Health Laboratory Service, 1992). Approximately 85 per cent of cases were related to *Salmonella* sp, with the upward trend in numbers of food poisoning cases being almost entirely attributable to *Salmonella* sp (Social Services Committee, 1989). The number of cases of *Salmonella* poisonings rose from 11,986 in 1982 to 31,516 in 1992. A particularly significant rise occurred with respect to one strain of *Salmonella, S. enteriditis* PT4 (2,246 cases in 1982 to 17,128 cases in 1992) (Adak, 1993, pers. comm.). This organism is associated with eggs. The number of cases of *Campylobacter* poisoning have also increased, from 12,797 in 1982 to 38,556 in 1992 (Adak, 1993, pers. comm.). Where a source is suspected, milk and poultry are most often implicated (Pearson and Healing, 1992).

Caterers have been implicated in the majority of food poisoning outbreaks, and numbers of cases associated with caterers have been said to be increasing faster than others. For instance, between 1986 and 1988 caterers were said to be responsible for 438 out of 537 general outbreaks (Anon., 1991). It has been suggested that this is, in part, attributable to the larger numbers of people eating out (Sheppard *et al.*, 1990). From 1984 to 1990 the average number of meals taken outside the home (per person per week, including midday meals) increased from 3.29 (MAFF, 1985) to 3.76 (MAFF, 1991). Although the figure for 1990 represents a slight fall compared with data for 1989, this probably reflects the general economic recession of the early 1990s. It is likely that the figure will not reduce further, but increase, as the UK comes out of recession. The caterer thus has a responsibility for consumer health. The increasing number of food poisoning cases also indicates that the traditional methods of ensuring safe food are not adequate and that a new approach is required. Table 22.1 shows the

Table 22.1   Number of general outbreaks of food-borne disease associated with the catering industry, 1986–1988

Restaurants	253
Hospitals	80
Institutuions	61
Staff restaurants	27
Schools	17

Source: Anon. (1991).

number of food poisoning outbreaks associated with different catering outlets.

The rise in the number of cases of food poisoning has been said to be the result of increased reporting, in part as a result of media attention. For instance, if illness follows the consumption of eggs, *Salmonella* is more likely to be suspected and tested for. This is not believed to be the entire cause of the rise. It is also, however, widely accepted that the number of reported cases is an underestimate of the actual incidence, with the actual incidence being ten to 100 (or more) times greater than that actually reported (Varnam and Evans, 1991). The extent of under-reporting is likely to be dependent on the origin of the poisoning. A group of people all suffering illness after a summer buffet is more likely to report the fact than an individual infected in the home, and the cause of the outbreak is more likely to be investigated and more easily identified. It is therefore thought that the number of reports associated with catering outlets is a more accurate reflection of actual incidences (Sheppard *et al.*, 1990).

It has also been suggested that the massive rise in the number of apparently unconnected cases may underlie poor control measures in food processing industries, supply chains or retail outlets (Sheppard *et al.*, 1990). The origins of some such outbreaks have been traced, particularly where serious illness is involved. For instance, an outbreak of *Clostridium botulinum* poisoning (botulism) arising from the consumption of hazelnut yoghurt (UK, 1989, affecting twenty-seven people) was traced to inadequate processing of the hazelnut purée used to flavour the yoghurt (Sockett, 1991).

New food processing technologies have also been proposed as a reason for the increasing number of food poisoning cases; in particular, the increasing use of cook-chill, where products may be stored for extended periods, combined with the emergence of pathogens able to grow at chill temperatures, e.g. *Listeria* and *Yersinia* (Varnam and Evans, 1991). The number of cases of *Listeria* poisonings peaked in 1988–89, but dropped considerably after warnings were given about pâtés, cook-chill products and soft cheeses. Approximately a quarter of cases are pregnancy related (Newton *et al.*, 1992), having serious consequences for that sector of the community.

The majority of food poisonings arise through the principles of good hygienic practice being ignored. Eight hundred and eighty-eight cases of *Salmonella* poisoning in the UK in 1989 (in four unrelated cases, but all arising from the consumption of cooked meats) were attributable to poor hygienic practices (Varnam and Evans, 1991). A number of failures in control are, however, usually involved in each food poisoning outbreak. For example, in an outbreak of poisoning caused by enteropathogenic *Escherichia coli* 0157:H7 (associated with hamburgers sold by the Jack-in-the-Box chain in the USA, 1993), with 475 cases across the USA and three deaths, the hamburgers were contaminated during production, and then did not reach a high enough temperature during cooking to destroy the organisms present (Mermelstein, 1993). This is representative of the usual situation where infected food reaches a kitchen, and poor temperature control or food-handling practices result in proliferation or survival of organisms present (Public Health Laboratory Service, 1992).

Overall, the most common (and preventable) causes of food poisoning are lapses in temperature control, including inadequate heating or storage at ambient temperatures (Anon., 1991; IFST, 1992). It is notable that the number of cases of food poisoning increase during the warmer summer months (Social Services Committee, 1989). The single most important cause of food poisoning is preparation of food too far in advance. This is often a feature of catering operations where trade may be irregular and at unsocial hours; thus to make best use of staff and facilities, foods are prepared in advance (Anon., 1991). Contamination through food handlers is less common, except in the case of staphylococcal intoxications (Varnam and Evans, 1991).

The most frequently isolated causal agents in outbreaks from hotels, restaurants and receptions between 1986 and 1988 were *Salmonella* sp and *Cl. perfringens* (Anon., 1991). Of 900–1000 outbreaks in England and Wales each year, 90 per cent are due to *Salmonella* infection (Public Health Laboratory Service,, 1992). Five outbreaks of Salmonella in 1992 were associated with a single type of dish, tiramisu, which contains raw egg (Public Health Laboratory Service, 1993). Other cases (Anon., 1991) were caused by *St. aureus, B. cereus* and other *Bacillus* species. The food vehicles responsible were more often detected in outbreaks caused by *B. cereus, St. aureus* and *Cl. perfringens*, probably owing to the short incubation times in these types of food poisoning and consequently the availability of food remnants. Poultry and other meats were most commonly implicated, and almost all cases of *B. cereus* poisoning were associated with reheated rice dishes.

The financial implications of lapses in hygiene are not always easy to calculate. There are immediate costs associated with fines (fines in excess of £10,000 are not uncommon for catering outlets – Knowles, 1994) and the payment of legal fees, the replacement of defective equipment or the destruction of defective stock, but also less tangible costs such as loss of business. The overall costs of food poisoning outbreaks can be substantial. For instance, the overall cost of a typhoid outbreak associated with canned corned beef in 1964 was estimated at £25m (Varnam and Evans, 1991).

The catering sectors most likely to suffer are theoretically the fast food and other restaurant chains, where brand image would (if branding has been successful) result in an association between an outbreak of food poisoning in one outlet with all others (Sheppard *et al.*, 1990). An outbreak in an individual restaurant would be expected to result in avoidance of the establishment, although research has shown that 34 per cent of consumers said that they would not change their eating habits (including avoidance of a particular establishment) following a bout of food poisoning (MAFF, 1988). An outbreak at a function, however, has been known to result in the loss of regular contracts between the caterer and the host organization (Sheppard *et al.*, 1990).

The legal requirement for hygiene

In the wake of reports of increased numbers of food poisoning cases, and of scares over the safety of eggs and soft cheeses, the UK government introduced the Food Safety Act 1990, which came in to force on 1 January 1991. This is the main piece of legislation of importance to the food industry (including caterers) and in general has been well received. The Act contains enabling powers, which among other things will allow the Act to be brought in line with EC legislation. The EC directive on the hygiene of foods was adopted in 1993 (Knowles, 1994).

Offences under the Act relate to food safety and consumer protection; it is the former that is of concern in the context of hygiene. The act includes a revision of the previous offence of rendering food injurious to health with the intention that it should be sold for human consumption; with the important change that it is no longer necessary for there to be the intention that the food should be consumed in that state. Two further offences are included of selling food that does not comply with food safety requirements (i.e. if it is injurious to health, unfit for human consumption or so contaminated that it would not be reasonable to expect it to be eaten in that state) and selling to the purchaser's prejudice any food for human consumption that is not of the nature, substance or quality demanded by the purchaser.

The hygiene elements of the legislation are enforced by local authority Environmental Health Officers (EHOs), who have been given new powers under the Act. In particular, they can now serve emergency prohibition orders, closing a premises immediately if they feel that there is an imminent risk of injury to health by its continuing to operate. The emergency prohibition order must be confirmed as an order before a magistrates court within three days. Officers also have the power to serve detention notices and seize unfit food (it will also be assumed that the whole batch is unfit unless proven otherwise), to issue improvement notices on premises where there is no imminent risk to health and to issue prohibition notices – including prohibiting the owner/manager from participating in the management of a food business again (Jacob, 1992).

There is now a strict requirement for food premises to be operated hygienically, and a food manufacturer or caterer does not have to be implicated in a food poisoning outbreak, or intend to sell unfit food, to be prosecuted under the UK Food Safety Act 1990. If a prosecution is made, the owner must show that he has taken all reasonable precautions to prevent the food he is producing from posing a health risk, i.e. the defence of due diligence. It is not yet known exactly what is required for a defence of due diligence to be successful, but there are factors that would seem necessary for such a defence to be credible; training of staff in hygiene and the existence of a safe and efficient system of food handling, for example, along HACCP lines.

Although the Food Safety Act 1990 includes powers to issue regulations on food hygiene training (Jacob, 1992), training is not mandatory in either the Food Safety Act or the EC directive on food hygiene, which the UK government has adopted. It is, however, recommended in both pieces of legislation, and it is difficult to see how a defence of due diligence would be successful if staff had not been trained. A relationship was found between the proportion of staff with adequate training and the proportion of the type of premises thought to present a high health risk (Audit Commission Survey, 1990). Overall, 12 per cent of premises examined were thought to present a significant health risk, and 19 per cent of takeaways fell into this category. The takeaways were noted as having the highest proportion of staff with poor training. Lack of training implies the presence of staff who may be unaware of the principles of good hygiene, but also indicates a lack of commitment from the owners to ensuring good hygienic practices.

Also recommended in the UK regulations, and a focus of the EC directive, is the implementation of a structured approach for the identification of potential hazards and their management, HACCP being one method of achieving this. The implementation of such a strategy should endorse the commitment of the operator to producing a safe product, and thus may help in the development of a defence of due diligence (Majewski, 1992). It has been accepted that HACCP in its entirety is not appropriate to all situations, thus an alternative approach, 'Assured Safe Catering' is proposed for the catering industry. This is based on the principles of HACCP and was published by the UK Department of Health in 1993. The Institute of Food Science and Technology (IFST) has also produced 'Guidelines to Good Catering Practice', based on the principles of HACCP (IFST, 1992), and the Hotel and Catering Industries Management Association a technical brief on the subject (HCIMA, 1987).

HACCP

Hazard analysis and critical control points can be described as a management tool to ensure the quality of a product by controlling the potential hazards in food operations (Majewski, 1992). In this context we are concerned with the production of a microbiologically safe product, but the system can also be applied to the maintenance of sensory or nutritional quality or to the assurance of chemical safety or the prevention of foreign bodies (Thorpe, 1991); in fact, most dynamic quality control systems would be based on such principles. The objective is to ensure a safe food through good management (i.e. control of raw materials and process operations) rather than to rely on end product testing. It is generally accepted that this is the better approach, as no end product testing regime can be entirely effective. Organisms may not be evenly distributed through the food, and thus a sampling regime could fail to identify contaminated materials. In addition, most routine microbiological testing takes 1–2 days to obtain a result (Majewski, 1992). The time delay does not present a problem for foods that are held for this period or longer prior to distribution, but in a catering outlet is totally impractical as foods are generally produced and consumed on the same day.

HACCP was originally designed for use on the nuclear and chemical industries, and was adopted by NASA in the 1960s (in conjunction with the Pillsbury Corp. and the US Army Natick Laboratory) to assure the safety of foods for its space programme (Majewski, 1992). More recently, it has been applied to food manufacturing industries, and it is suggested that a similar scheme should be adopted by caterers.

HACCP describes a system of control for assuring food safety, providing a structured and critical approach to the control of identifiable hazards. In this way it should be possible to identify areas of concern where failure has not yet been experienced (Thorpe, 1991).

A hazard can be defined as something that has the potential to cause harm to the consumer (safety) or damage to the product (spoilage) (Varnam and Evans, 1991). Hazards can be specific (e.g. staphylococcal enterotoxin) or relate to operational malpractice (e.g. cross-contamination) (Thorpe, 1991). A hazard analysis estimates risks in producing, processing or preparing foods by assessing all possible hazards and the likelihood of them occurring (Bryan, 1981). Risk is the likelihood of the hazard being realized. A critical control point is a location, a practice, a procedure or a process that, if not controlled, could result in an unacceptable risk (Sheppard *et al.*, 1990). In some systems, two types of control point are identified: one that will eliminate a hazard, and one that will minimize a hazard, but will not eliminate it (Varnam and Evans, 1991).

HACCP and food manufacturing

While it is suggested that HACCP principles should be applied in the food service or catering industries, it will initially be discussed in some detail in the environment where it was first applied in relation to food – food manufacturing.

The HACCP approach consists of describing and assessing the hazards associated with all stages of the food manufacturing operation – from raw material acquisition to the sale and consumption of the product. The critical control points required to control the hazards are identified and procedures established by which these critical control points can be monitored. Each HACCP analysis is specific to a particular operation and product, and must be reassessed each time a change is made to either ingredients or process (Thorpe, 1991).

HACCP requires a multidisciplinary approach to cover all aspects of the operation. The personnel involved would be primarily internal, with access to the necessary information. The HACCP team should ideally include a chairman, a production specialist, a technical specialist, a process engineer and others, such as raw materials buyers (Thorpe, 1991).

There are four stages in the preparation of a HACCP system:

1 Preparation of a detailed flow diagram for the process, including details of management routines, process details (including sanitation routines) and production unit operations (including design, storage areas and security). Where production practices change to accommodate differing circumstances, alternative procedures should be included in the flow diagram, and also the circumstances under which they would be used. A list of all food ingredients used should also be prepared, including alternatives where appropriate (Thorpe, 1991). A flow diagram for the production of beef stew and dumplings (cook-freeze system) is shown in Figure 22.1.
2 Identification of the characteristics of production to enable definitive conclusions to be drawn regarding hazards to the consumer or the product, including raw materials, final product storage, formulation and preservation systems, packaging and consumer handling practices. The basis on which conclusions are drawn should be recorded. A structured approach to this process could be to first examine food product factors (such as storage, formulation and packaging) and then hazard-related parameters (such as temperature, pH value, or damage resistance of packaging).
3 Consideration of each operation in the manufacturing process with respect to the identified hazards, and identification of the stages in the process that are critical and need to be controlled adequately to assure safety – critical control points (Thorpe, 1991) (see Figure 22.1). A HACCP decision tree has been developed to assist in the identification of critical control points (Majewski, 1992). Three main criteria should be determined for each operation: can micro-organisms be introduced, and if so can they grow; will organisms already present in the food be able to grow; are the organisms destroyed? A judgement of the severity of the risk should be made, in terms of the seriousness of failure (Thorpe, 1991). Many users define four levels of concern from none to high, where none indicates no risk of poisoning and a high life-threatening risk (Varnam and Evans,

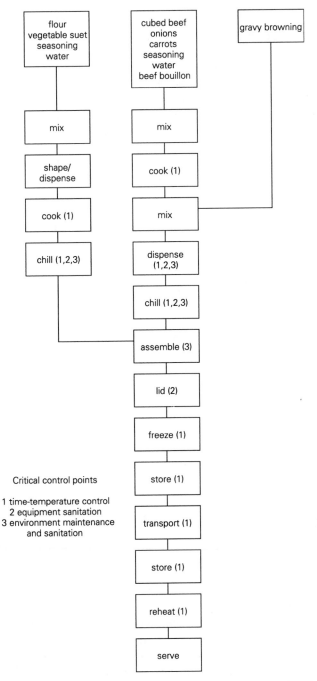

Figure 22.1 A process flow diagram for beef stew and dumplings (cook-freeze system) indicating critical points (*Modified from*: Sheppard *et al.*, 1990)

1991). Assessment of risk can be based on probabilities, on comparisons with similar products or on experience – in the absence of hard data (Thorpe, 1991). The basis on which the level of risk has been determined should be recorded.

4 Control options are devised for the monitoring of each CCP. These are criteria that indicate whether an operation is in control. They may include monitoring microbiological, chemical or physical parameters or the expertise required of personnel (Thorpe, 1991). Target levels and tolerances should be established for each measurement, and the corrective action to be taken if a CCP is out of control defined (Majewski, 1992). In addition, data recording and product recall procedures are determined. It is important that the monitoring system itself does not compromise food safety (e.g. the use of glass or mercury thermometers), and that procedures are laid down to prevent this (e.g. for the disinfection of temperature probes between samples) (IFST, 1992).

At this stage, changes may be made to the process/ingredients to reduce the risk, or make control more effective. Possible changes must be discussed with relevant personnel, as a change in a processing parameter to increase a time-temperature combination for instance, may change the organoleptic characteristics of the product. If changes are agreed, a modified flow diagram should be prepared.

Monitoring involves five types of procedure: documentation of control (e.g. affirmation by operatives that controls have been set correctly); monitoring of process parameters (e.g. temperature); validation of control equipment (e.g. the performance of the equipment, calibration, etc.); analysis of the monitoring of control points; end-product testing for verification that the HACCP system is being correctly applied and is effective.

The HACCP system should be continually reviewed to assess its effectiveness, and to modify it in the light of changing process or ingredients, or in the light of failures to control a hazard.

Application of HACCP in catering operations

There are a number of reasons why the application of full HACCP procedures are not appropriate to caterers. HACCP principles should, however, be applicable in any system where food is being prepared. Indeed, HACCP has been investigated as a means of hygiene control for street vendors in developing countries, although its implementation in such circumstances is unlikely (Bryan, 1993)!

To be effective, a HACCP system requires standardization of operations and such standardization is not common in catering systems. The application of HACCP to cook-chill systems is easier to envisage, and is recommended in the Department of Health's guidelines on cook-chill (Department of Health, 1989). In addition, production is rarely planned, foods are produced using batch processes and often the quantities produced are not matched to the equipment available (Sheppard *et al.*, 1990).

A further problem for catering operations is the availability of adequate expertise and staff resources to obtain the necessary data (Thorpe, 1991). Even the smallest units should, however, be able to adopt a HACCP approach by considering hazards that might occur at each stage of preparation, new hazards that could be introduced at any stage, and the implication of a change in preparation methods. Of particular importance will be handling procedures both during preparation and of the final product, holding times and temperatures and cooling times. A simple approach is to define hazards critical to food safety in relation to the most common causes of food poisoning. The manager should therefore look critically to determine where these sources of food poisoning are likely to originate and the measures to be taken to prevent them happening. In particular, the manager should consider: food supplies, food temperatures and the times food is held at these temperatures, working practices, staff hygiene, and equipment and general kitchen hygiene. This approach forms the simplified procedures laid down in the IFST publication 'Guidelines in Good Catering Practice' (IFST, 1992).

The difficulty in applying HACCP to catering operations has been recognized and a modified system, Assured Safe Catering has been developed (DOH,1993). Assured Safe Catering aims to help the caterer to construct a written, safe system of food production within any catering department, which will be effective and appropriate for that operation. It identifies certain hazards/critical controls common to most catering operations, namely: purchase of prepared foods, receipt of food, storage of high-risk (able to support the growth of bacteria and not cooked prior to consumption) foods prior to preparation, preparation, cooking, cooling, hot holding, reheating, chill storage and service. Figure 22.2 shows a typical flow diagram indicating the use of HACCP principles in the production of fried chicken in a fast food restaurant. Assured Safe Catering accepts that some companies will not be able to create a team to establish HACCP. In these instances, management is advised to develop its own system, but it is noted that knowledge of basic hygiene principles is essential. Indeed, it has been said that HACCP is only likely to be effective where the principles of good hygiene are already in place (Majewski, 1992). In addition, the manager will need to be familiar with all operations from purchase of raw materials to service of the finished product. In areas where sufficient expertise does not exist, it is suggested that advice should be sought from outside, e.g. from EHOs in the local Environmental Health Department. The document notes that controls should be adequate and feasible, and should

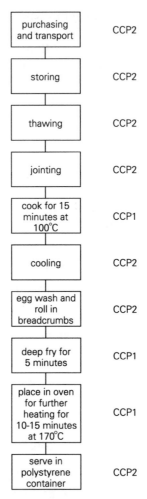

CCP1 critical control point that will ensure the control of a hazard

CCP2 critical control point that will minimize, but not control, a hazard

Figure 22.2 Flow diagram for the production of fried chicken

not be restricted to those already in place, but other more effective alternatives should be considered. It emphasizes the importance of implementing the controls and of recording measurements – first, so that failures in control can be identified, and secondly, so that such records can be used to show that all necessary steps had been taken to control the hazard. All procedures should be documented so that staff are aware of their responsibilities.

Implementation of HACCP principles

Implementation of any HACCP-based system requires co-operation at all levels, from the operative required to record control measurements, to the managers to ensure that the system is being correctly implemented and monitored. This may require a change of attitude by some managers, as recent research indicates that managers only consider food hygiene as being significant when something goes wrong (Guerrier *et al.*, 1992). The proactive approach required by HACCP may thus be quite contrary to their current thinking.

Implementation of HACCP, or the Assured Safe Catering equivalent, may require training of staff in HACCP principles, in hygiene, or in the methods to be used for monitoring control points. Training should also include actions to be taken in the event of measurements being outside of agreed tolerances. The responsibilities of each member of staff and the reasons for taking control measurements should be explained.

It has been suggested that the system should be introduced gradually (Department of Health, 1993); for instance, implementing controls relating to one operation in the flow diagram at a time, and when the kitchen is not busy. Once the system has been implemented it should be verified and checked at frequent intervals and modified if necessary.

Conclusions

The numbers of food poisoning cases are increasing rapidly and it has become clear that traditional methods of ensuring food safety are not adequate. This is recognized in recent legislation, which encourages the use of a structured approach, such as HACCP, to ensure food safety. This legislation also includes a new defence of 'due diligence', where a food manufacturer or caterer (if prosecuted) is required to prove that he has taken all possible precautions to prevent his products becoming unsafe. It is suggested that the establishment of a HACCP-based system will help in the development of such a defence.

It has been recognized that HACCP in full is not appropriate to catering operations, and an alternative, based on HACCP principles (Assured Safe Catering), has been published. A change in the attitudes of catering managers is necessary, however, as hygiene and safety are currently only considered significant if something goes wrong. It is possible that such a change in attitude may emerge as a result of the requirements of the Food Safety Act 1990, and increased public awareness of food safety issues. It is important that the caterer provides the levels of protection that the customer has every right to expect (Ramsden, 1991).

References

Adak, G. K. (1993), *Personal communication*. London: Public Health Laboratory Service.

Anon. (1991). *The microbiological safety of foods, part II*. Committee on the Microbiological Safety of Foods. (Chairman, Sir Mark Richmond). London: HMSO.

Audit Commission Survey (1990). *Environmental Health Survey of Food Premises*. London: HMSO.

Bryan, F. L. (1981). Hazard analysis in food service operations. *Food Technology*, **35**(2), 78–87.

Bryan, F. L. (1993). HACCP – street vending in developing countries. *Food in Australia* **45**(2), 80–84.

Department of Health (1993). *Assured Safe Catering*. London: HMSO.

Department of Health (1989). *Chilled and Frozen: Guidelines on Cook-Chill and Cook-Freeze Catering Systems*. London: HMSO.

HMSO (1990). *Food Safety Act 1990*. London: HMSO.

Guerrier, Y., Kipps, M., Lockwood, A. and Sheppard, J. (1992). Perception of hygiene and quality in food service operations. In C. P. Cooper and A. Lockwood (eds), *Progress in Tourism, Recreation and Hospitality Management*, Vol 4. London: Belhaven Press, pp. 182–194.

HCIMA (1987). *HACCP – The Effective Approach to Food Hygiene and Safety*. HCIMA Technical Brief, Sheet No. 5 London: HCIMA.

IFST (1992). *Guidelines to Good Catering Practice*. London: Institute of Food Science and Technology.

Jacob, M. (1992). Food Safety: action to protect the consumer. *Communicable Disease Report 2* (Review Number 7), R78–R81.

Knowles, T. (1994). Some aspects of UK and European food legislation. *International Journal of Hygiene and Nutrition in Food Service and Catering*, **1**(1), 49–62.

MAFF (1985). *Household Food Consumption and Expenditure 1984*. London: HMSO.

MAFF (1988). *Food Hygiene: Report on a Consumer Survey*. London: HMSO.

MAFF (1991). *Household Food Consumption and Expenditure 1990*. London: HMSO.

Majewski, M. C. (1992). Food safety: the HACCP approach to hazard control. *Communicable Disease Report 2* (Review Number 9), R105–R108.

Mermelstein, N. H. (1993). Controlling E coli 0157:H7 in meat. *Food Technology*, **47**(4), 90–91.

Newton, L., Hall, S. M,, Pelerin, M. and McLaughlin, J. (1992). Listeria surveillance 1992. *Communicable Disease Report 2* (Review No. 12), R142–R144.

Pearson, A. D. and Healing, T. D. (1992). The surveillance and control of Campylobacter infections. *Communicable Disease Report 2* (Review No. 12),

R133–R138.

Public Health Laboratory Service (1992). Outbreak Forum V. *Communicable Disease Report 2* (Review No. 11), R121.

Public Health Laboratory Service (1993). Recent outbreaks of salmonellosis. *Communicable Disease Report 3*(3), p. 9.

Ramsden, E. (1991). The Food Safety Act: implications for the Environmental Health Officer. *British Food Journal* **93**(8), 12–13.

Sheppard, J., Kipps, M. and Thomson, J. (1990). Hygiene and hazard analysis in food service. In C. P. Cooper (ed.), *Progress in Tourism, Recreation and Hospitality Management*, Vol II. London: Belhaven Press, pp. 192–226.

Social Services Committee (1989). *Food Poisoning, Listeria and Listeriosis.* London: HMSO.

Sockett, P. N. (1991). Food poisoning outbreaks associated with manufactured foods in England and Wales: 1980–1989. *Communicable Disease Report 1* (Review Number 10), R105–R109.

Thorpe, R. A. (1991). HACCP in catering. In *Catering for the '90's*. Campden Food and Drink Research Association, Symposium Proceedings.

Varnam, A. H. and Evans, M. G. (1991). *Foodborne Pathogens – An Illustrated Text.* London: Wolfe Publishing.

Part Five

Panel Questions

23 The view from the industry

Colin Clark, Bob Cotton, Mike Henderson, Darrell Stocks and Barry Ware-Lane

---

Question 1: What do you consider have been the major changes that have affected your sector of the industry over the past few years? How have these changes affected your organization?

Commercial catering: Barry Ware-Lane

The major changes affecting commercial catering operations over the last five years have been:

The state of the economy and the resultant recession, leading to record levels of business receivership and high unemployment. In turn, lower levels of disposable income, fear of redundancy and the negative equity trap has led to reduced eating out and trading down. The economic downturn has inevitably increased the need for catering operations to control operating margins even more and reduce purchase and payroll costs in particular.

Government legislation in terms of the Food Safety Act/Food Hygiene Regulations 1990/1, Transfer of Undertakings (TUPE) and the introduction of the Uniform Business Rate, increasing costs to the caterer both in the implementation and current operation.

Increased competition, particularly as a result of the Monopolies and Mergers Commission Report into the supply of beer, has prompted the major brewing groups to reorganize their pub estates and strive to increase catering revenue. The retail and leisure sectors have also invested heavily in the provision of catering facilities both as profit and service centres in their own right.

Catering consumers are increasingly willing to experiment with different types of food due to increased travel and knowledge gained from television programmes, etc. This has led to higher expectations in terms of value and quality with a move to more informality when dining out.

Catering operations have responded to these changes in the following ways:

A greater emphasis has been placed on promotional activity and niche marketing. Promotional offers linking discounts and loyalty incentives have been used to increase volumes, together with food promotions from different parts of the world. Awareness of healthy eating trends, green issue aspects and demographic changes have also been utilized by marketers.

The creation of customer care programmes and the growing attention to quality assurance has been paramount to the retention of existing customers, upselling and satisfying customer expectations.

As operating costs have been reduced to the minimum, catering operators have invested more carefully in both refurbishment and new premises, with greater attention to design aspects and the 'eating experience'. Themed restaurants have grown which are aimed at younger, more affluent consumers.

Local management have been required to become more commercially orientated and focused, with emphasis placed on customer satisfaction and financial returns, together with more marketing awareness.

Contract catering: Bob Cotton

There are six changes:

The feeding of staff is no longer a fully subsidized employee benefit. Instead, it has become a service available for the convenience of staff if they wish. In addition, food is no longer seen as a commodity characterized by the phrase 'meat and two veg'. The canteen has been replaced by a staff restaurant, and it now has to attract the employee as a customer.

The decision to use contract caterers was once the responsibility of the personnel manager. Now most clients see the decision as a commercial one requiring the services of a professional purchasing manager.

The management fee, or cost plus, contract is giving way to the fixed price contract. Clients, at a time of recession and cost-led competition, see the use of contractors more as an economy measure rather than a move to raise quality.

Employees at all levels have much higher expectations about food, thanks to travelling and the increase in eating out. Contractors need to invest in food promotions to attract customer take-up.

Increased competition is another major change. There are many more contractors pursuing contracts. The new competition comes from fast and convenience food outlets located in every high street.

Public service contracts have become a significant proportion of the large contractors' turnover and a very high proportion of new business. Public sector contracts tend to be large, averaging over £1m per year, compared with commercial contracts averaging £250,000. They are complex to manage with stringent monitoring by the client in a highly political environment.

The organization has changed in three ways to tackle these changes:

Niche market selling and operating have been developed to make sure that our services are sensitive to client needs. Operations like staff restaurants are giving way to management teams dedicated to the NHS.

Investment in the specialist support activities like training, hygiene, sales, marketing and IT are needed to give clients better value and to differentiate ourselves from the competitors.

Much more attention is being given to commercial management rather than just catering issues to ensure service. All levels of GM management need to be commercially aware to ensure client satisfaction at the same time as a profitable outcome for Gardner Merchant.

Hospital catering: Colin Clark

Most of the significant changes that have occurred recently in Food and Beverage (Catering) Services in the NHS result from the radical reforms introduced in the 1991 government white paper, 'Working for Patients'. The establishment of NHS Trusts, that manage hospitals and other services, was part of a strategy that aimed to establish a competitive, internal market for health care. The impact of this market has been much greater than the introduction (1983) of competitive tendering for hotel services.

District Health Authorities (DHAs) no longer have a management responsibility, but purchase the services they consider appropriate to the health needs of their local population and other providers of care. The direct impact on catering services of these management changes is minimal, as most DHAs deleted their District Catering Management posts in 1984 following the publication of the white paper 'Patients First'.

The trigger for change has been the reduction in funding of hospital-based care that reflects the switch in resources to primary (GP) and community care that was implicit in the reforms. Occupancy levels are now of great concern to many Providers and the realities of a market 'in slump' are being faced by NHS managers. Costs are being cut using the measures traditionally encountered elsewhere in the industry. Wage cuts, redundancies and other economies in fixed costs are being forced on catering departments. Food budgets continue to be flexed against occupancy and sales.

The Health and Medicines Act 1988 gave a new freedom to Health Authorities to generate income. They were encouraged (1990) to introduce a broad range of 'hotel services' in order to generate income and reflect the value placed on patients' choice. Profit from new food and beverage sales is now actively sought by many Trusts. Ventures include opening staff restaurants to the public and revamping facilities in outpatients departments to increase turnover. Catering for private functions on NHS premises and outside is no longer unusual.

The focus on the individual consumer, spelled out in the Patient's Charter, has resulted in a wider recognition that marketing is central to the NHS manager's role.

The development of patients' hotels and private suites illustrates a battle for increased business and efficiency in which the quality of food and beverage services is accepted as being important, but not ultimately significant, influences on success or failure in the market.

Hotels: Darrell Stocks

The ever increasing importance of the international traveller

The continued globalization of the industry has had a number of effects on Forte. Pride was hurt with British ownership of the two major international brands of Holiday Inn and Hilton, but more important was the effect on the segmentation of the Forte portfolio.

The global traveller requires global brands where he can be certain of his required standards wherever he goes. Until the recent rationalization, Forte stood for little other than perhaps a certain minimum standard in its hotels.

Forte's brands and collections since recent formation are now being communicated to the appropriate markets and Forte Crest is targeted at the international traveller, with its site criteria of major city centres and airports around the world.

The very name change from THF was driven by this factor of marketing the name Forte and its umbrella brands around the world.

Origination of the budget sector and its exploitation

While there was much discussion of the budget sector during the late seventies and early eighties and the proposed entry into the UK by the

French companies, it was not until Little Chef opened the first lodge in 1985 that the opportunity began to be exploited.

It was originally formulated to exploit spare land adjacent to Little Chefs, but its rapid success and acquisitions of other brands with location capability – Happy Eater, Harvester and Welcome Break – quickly led to the name change to the Travelodge brand. Travelodge has been a major success story and is operational in Ireland, with plans and sites identified for Spain, France and Germany.

Forte's success has opened the way for much competition and it is a major strategic issue for the company to retain the market leadership in the UK and develop the brand worldwide.

Growth of non-hotel restaurants

This trend is, of course, well established but there has been a positive explosion in the numbers and range of types of restaurant. This factor, coupled with the growth in the mass market hotel user, i.e. not just expense account senior businessmen – who wants better value and informality – means that in many cases the majority of hotel guests eat and drink outside of the hotel. This has led to the hotels repositioning their outlets from 'dining room' to retail restaurant. To capitalize on the trend, Posthouse have developed the 'Traders' concept and the other brands and collections have developed a much more retail-orientated approach.

Information technology and channels of purchase

The growth in the sophistication and power of computers, plus the internationalization of the traveller, has led to a concentrating of reservation systems outside of the hotels themselves. Airlines, car hire and travel agents particularly have assumed greater importance.

This, plus other factors, has caused hotels to develop their own better central reservations systems with all hotels on line. Forte's Travelodge operates through a central reservations system only. A member of the public can only book a room through central reservations and not a hotel direct.

The importance of branding and communication with the customer

The growth of the market, the complexity of the product and customer choice, together with the need for reassurance, has led to the further development of brands, and brand extensions. Having developed the brands their values need to be communicated to the customer.

Forte have done this quite successfully to their different segments, but none more so than the Posthouse TV campaigns targeted at both leisure and business markets with different advertisements.

Public houses: Mike Henderson

The major change that has affected the pub industry over the past five years is the Beer Order Act. This, in simple terms, restricted a company that brewed beer, to directly managing no more than 2,000 pubs. The Act was principally aimed at the big six breweries, i.e. Bass, Whitbread, Allied, Courage, Grand Met and Scottish and Newcastle. Bass, Whitbread and Allied decided to remain in brewing and retailing and, as a result, had to dispose of or lease thousands of pubs over the 2,000 limit. Courage and Grand Met decided to swap pubs for breweries, so that Courage is now only a brewer with no directly-owned pubs, while Grand Met decided to become a pub owner with no brewing capacity and thus the 2,000 limit did not apply to them.

Scottish and Newcastle owned slightly over 2,000 pubs and quickly decided to dispose of the surplus so they could remain both a brewer and a retailer. The situation as of today is now more complicated, as Scottish and Newcastle have bought Grand Met's pub estate and are now well in excess of the 2,000 limit – they are going to have to make large disposals.

The Beer Orders Act has resulted in hundreds of pubs flooding the free house market, thus depressing even further already depressed property prices, but has also led to the formation of numerous pub-owning companies, e.g. Enterprise and Centric, which have estates of a few hundred, low barrelage (under five a week), poorly maintained tenanted pubs.

At the same time, some of the regional brewers, e.g. Greenalls, though not legally obliged to do so, took a closer look at their strengths and weaknesses and decided to opt out of brewing and remain purely as pub retailers.

This Act caused the large brewers a vast amount of work over a two-year period and, as a result, they neglected their mainstream estate in terms of investment and, only now, are they beginning to catch up while competing leisure interests, e.g. ten pin bowling and multiplex cinemas, have rapidly developed.

The aim of the Beer Orders Act was to reduce the power of the big six and give the pub customer more choice. In fact, the act has had the opposite effect and customers now have less choice. From all points of view, the Beer Orders Act has failed completely and the one dissenting member, Leif Mills, of the original Monopolies Commission investigation, is now fully justified in his dissenting view.

In addition, the public house sector has suffered its share of the recession and beer sales have continued to decline year on year. While some retailers have been able to replace lost beer sales with increased food sales, the latter pound for pound is only half as profitable as the former.

Over the past five years, pub catering has matured and as a result there are now a number of strong brands both for formal restaurant operations, e.g. Beefeater and Harvester, and informal family dining, e.g. Brewers Fayre and Millers Kitchen. The industry has moved a long way from chicken and scampi in the basket – the only offering until the early seventies.

In my own company over the past five years, we have mirrored a lot of these changes. In 1991, having had falling beers sales over a number of years, we decided to exit from brewing and concentrate on being a pub retailer. In 1990, we decided to form a branded catering division, Premier House, which currently has three main brands (Millers Kitchen – family dining, Hudsons – formal mid-spend restaurant, and Quinceys – American-style diner). Premier House has recently developed a chain of budget accommodation.

At the same time, the tenanted estate which had been neglected was reformed as Inn Partnerships and licensees are now franchisees not tenants.

All in all, the past five years have been the most turbulent ever for the industry and I am sure there are further changes still to happen.

Question 2: What do you feel will be the major influences on your sector of the industry over the next five years? What opportunities does this offer your organization?

Commercial catering: Barry Ware-Lane

Gradual economic growth, both in the UK and subsequently in Europe, will positively impact on consumer spending. The maintenance of lower interest rates will enable investment and refurbishment of catering facilities hitherto delayed, and with the spread of free trade, expansion both from and into Europe will increase.

Further EC legislation will affect the way companies operate, particularly with regard to labour issues and health and safety. However, deregulation in the UK, as seen on the motorways, will benefit catering operators and present future opportunities for growth. The satisfactory signing of the GATT agreement will terminate trade wars.

Competition will increase from American and European operators keen to gain a presence in the UK. Company-owned branded outlets will spread nationally/internationally by virtue of partnerships and mergers in order to achieve greater brand awareness and its associated sales benefits in addition to achieving economies of scale. Competition from other sectors of the consumer catering market will influence all levels of trade and possibly depress growth with the need to continue budget offers.

The main demographic trends of contraction in the 16–24 age group and ageing population will influence the labour supply and increase the flexible use of part-time workers. Coupled with the increase in the child population, family targeted catering will grow.

Increased use of technology will aid operators in terms of effectiveness. Additional management information will allow specialized sales and marketing departments to measure promotional productivity and target segments more effectively.

These changes will present the following opportunities:

Branded outlets will develop across the catering sectors and franchise outlets will offer the opportunity to achieve rapid company growth.

Demographic changes present opportunities to target market families and older consumers and menus will reflect further moves toward healthy eating.

Catering operations will increase opening hours more in line with their continental counterparts and opportunities exist to further extend the home delivery market.

Companies will become 'market orientated' and diversify/spread the range of catering outlets within their portfolios to reduce the risk and increase the opportunities for volume growth.

Contract catering: Bob Cotton

Catering-only contracts will in the future be replaced by support service contracts. Catering will be just one service put out to tender alongside the cleaning, building maintenance, secretarial and reception, etc. A full support service contract for a hospital could include over fifteen disciplines. As a result, contract management will need to be multi-skilled.

The internationalization of the contract catering industry will increase. A striking feature of the world economy is the spread of free trade. Former Communist countries, for example, are opening up to the Western contract caterers as they strive to become competitive in world markets.

In return, the UK domestic market will attract competition from successful companies from overseas. Similarly, UK companies reinforced by overseas earnings will have the resources to invest in specialist catering support services previously restricted to the largest contract caterers.

The proportion of public sector business will increase as the squeeze on public expenditure linked to compulsory competitive tendering leads to a greater use of contractors.

The introduction of EC legislation will affect the way the company operates. The application of the Transfer of Undertakings legislation (TUPE) has adversely affected the company's approach to compulsory competitive tendering. Despite the UK opting out of the Social Chapter, the management of labour could be affected by EC legislation in fields of health and safety.

The changes over the next five years will offer three opportunities. The profitability of the business will rise in line with the increase in contract size, thanks to the increase in public sector work and the effect of support service contracts. The stability of the business will be increased by the growth of international business. The more markets in which the company operates, the less the impact of recession or a business setback in any one country will affect the company. Trends in the marketplace require ever more sophisticated management at all levels of the business. A large well-resourced contractor will do better than those smaller companies which largely sell on price.

Hospital catering: Colin Clark

Competition between NHS Trusts will continue to increase, particularly in the acute sector. Institutions for the mentally ill and people with learning difficulties will continue to reduce in size and close. Changes in the pattern of care will increase the number of small units, which will make the use of cook-chill attractive. Realization that cook-chill is not financially viable in large units will cause a surplus in production capacity within the NHS and in the commercial sector.

The establishment of the National Supplies Authority (in 1992) and its divisional organization will have considerable impact. The move to centralize purchasing and rationalize distribution will increase costs attributed to catering, but hopefully will reduce total NHS spend on the supplies system. On-cost changes are a real concern to catering managers, particularly when faced with competition from private contractors.

Closure of local stores will increase response times and reduce control at the point of usage. Balancing bulk purchase, storage and delivery with fluctuating customer demand will become an issue between the two professions as the self-funding supplies organization seeks to optimize its efficiency.

The rigorous appraisal of effectiveness, combined with a commitment to improving the quality of services, will offer opportunities to the competent professional. Commercial contractors who have learnt the skills of working within tight specifications and predetermined costs are increasingly prepared to tender for hospital catering contracts. The risks involved in capturing these contracts that measure value for money will continue to be attractive until the economic climate improves.

The National Audit Office has undertaken a survey (1993) of catering in the NHS and has identified significant weaknesses in the management of the services. Lack of standard setting, performance measurement and meaningful indicators within the service reflects the wider conflict inherent in a commitment to giving Provider Units (Trusts) independence in a sensitive public service for which the Secretary of State is politically answerable. The reaction of the NHS Management Executive to these criticisms is, at the time of writing, unknown. It is however certain that the responsibility of the Purchasing Authorities to specify the safety and quality of catering services will be reinforced. It is against this background that decisions relating to the management and funding of catering services will be determined.

Hotels: Darrell Stocks

Many of the influences of the past five years will continue to have major effects on the industry.

The globalization issue will allow Forte to expand worldwide. Growth will initially focus on two brands : Travelodge in the budget sector and Crest in the senior businessman market. The requirement for rapid expansion will put pressure on capital resources and development will occur through management contracts.

New customer markets, especially leisure, will provide opportunities for resort-type hotels around the world. These hotels will also attract the conference and convention markets. Forte will take advantage through the sheer virtue of its size.

The trend to eating outside the hotel will continue. Ultimately the market could end up, as in the USA, with very few hotel restaurants except at the luxury end. Forte will either respond by developing retail outlets in hotels either alone or by joint venture or lease off the space and concentrate only on accommodation sales.

Once the economy recovers there will quickly be a shortage of skilled people again putting pressure on catering operations. These will continue to polarize between expensive fine dining and good value 'system' catering, the latter allowing the brand to override to some extent the lack of fine quality food. More opportunities will therefore arise in mass market catering and Forte, by offering better career structures, will ensure a larger share of qualified personnel.

Technology and especially video conferencing may alter the demand for overnight stays from an important segment. The demand will require major capital investment which large companies like Forte can provide.

The recession has meant almost a commodity approach to the daily selling of hotel rooms – such has been the excess of supply to demand. The key issue in the future will be to differentiate companies and brands and communicate the differences. Forte, as the largest UK operator, has a major problem but also is best placed to capitalize on the opportunities.

Public Houses: Mike Henderson

Over the next five years, beer sales will continue to decline and food sales will continue to increase. In branded operations only the best will survive – Harvester will either expand or disappear, having merged with another brand. Who would have envisaged that Berni, *the* brand of the sixties and seventies, would have disappeared by the nineties?

Despite the effect of the Beer Orders Act there are still far too many poor-quality wrongly-sited public houses. At a conservative estimate there are at least 10,000 too many pubs which neither provide a return for the pub owner or the pub operator. If and when the property market recovers, then there will be a surplus of pubs for sale.

Up until the late 1980s, housing estate sites were highly sought after by brewers – now these are the least favoured sites and most operators have or will be disposing of these when circumstances allow.

Pubs, from being male dominated, are rapidly becoming attractive to families and the government is shortly to announce a change in the law that we legally allow children under 14, without the need to dine, into public houses that have a Children's Certificate. This will cause pub retailers to have a major strategy rethink and call for substantial investment in designated properties.

The greying population is increasing over the next five years and what is currently a neglected market is going to have to be focused on. What does this population want: early evening food, quieter areas, disabled parking space, full waitress service for drinks and food, etc.?

At the same time, the pub is competing with other leisure interests and no longer is a visit to the pub the only evening entertainment – the video at home with a takeaway and a bottle of wine is strong competition as well as the resurgence in cinema going.

Fun pubs, the fashion in the late eighties, are now out of vogue and traditional ale is now back in fashion, but the 18–25 age group is decreasing and is not finding pubs as attractive as previous groups of their age.

What are we going to do? An increasing emphasis is being put on food both branded and unbranded. Pubs with no long-term potential, e.g. estate pubs, are being disposed of. Managers are being paid a sensible salary with a bonus on performance and are far more aware of their own pub's profitability, and are being enabled to make more of their own decisions relating to their pub's performance.

Europe is neither a threat nor an opportunity – the UK pub industry is so different from that of Europe that it is very difficult to transfer retailing concepts.

Undoubtedly the pub industry is in for a very difficult five years, at the end of which there will be far fewer pubs – but those that remain will have much higher standards – and there will be fewer brewers in the field of play – some family-owned companies will not survive.

Question 3: What are the key features of customer expectations in your sector now and how do you satisfy these requirements through your food and beverage provision?

Commercial catering: Barry Ware-Lane

Customers now have much higher expectations with regard to the provision of food and beverages, not only in terms of choice and quality but also with regard to price competitiveness and the service environment. Convenience, ease of parking and security aspects now influence choice. The 'value for money' requirement encompasses many factors, with cleanliness/hygiene emerging as a key criterion.

The interest in 'healthy eating' and the decline in red meat consumption have been mirrored in terms of menu choice, with the introduction of self-help salad bars, the introduction of vegetarian/vegan dishes and choice of mineral waters, etc. The increase in the awareness of green issues has also prompted the need to recycle whenever possible and reduce energy costs. Environment friendly products are now a prerequisite and no-smoking areas are now being extended to cover the whole dining area.

Increased travel and knowledge of foods have enabled customers to become more confident and adventurous when dining out. Foreign cuisines now feature strongly as individual dishes on menus as well as special promotions, or as specific destination venues in their own right.

Informality and the trend to 'snacking/grazing' has seen a relaxation of dress codes and less of a requirement to partake in the traditional three-course meal. However, the fixed price menu choice still satisfies the value for money requirement.

Quality is no longer relevant just to food and beverage products, but is now applicable to the total experience received by the customer.

Discounts, special offers and promotions are now expected as a norm by customers and each catering operation must be seen to actively seek new custom to maintain interest and repeat business or lose its competitive edge.

Added value, through merchandising and product enhancement, satisfies the customer searching for something new and different and those restaurants adding 'theatre' to the meal experience reap the rewards.

Contract catering: Bob Cotton

Customers have higher expectations with regard to every aspect of food and beverage provision. Choices in eating are much wider than hitherto. There are the effects of increased interest in healthy eating. Salads and a variety of low-calorie, vitamin-rich dishes are needed. The interest in animal welfare has led to a growing demand for vegetarian food, particularly among the young.

Travel has encouraged people of all ages to respond positively to foreign cuisine. Indian, Chinese, Italian, Spanish food dishes can often feature as both staple dishes and as a special promotion.

Convenience and fast food products like hamburgers, baked potatoes and pizzas are expected to be on offer, along with more traditional food. The contract caterer has to be prepared to offer the full range of possible eating choice and experience.

Quality is as important as variety. Interest in food and its quality is growing with the spread of eating out. Contractors have to offer quality food, whether in the directors' dining room or in the low-price items in the staff restaurant.

Price competitiveness is a constant concern for contract management. Clients increasingly compare food purchasing costs of contractors with the cost of buying similar produce in the high street. Value for money is essential to a company's success.

More clients want the provision of food and beverages to be an integral part of the company's business activities : entertaining in the evening, linked to a business event, and the support of food and drink throughout the day rather than at regular meal times. The supply of food is seen as a business tool which can be used to assist the core activities of the client.

Investment in national teams of technical and business specialists has helped local contract management to respond to the demand from clients for variety and quality food. Merchandising specialists help with food promotions and menu development. Residential training courses help chefs to improve their technical skills at the same time as their ability to meet the contract budget and other commercial targets.

Hospital catering: Colin Clark

Changes in social attitudes have combined with the messages of the Patient's Charter to create a more critical and vocal customer. They are being actively encouraged in many hospitals, where regular surveys of customer views are undertaken. In some acute units, patients are offered the opportunity, on a daily basis, to comment on the services using the menu cards on which they select their meals. Surveys demonstrate that the

18–32-year-old customers are much less satisfied than the elderly who make up the majority of those served. The fashionable phase of quality assurance, characterized by a reliance on mission statements, has now passed and a real concern for the needs of individuals is becoming increasingly evident. Using customer satisfaction as the ultimate measure of success will become the norm in the NHS as elsewhere in the industry.

While in hospital, patients are often very aware of food as part of their treatment and reflect on their normal eating habits as an influence on their health. The recommendations, in 1983, of the National Advisory Committee on Nutrition Education (NACNE) and, in 1984, of the Committee on Medical Aspects of Food Policy (COMA) have been distorted by the media. Publication of the King's Fund report 'A Positive Approach to Nutrition as Treatment' (1992) has given encouragement to a more flexible and informed approach that recognizes the differing nutritional needs of individuals and is reflected in the menu planning and meal production methods in most hospitals.

Flexibility and a ready response to the expression of food preferences are important throughout the industry, except where a well-defined, standardized product is offered. The use of advanced meal ordering and centralized plating or tray assembly is no longer regarded in many hospitals as the best style of service. Bulk food distribution, common in earlier times, is being reintroduced utilizing hostess trolleys to provide choice at the point of service.

Facilities and services provided for staff and visitors reflect a more sophisticated and demanding clientele. Stainless steel cafeteria counters are being displaced by self-service units that are finished in a range of attractive materials. Attention to lighting and the ambience of the whole dining area is no longer considered inappropriate.

Hotels: Darrell Stocks

The major issue for catering outlets in hotels is how to address the basic customer need for refreshment when away from home which, depending on need, is either for substitute domesticity or enjoyment. These two factors are in basic conflict. The former require comfort food quickly and inexpensively served at a level appropriate to their budget. This budget may not be consistent with the hotel restaurant's pricing policy.

Leisure diners require good value appropriate to their requirements and expectations. If the single hotel restaurant offers the 'traditional' dining room, then the leisure users go elsewhere. If the restaurant offers a leisure experience, the other diners are dissatisfied and the repeat overnight stay is put at risk.

Where demand allows, the solution is to offer at least two restaurants, but, with the current emphasis on minimal overheads, part of the answer is room service or lounge service provision.

Forte is pursuing the sensible long-term approach through its branding. Ultimately the brand will communicate exactly what the customer can expect, including the catering experience. For example, Heritage Hotels are targeted at older couples who can expect traditional catering in traditional restaurants. Crest hotels are targeted at senior businessmen with modern and stylish restaurants. The conflict arises when the older couple find themselves in a Crest restaurant.

Customers require the following: value for money, appropriate style of service, atmosphere, appropriate menu range, appropriate food quality. Customer expectations are directed by brand values and Forte have developed catering concepts to reflect these values. For example, Posthouse targets junior/young businessmen and families. The menu content, range, pricing, décor theme and informal style of service entirely reflect brand values.

Customer requirements are also linked to price – what customers are prepared to pay. For example, room service : Posthouse, a three-star brand, does not offer room service; Crest, with four stars, provides moderate room service; but Grand, with five stars, offers private dining service with a personal butler.

Given that many hotel residents eat out because they prefer the non-hotel competition and that most locals never eat in their local hotel, the future challenge is to provide a retail-oriented restaurant without alienating the resident wanting a substitute domestic meal. Posthouse have recently conducted a trial of a newly-created branded restaurant which has met considerable success at increasing the sleeper–diner ratio and attracting non-residents.

Public houses: Mike Henderson

Public house customers now expect a far greater choice of food with the appropriate level of service – with the same 'value for money' image that pubs project.

Pubs have moved heavily into the family market with the provision of children's menus, not only for young children but also menus for the young adult. Pub kitchens are now fully equipped and demand the appropriate level of investment – a microwave and a deep fat frier are no longer adequate!

Customers are beginning to move on from steak and chips and want 'restaurant meals' in pub surroundings at pub prices. How are pubs going to provide this without paying the wage a skilled chef demands? One answer is to look at sous-vide – this is going to increase rapidly over the next five years.

Standards of service in pubs have been and still are appallingly low and until recently customers have accepted these and no retailer has tried to improve them. However, customers are now quite rightly demanding better standards of service on the beverage side and retailers are having to respond. Nearly every company has some sort of 'mystery customer' scheme to monitor service levels and the abolition of the Wages Act is enabling retailers to pay differential rates according to ability. There is a long way to go and the retailer that succeeds in their service standards will win market share from the others.

Question 4: Organizational structures and management roles have changed significantly over the past few years; for example, the decreasing need for middle management positions. How have these changes affected your sector of the industry?

Commercial catering: Barry Ware-Lane

In the quest to reduce central overheads, area managers have been replaced by regional managers/team leaders. Unit managers have thus been 'empowered to manage' and by virtue of a flat organization structure, the needs of the customer are immediately responded to and communication lines shortened. Decision-making is quicker and operates much more at the customer interface, ensuring guest satisfaction.

Unit management responsibilities have been widened, with greater responsibility for the commerciality of the business operations. Training in management skills has therefore developed, with technical and health and safety functions devolving to specialists to assist the unit manager.

The use of consultants is now more widespread in order to satisfy a short-term objective, with many senior redundant executives being commissioned on special projects.

Senior and junior management have become more profit orientated and salary levels have been enhanced with bonus and incentive schemes related to performance levels.

Market-led operations require management information and therefore the use of technology has increased. Electronic data interchange is now commonplace with unit and supplier information directly linked to head office. The processing of information is thus quicker and trends are reacted to more speedily.

Contract catering: Bob Cotton

The need to be more sensitive to the different needs of each client has dictated changes in the organization. Layers of middle management engaged in supervising local contract managers have been removed. The emphasis is now for management at all levels to meet the client as frequently as possible.

The centre of gravity of the organization has moved to the contract managers. They are responsible on a day-to-day basis for the quality of the service delivered to the customer. No amount of middle or senior management supervision can achieve success without an effective contract manager.

The responsibilities of contract managers have increased following the rise in public service contracts. They could be responsible on a day-to-day basis for £2m worth of work a year. Political and commercial skills are as important as professional training in catering. Many former middle managers have been redeployed as front-line catering management.

Large contracts like hospitals have complex technical as well as managerial requirements. Hygiene and dietetics are two areas of special interest in a medical environment. A programme of investment in a national team of specialist technical staff and facilities in a position to meet the request of local contract management has taken place.

These technical teams are required to see themselves as profit centres selling their services independently rather than as overheads. The need to think commercially is important for all parts of the company – even for technical specialists.

The one management overhead to flourish in the new competitive climate has been the sales and marketing area. In particular, those involved in producing tender documents have been very busy. Not only does Gardner Merchant have to tender for more contracts to convert into sale, but the work itself is more complicated. Public sector tenders, in particular, are more demanding than commercial ones. Retendering is still undertaken by the contract manager concerned. They require the support of national specialists to succeed.

The sales force has been upgraded in line with the definition of the business into niche markets. The more the sales person is aware of the special characteristics of the niche market, the more successful they are. The sales force is helped by national co-ordinators, who research the niche market for which they are responsible and guide the thinking of those sales forces and those preparing tenders.

Thus the responsibility of front-line operations and sales staff has increased, with a new feel for the commercial and marketing characteristics of their work as their professional concerns. At national level, the growing complexity of the business has necessitated investment into specialist technical services.

Hospital catering: Colin Clark

Management arrangements for catering are inevitably conditioned by changes in the organizational structure of the NHS. When hospitals were administratively grouped together in the 1970s, the management of catering was established on a district wide (functional) basis. Area Health Authorities, that had been established in 1974, were abolished in the early 1980s. At the same time, functional management was swept away as part of the 'small is beautiful' movement.

During the late 1980s, the need to offer career prospects to catering and domestic managers, who could no longer look to district appointments, coincided with a drive to reduce management costs. The King's Fund report of 1984, prepared with the Hospital Caterers' Association, on the management of catering services, supported the integration of the management of catering and domestic services. Many hospitals introduced hotel services or facilities management structures. The catering managers' posts were deleted, leaving only an assistant grade in charge.

The immediate effect of this has been to significantly reduce the level of competence of those directly responsible for food and beverage services. Working Paper No.10, issued in 1989 by the NHS Management Executive, deals with the responsibilities for training and development in the reformed NHS. No reference is made to the needs of catering or other managers of the hotel services professions.

The National Catering Management Trainee Scheme no longer exists. It was modified to reflect the policy of switching to hotel services management during 1986 and major elements of the former course programme were deleted in favour of general management issues. Support for the scheme in its new form withered. The decision to move to a National Vocational Qualification (NVQ) focused programme is not suited to the needs of graduate recruits who traditionally have entered the NHS through the training programme.

In the long term the reduced level of coaching by senior professional managers and the absence of formal training and development programmes presents a very real danger for a service that is subject to increasing demands for quality and efficiency.

Hotels: Darrell Stocks

Smaller, flatter structures originally emerged in response to the shortage of quality people and progress continued in the recession with the need to reduce the cost base. As a generalization, one layer of management has been removed at head office and one layer in the hotels. Additionally, remaining staff have had to accept increased responsibilities.

Responsibility has been moved nearer the customer by the formation of single business units (SBUs). Responsibility rests with operational management rather than with the corporate centre. Both of these factors have meant that better quality people in position are required.

Rather than carrying experts at the centre, e.g. trainers, these work operationally in the hotel and are seconded to the centre when the need arises. Some hotel-based roles, e.g. engineers, personnel, accountants, are now combined in a region when it is not necessary for each hotel to have its own.

Public houses: Mike Henderson

Management changes have not had a large effect on the industry – most changes have been as a result of the Beer Orders Act. In Greenalls, one tier of middle management has been removed and area managers report directly to a regional director who is responsible to the managing director.

Traditional brewery retailer roles have been revised and cellar service technicians and stocktakers are now often self-employed rather than employed by the brewer/retailer.

Unit managers are now regarded as more professional than just dispensers of beer and are better rewarded but have to perform accordingly. They are often running an asset worth in excess of £1m, turning over £15,000 to £20,000 a week, with thirty full- and part-time staff. Managers that do not perform are no longer moved sideways within the company but are moved out of the company.

The area manager's role is changing from being that of a 'policeman', as EPOS technology has largely replaced that need, to being one of a business development manager. From being a traditional male role, more and more area managers are female – a refreshing change.

At one time, being an area manager was the apex of one's career – now it is the first step for a graduate.

In large companies, the 'company policy' often has a detrimental effect at unit level and in order to achieve the optimum profit at unit level, company rules have to be relaxed and the professional unit manager allowed to run his business with a greater degree of freedom.

Question 5: What do you consider are two or three issues which will influence the development of the industry as a whole?

Commercial catering: Barry Ware-Lane

Political stability and economic growth: As the UK recovers from the recession and confidence returns, the hotel and catering industry will develop in both the domestic and international arena. Political stability is essential to this development, with new market opportunities creating international expansion and growth. Increased leisure time presents further opportunities for development.

Professional recognition: Government recognition of the importance of tourism and the hotel and catering industry to both the country and the economy will 'professionalize' the industry. Unified representation is gathering momentum and, as a lead employer, professional management qualifications will further enhance the standing of the industry as a profession and career progression provider.

Creativity: Creativity within the industry in terms of design, theming, marketing, and 'theatre' will influence development. Eating out will become more of a way of life and enjoyed by all socioeconomic groups.

Contract catering: Bob Cotton

Three factors will determine the future shape of the food and beverage contracting industry : politics in the UK and EC, the speed of the spread of support service contracts, and the participation of the industry in the world market and internationalizing of their business.

The rise of the public sector market to dominate our new business in the UK and to rival the turnover of our commercial contracts is the direct result of decisions by politicians. The introduction of CCT came about almost despite the wishes of industry. The unwilling buyer has always been bad news for contractors. Now that the business is there, our business is to depoliticize the issue. The use of contractors to supply public services should be as acceptable to opposition politicians as to the present government. Quality performance on the job will be important. Investment in the development of ideas in support of the use of contractors will be equally important.

Support service contracts requiring catering contractors, among other disciplines, to supply other related activities like cleaning, security and building maintenance are spreading slowly. The public sector developed the idea to make possible a new flow of savings on retendering once the first efficiency savings had been realized. The private sector has been much more reticent. The ostensible reason is their desire not to put 'all their eggs in one basket'. The real reason is the wish to avoid creating internal management upheavals in pursuit of a low priority management issue.

The growth of international business will directly affect the company's ability to insulate itself from the effect of UK politics and the economy. The world is a large market, and provides unlimited opportunity for growth. Retaining senior top-quality staff is easier if the company is growing. Expansion overseas, although complex and expensive, allows the company to insulate itself from the long-term changes in UK politics and the economy.

Hospital catering: Colin Clark

The report of the National Audit Office on Hospital Catering will be published at a time when the management of the NHS is going through another phase of its continual restructuring cycle. Regional Authorities are being abolished and regional offices established within the NHSME. They will adopt a 'light touch' approach to their responsibilities which include the management of the internal market for health care. District (Purchasing) Authorities will be merged into large consortia and amalgamated with Family Health Service Authorities. These will be powerful public bodies with an inherited (HSG(92)34) responsibility for specifying the nutritional value and safety of the food and beverage services that they purchase.

The NAO report will, for a moment, draw attention to the importance of food and beverages as part of the total health care provided by the NHS. It will challenge the NHS to find ways of improving the performance of the managers of this £491m food and beverage business.

Improvement will not occur unless stimulated and supported. It must be hoped that Purchasers, if not the NHSME, will recognize that this can only be achieved through performance measurement that includes the quantification of consumer satisfaction. This must be supported by professional training and development programmes.

The traditional shelter from market forces enjoyed or suffered by NHS catering will continue to be eroded. Our Purchasers will change and have less to spend: our large institutions will diminish and reduction in the length of average stay will demand more service flexibility; our consumers will become more discerning and demanding. The challenges to the food and beverage manager will increase and the opportunities to excel will multiply. The future will be exciting.

Hotels: Darrell Stocks

Brands: Segmenting the market, globalization of brands, maximizing distribution through a larger number of locations and communication with the target markets.

Central reservations: Information technology sophistication will enable simple worldwide reservations systems to maximize yield, in order to achieve what the airlines can already do.

Ageing population: As video conferencing, etc., grows, the requirement for leisure-based accommodation and resort hotels will increase with the ageing and wealthy population.

Public houses: Mike Henderson

Not being taken seriously by the government and still regarded as a Cinderella industry because we don't make anything that is visibly exported.

A poor image as a profession – low pay, long hours and lack of recognition makes it difficult to recruit quality employees. If all else fails you can always get a job in catering!

The recession! Customers now expect special offers in pubs/restaurants, and they are quite prepared to haggle over room rates. In future, value for money will become essential – those that don't offer it will suffer.

Increasing competition for the 'leisure pound' – why go out to drink and eat when you can go ten-pin bowling, to the cinema, stay at home with a video, etc.?

Index